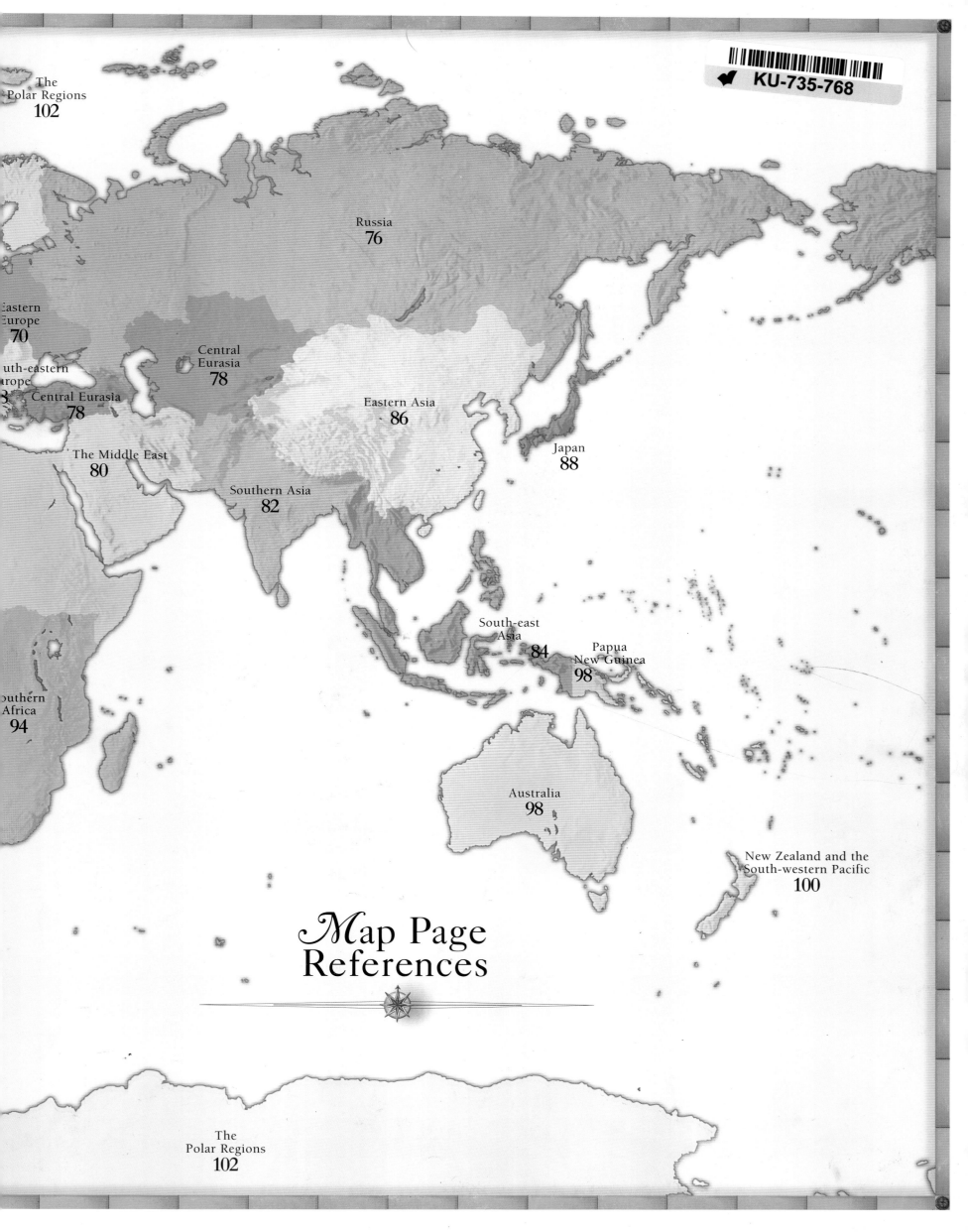

The
Polar Regions
102

Russia
76

Eastern
Europe
70

South-eastern
Europe

Central
Eurasia
78

Central Eurasia
78

Eastern Asia
86

Japan
88

The Middle East
80

Southern Asia
82

South-east
Asia
84

Papua
New Guinea
98

Southern
Africa
94

Australia
98

New Zealand and the
South-western Pacific
100

Map Page
References

The
Polar Regions
102

THE READER'S DIGEST
Children's Atlas
of the World

Cameron

$\mathcal{T}$HE READER'S DIGEST
Children's Atlas of the World

A Reader's Digest® Children's Book
First published 1998.
Reprinted 2000 by
Reader's Digest Children's Publishing Ltd,
King's Court, Parsonage Lane, Bath BA1 1ER,
a subsidiary of The Reader's Digest Association, Inc.

Conceived and produced by **Weldon Owen Pty Limited**
59 Victoria Street, McMahons Point, NSW, 2060, Australia
A member of the Weldon Owen Group of Companies
Sydney • San Francisco

READER'S DIGEST CHILDREN'S BOOKS
General Manager: Vivian Antonangeli
Creative Consultant: Michael J. Morris
Group Publisher: Rosanna Hansen
Senior Editor: Cathy Jones
Editor: Louise Pritchard
Assistant Editor: Sarah Williams
UK Consultant: Deborah Hall

WELDON OWEN PTY LTD
Chief Executive: Officer: John Owen
President: Terry Newell
Publisher: Sheena Coupe

Design Concept: John Bull
Managing Editor: Ariana Klepac
Art Director: Sue Burk

Project Editor: Scott Forbes
Consulting Editor: Colin Sale
Editorial Assistant: Anne Ferrier
Text: Scott Forbes

Senior Designer: Hilda Mendham
Designer, Thematic Spreads: Lena Lowe
Pre-press Co-ordinator: Jocelyne Best
Computer Production: Laura Sassin, Amanda Woodward
Computer Graphics: Stuart McVicar
Jacket Design: John Bull

Senior Picture Researcher: Anne Ferrier
Picture Researcher: Peter Barker
Archives: Rita Joseph

Illustrators: Susanna Addario,
Andrew Beckett/illustration, André Boos,
Anne Bowman, Greg Bridges, Danny Burke,
Martin Camm, Fiammetta Dogi, Simone End,
Giuliano Fornari, Chris Forsey,
John Francis/Bernard Thornton Artists, U.K.,
Jon Gittoes, Ray Grinaway, Terry Hadler/Bernard Thornton
Artists, U.K., Tim Hayward/Bernard Thornton Artists, U.K.,
David Kirshner, Frank Knight, Mike Lamble,
James McKinnon, Peter Mennim, Nicola Oram,
Tony Pyrzakowski, Oliver Rennert, Barbara Rodanska,
Claudia Saraceni, Michael Saunders, Peter Schouten,
Stephen Seymour/Bernard Thornton Artists, U.K.,
Marco Sparaciari, Sharif Tarabay/illustration,
Steve Trevaskis, Thomas Trojer, Genevieve Wallace,
Trevor Weekes, Rod Westblade, Ann Winterbotham

Maps: Digital Wisdom Publishing Ltd
Flags: Flag Society of Australia

Production Managers: Helen Creeke, Caroline Webber
Production Assistant: Kylie Lawson
Vice President International Sales: Stuart Laurence

British Library Cataloguing in Publication Data
A catalogue record for this book is available from
the British Library.

Color Reproduction by Colourscan Co Pte Ltd
Printed by Toppan Printing Co, (H.K.) Ltd
Printed in China

A WELDON OWEN PRODUCTION

THE READER'S DIGEST
Children's Atlas of the World

Consulting Editor: Colin Sale

A Reader's Digest Children's Book

Contents

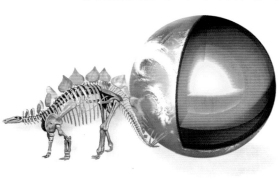

NORTH AMERICA 32

SOUTH AMERICA 48

EUROPE 54

ASIA 74

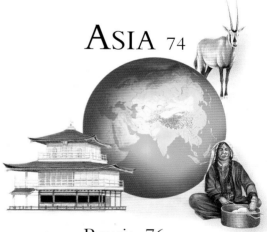

AFRICA 90

AUSTRALIA AND OCEANIA 96

How to Use This Atlas

THE READER'S DIGEST CHILDREN'S ATLAS OF THE WORLD takes you on a fascinating tour of our extraordinary world. Before you start, read the sections called Maps and Mapmaking and How to Read a Map. There you will find out about different kinds of maps and how they are made, and learn how to read and use maps. The remaining introductory pages are a guide to our planet, Earth. They show you where it is located in the Solar System, what it is made of, how its landscapes have been shaped and how weather, wildlife and peoples vary around the world. The atlas maps are divided into seven parts – one for each of the continents of North America, South America, Europe, Asia, Africa, and Australia and Oceania, and one for the polar regions. Each part begins with a continent map that includes country lists and shows the most important features of the landscape. The continent map is followed by a series of illustrated maps which are packed with facts, pictures and activities. The sample maps and notes on these two pages explain the features on both types of map. At the back of the atlas you will find the World Fact File. This provides useful information on all of the world's countries and major territories. Finally, there is a glossary of terms used in this book, as well as a gazetteer – a geographical index that helps you to find places on the maps.

Continent Facts Includes the size of the continent, its population and the names of its countries.

ILLUSTRATED MAP

Country list A list of the countries or states on the map, their populations and capital cities.

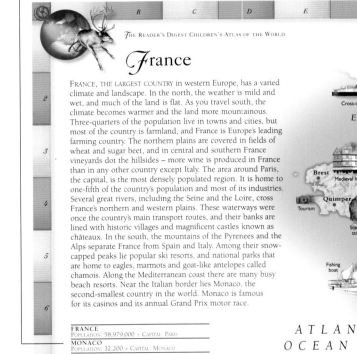

France

FRANCE, THE LARGEST COUNTRY in western Europe, has a varied climate and landscape. In the north, the weather is mild and wet, and much of the land is flat. As you travel south, the climate becomes warmer and the land more mountainous. Three-quarters of the population live in towns and cities, but most of the country is farmland, and France is Europe's leading farming country. The northern plains are covered in fields of wheat and sugar beet, and in central and southern France vineyards dot the hillsides – more wine is produced in France than in any other country except Italy. The area around Paris, the capital, is the most densely populated region. It is home to one-fifth of the country's population and most of its industries. Several great rivers, including the Seine and the Loire, cross France's northern and western plains. These waterways were once the country's main transport routes, and their banks are lined with historic villages and magnificent castles known as châteaux. In the south, the mountains of the Pyrenees and the Alps separate France from Spain and Italy. Among their snow-capped peaks lie popular ski resorts, and national parks that are home to eagles, marmots and goat-like antelopes called chamois. Along the Mediterranean coast there are many busy beach resorts. Near the Italian border lies Monaco, the second-smallest country in the world. Monaco is famous for its casinos and its annual Grand Prix motor race.

FRANCE
POPULATION: 58,979,000 • CAPITAL: Paris
MONACO
POPULATION: 32,200 • CAPITAL: Monaco

Amazing Fact This box contains fascinating facts about the area on the map.

• AMAZING FACT •

France is now connected to Great Britain by an undersea rail link known as the Channel Tunnel. The tunnel took seven years to build and includes two rail tracks. Trains take 35 minutes to pass through the tunnel. People can travel from London to Paris in about three hours.

BOULES
Boules is a bowling game that is popular in France. It is played with metal balls on a hard dirt surface.

CONTINENT MAP

North America

THE CONTINENT OF NORTH AMERICA extends from just south of the North Pole to just north of the Equator. It includes almost every kind of environment, from ice-caps to forests, mountains, deserts and rainforest. In the west, an almost unbroken chain of mountains stretches from Alaska to Costa Rica and includes the Rocky Mountains, one of the world's most famous mountain ranges. The United States of America (U.S.A.) and Canada are the largest of the continent's 23 countries. Canada is made up of ten provinces and two territories, while America includes some of the world's biggest cities, but also vast areas of wilderness. Most Americans are descendants of European immigrants, but there are also many people of African and Asian origin, as well as native peoples.

Records A list of the tallest, longest and largest features of the continent.

Size comparison Shows how the continent's most important mountains and rivers would compare if you could see them side-by-side.

Political map Shows all the countries within the continent.

Physical map Shows the main features of the landscape.

Coloured border
Each part of the atlas has a different coloured border.

Map reader's grid The letters and numbers on the border help you find places on the map. See page 10 to find out how to use the grid.

Projects By trying these activities and experiments, you can learn more about a topic or a part of the world.

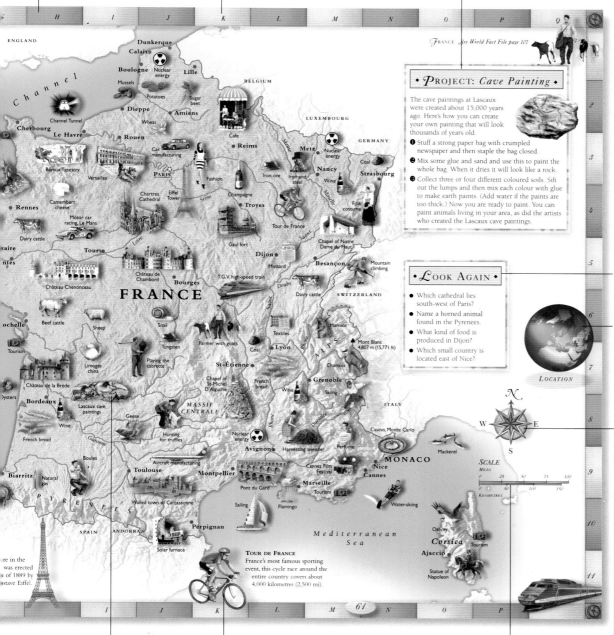

*F*RANCE *See World Fact File page 107*

• *P*ROJECT: *Cave Painting* •

The cave paintings at Lascaux were created about 15,000 years ago. Here's how you can create your own painting that will look thousands of years old.

❶ Stuff a strong paper bag with crumpled newspaper and then staple the bag closed.

❷ Mix some glue and sand and use this to paint the whole bag. When it dries it will look like a rock.

❸ Collect three or four different coloured soils. Sift out the lumps and then mix each colour with glue to make earth paints. (Add water if the paints are too thick.) Now you are ready to paint. You can paint animals living in your area, as did the artists who created the Lascaux cave paintings.

• *L*OOK AGAIN •

● Which cathedral lies south-west of Paris?
● Name a horned animal found in the Pyrenees.
● What kind of food is produced in Dijon?
● Which small country is located east of Nice?

Look Again
To answer these questions, you'll need to look closely at the information on the map.

Locator globe
This globe shows where the area on the map is located.

LOCATION

TOUR DE FRANCE
France's most famous sporting event, this cycle race around the entire country covers about 4,000 kilometres (2,500 mi).

Illustrations These show the people, places, wildlife and activities in the area on the map.

Feature illustrations These illustrations provide extra information about some of the map illustrations.

Scale The scale bar helps you to calculate distances on the map. To find out how to do this, see page 10.

Compass The compass helps you find north. To find out how to use the compass, see page 10.

*K*EY TO MAP COLOURS

Desert and semi-desert

Forest and grassland

Tundra

Ice-cap

country border

regional (state) border

disputed border

CHANNEL ISLANDS (U.K.)

territory, and country to which it belongs

●**Baltimore**
◉**ANNAPOLIS**
✪**WASHINGTON, D.C.**

✪ national capital
◉ regional capital
● city or town

Arno

river

Lake Ontario

lake

▲ Ben Nevis
1,343 m (4,406 ft)

major mountain

ⓔ African elephants

ⓔ endangered animal

Maps and Mapmaking

A MAP IS A PICTURE that represents an area of land on the Earth's surface. Any area, no matter how large or small, can be drawn as a map. Some maps show a small area such as a town; others show the whole world. Maps usually show areas that are much larger than the page they are printed on, so features are drawn much smaller than they really are. This is called drawing to scale. The bigger the area of a map, the smaller the features have to be drawn. Maps that show a small area and a large amount of detail are called large-scale maps. Maps that show a large area and a small amount of detail are called small-scale maps. On most maps, features are represented by lines, colours and symbols. For example, on a map of a town, black outlines may indicate streets, and coloured shapes may show buildings. On a map of a country, towns may appear as simple black dots, and rivers as blue lines. A book of maps – like the one you are reading now – is called an atlas. An atlas usually contains maps of the whole world as well as maps of countries and continents.

• AMAZING FACT •

In Greek mythology, Atlas was a man who led a rebellion against the gods. As a punishment for this act, he was made to support the world on his shoulders. When the first books of maps were published in the 16th century, many had an illustration of Atlas carrying a globe on their covers. As a result, a book of maps soon became known as an atlas.

MAPPING THE WORLD

Each of these maps shows the location of Riverford School, but each is drawn to a different scale.

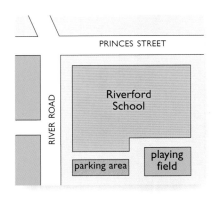

In this map of Riverford School, lines, coloured shapes and labels are used to show the school, nearby streets and other features. Maps of small areas like this are often called street maps.

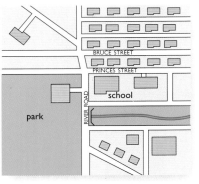

This is a map of Riverford town. Because the area of the map is larger, less detail can be shown. You can now see that the school is near houses, a park and a river, but you can no longer see the school parking area or playing field.

This map shows the region around Riverford. The town is now represented by a simple black dot, so you can no longer see the school or the streets. But you can see that Riverford is near water, and that it is linked to other towns by major and minor roads.

• PROJECT: *Mapping Your Neighbourhood* •

You can draw a map of your neighbourhood. To do this you will have to think about where places are, how far apart they are, and what shape they are. You may need to go for a walk and make a list of the things you want to show on your map.

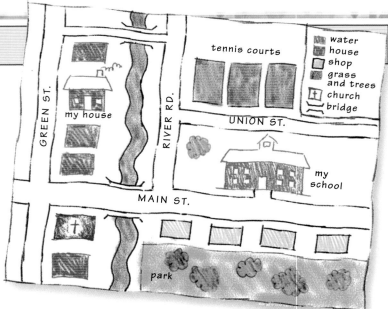

❶ Once you have decided what you are going to include, draw in the streets.

❷ Then add shapes to represent features such as buildings, parks and rivers. Label the streets.

❸ Now colour in your map. Use one colour for houses, one for streets, and so on. Draw a key to show what the colours represent. Finally, add labels for important places such as your home and school.

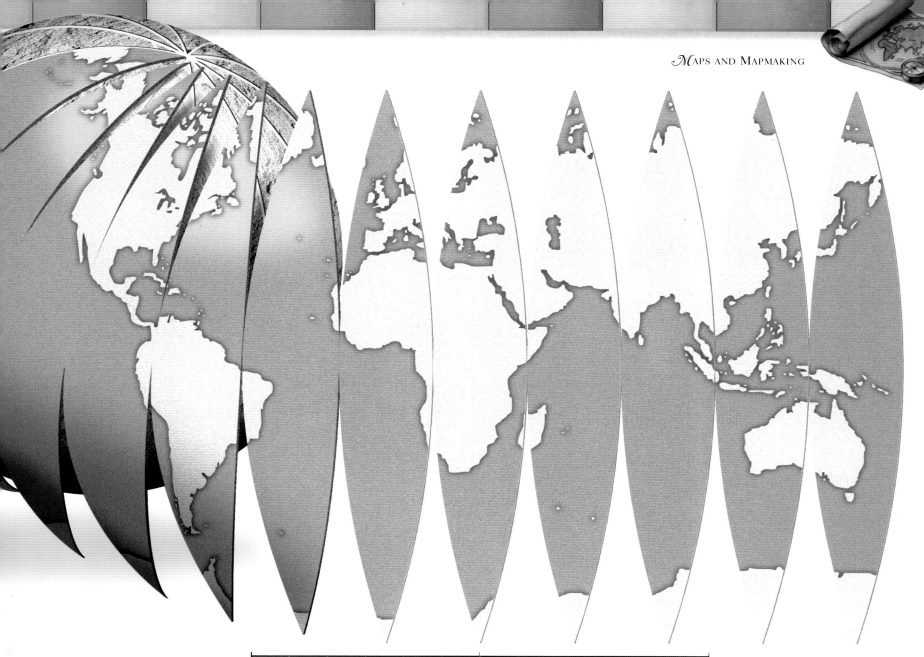

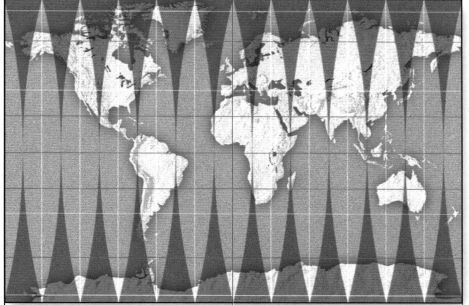

Arctic
Circle
(66.5°N)

Tropic of
Cancer
(23.5°N)

Equator
(0°)

Tropic of
Capricorn
(23.5°S)

Antarctic
Circle
(66.5°S)

180°   Greenwich Meridian (0°)   180°

MAKING MAPS

People who make maps
are known as mapmakers
or cartographers. Before
aeroplanes and spacecraft
were invented, mapmakers
used information supplied
by travellers and explorers to
make maps. Nowadays, most
maps are based on surveys
and on photographs taken
by satellites positioned in
space, high above the Earth.
Mapmakers face one major
problem: the Earth is round,
but most maps have to be
flat. A globe is the most
accurate kind of map because it is the same shape as the Earth.
But if you tried to create a flat map by simply peeling off the
surface of a globe, you would have to divide the peel into pieces,
or segments. You can test this for yourself by carefully peeling an
orange in one piece and trying to flatten out the skin. You will
find that it is impossible to make the peel lie flat without
breaking it. In order to create a flat map, mapmakers have to
stretch and squash the segments of the globe. The different ways
in which they do this are known as projections. There are many
types of projections, and each creates a slightly different map.

A FLAT EARTH

As shown above, the
surface of the globe
can be divided into
segments. To create
a flat, rectangular
map like the one on
the left, mapmakers
must fill in the gaps
between the segments.
To help them do this
and plot locations,
mapmakers use lines
of latitude (horizontal
lines) and longitude
(vertical lines).

LINES AROUND THE WORLD

Mapmakers use a grid system to plot locations on the globe.
Lines of longitude are drawn between the North Pole and
the South Pole and are measured in degrees east or west
of the Greenwich Meridian (0°). Lines of latitude are
drawn in a west-east direction and measured in degrees
north or south of the Equator (0°). The Equator
divides the world into the northern and southern
hemispheres. The Greenwich Meridian and the 180°
line separate the eastern and western hemispheres.

How to Read a Map

MAPS ARE PACKED WITH INFORMATION. Some maps show you where countries are, what size and shape they are, and where they are in relation to other countries. Maps can also tell you about a region's climate, landscape, vegetation, towns and cities, and transport routes. Once you have learnt how to read maps, you can use an atlas to find out many things about countries all around the world.

FINDING PLACES

Most maps and atlases use a gazetteer and a grid system to help you find places. You look for the place name in the gazetteer – an index of place names, which usually appears at the back of the atlas – and then use the grid reference to find the location on the relevant map. Normally, a map grid consists of a series of letters along the top and bottom of the page and a series of numbers down the sides. Take a look at the map of Australia on the right. The grid reference for the city of Melbourne is H8. To find Melbourne, look at the letters on the top or bottom border and find H. Then find 8 on the left- or right-hand border. Imagine a line running down the page between the two Hs and another running across the page between the two 8s. (You can use a ruler to help you line up the numbers.) You will find Melbourne near where these lines would meet.

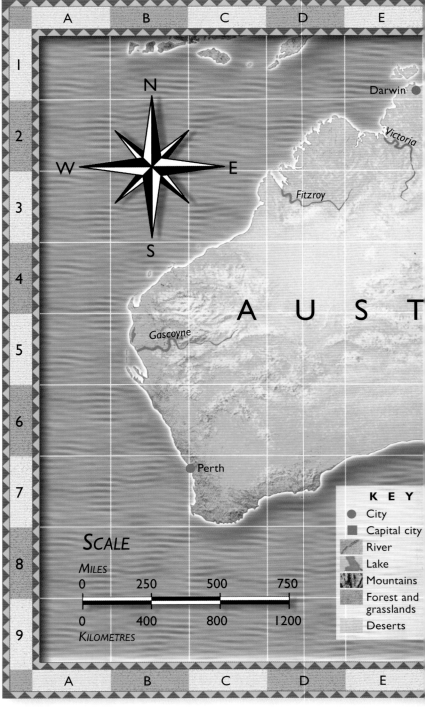

USING THE MAP GRID

In the gazetteer of this book, each place name is followed by a grid reference. The grid reference for the city of Nashville, Tennessee, in the United States is 41 L4. To locate Nashville, turn to page 41 and find L and 4 on the grid. Trace a line down from L and another across from 4. Nashville is near the intersection of the two lines.

DESCRIBING DIRECTION

A map usually has a compass symbol, which indicates the direction of north (N) on the map. Sometimes, as on the map above, it also shows the directions of south (S), east (E) and west (W). You can use the points of a compass to describe where places are. For example, on the map above you can say that Sydney is east (E) of Adelaide and that Brisbane is north (N) of Sydney. Brisbane is both north and east of Adelaide, so we can use a combination of compass points and say that Brisbane is north-east (NE) of Adelaide. But Brisbane is further to the east of Adelaide than it is to the north of it. So, if we want to be even more accurate, we can describe Brisbane as being east-north-east (ENE) of Adelaide. The compass above left shows all the combinations of compass points that you can use to describe direction.

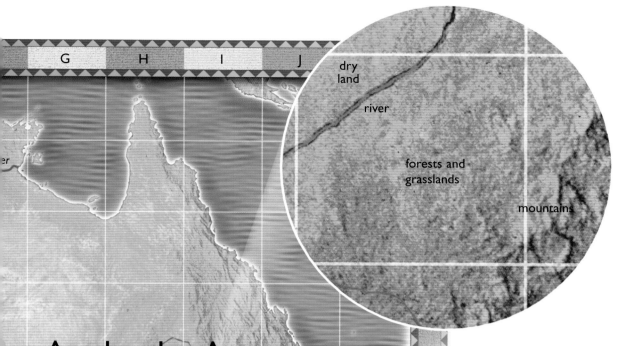

dry
land

river

forests and
grasslands

mountains

COLOUR KEYS
On this map of Australia, dark shading
indicates mountains. Green represents
forests and grasslands, and orange
shows desert and other dry land.
Areas of water such as oceans, lakes
and rivers are all coloured blue.

G   H   I   J

er

A L I A

Lake
Eyre   Cooper Creek

Darling

Lachlan

Adelaide   Murray

Melbourne

Hobart

Brisbane

Sydney

CANBERRA

5

6

7

8

9

G   H   I   J   K

THE LIE OF THE LAND
The colours of a map may tell you something about a
region's landscape, vegetation and climate. Often, shading is
used to show mountain ranges, and colours are used to
represent different kinds of vegetation. Green normally
represents forests or grasslands, while yellow or orange
indicates an area of dry land such as desert. On many maps,
a special symbol, such as a square or star, is used to indicate
a capital city. Most maps and atlases have a key that explains
these features. In this atlas, you will find the key on page 7.

♦ PROJECT: *Using a Scale* ♦

To measure the distance between
Perth and Sydney on the map at
left, follow these steps:

❶ Place the straight edge of a piece
of paper on the map so that it
lines up the dots of the two cities.
Mark their positions on the paper.

❷ Place the paper next to the scale so
that one of the dots lines up with
zero. The scale is shorter than
the distance, so mark the paper
where the scale ends and note
the distance it represents.

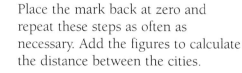

Place the mark back at zero and
repeat these steps as often as
necessary. Add the figures to calculate
the distance between the cities.

You can also use the scale to measure
distances along curved lines.

❶ Place a piece of string on the map
along the Darling River, bending it
to match the course of the river.

❷ Grasp the string at each end of
the river, then straighten it out
and measure it against the scale.
You can then calculate the length
of the river.

MEASURING DISTANCE

Most maps have a scale. This shows how distance on the map
compares with real distance. Many scales appear as a bar that
is divided into sections, as do the ones used in this book. In
the scale shown on the map above, each section on the top
part of the bar is equal to 250 miles, and each section on the
bottom of the bar represents 400 kilometres. The project on
this page shows you how to use this type of scale to measure
distances on a map. Scales can also be written like this:

1:1,000,000

This shows that the map has been reduced 1,000,000 times.
Distances on the ground are therefore 1,000,000 times greater
than they are on the map. Thus 1 centimetre on the map is
equal to 1,000,000 cm, or 10 km, and 1 in on the map is equal
to 1,000,000 in, or 15¾ mi. Other scales are written like this:

1 cm = 10 km

This shows that 1 centimetre on the map corresponds to
10 kilometres in real distance.

N

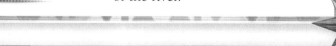

Planet Earth

WE LIVE ON A SMALL PLANET in a tiny part of a vast universe. Our part of the universe is called the Solar System. There are nine planets in the Solar System, and they move around, or orbit, a star that we call the Sun. Enormous groups of stars are known as galaxies. Our galaxy is called the Milky Way and it is made up of at least one billion stars. There are many millions of galaxies in the universe and each one is surrounded by a vast, empty space. The Solar System formed about 5,000 million years ago from a swirling cloud of dust and gases. The hot, central part of the cloud became the Sun, while further out, rocks and gases combined to form the planets. Other rock fragments became asteroids, or minor planets.

❖ AMAZING FACTS ❖

- Our galaxy looks like this. The faint, glowing arms of this galaxy are clouds of stars. Each of these stars is like our Sun and may have its own system of planets.

- Jupiter is bigger than all the other planets, moons, comets and asteroids put together. Yet, it is still only about a hundredth as large as the smallest star.

ROUND AND ROUND

As each planet orbits the Sun, it also spins, or rotates, on its axis – an imaginary line through its centre. Earth rotates once every 24 hours, and takes one year to orbit the Sun. Planets near the Sun orbit more quickly than those further away. Asteroids also orbit the Sun. Most are located between Mars and Jupiter, in an area known as the asteroid belt. The planets and asteroids are all held in their orbits by gravity, a powerful force that pulls them towards the Sun. Without this force, they would fly off into space.

THE PLANETS IN PERSPECTIVE

The illustration below shows the relative distances between the planets, as well as how long each planet takes to orbit the Sun (a year for that planet) and how long it takes to spin on its axis (a day for that planet).

Sun | Mercury Year: 88 Earth days. Day: 59 Earth days.

Venus Year: 225 Earth days. Day: 243 Earth days.

Earth Year: 365.25 days. Day: 24 hours.

Mars Year: 1.9 Earth years. Day: 24.6 hours.

Asteroid Belt

Jupiter Year: 11.9 Earth years. Day: 9.8 hours.

Saturn Year: 29.5 Earth years. Day: 10.2 hours.

Uranus Year: 84 Earth years. Day: 17.9 hours.

◆ PROJECT: *Space Mobile* ◆

You can make your own mobile of the Solar System to hang up in your bedroom or in your classroom at school.

❶ First, collect some paper, coloured pens, string or cotton thread, scissors and a coat-hanger.

❷ Draw the Sun and each of the planets and colour them. Make sure you copy the colours and relative sizes of the planets as shown in the illustrations on these pages.

❸ Carefully cut out each planet using a pair of scissors.

❹ Make a small hole in the top of each planet with the point of a pen or pencil and thread a length of string through the hole.

❺ Tie the Sun and the planets to the bottom of the coat-hanger. Place the Sun in the middle and arrange the planets on either side of it in the order shown in the illustration on these pages. Don't forget that some planets are closer together than others.

❻ When all the planets are in place, the mobile is ready to hang.

WORLD IN MOTION

As Earth turns on its axis, we move in and out of the Sun's light. Day begins as we move into the light. As we turn away from the Sun, night falls. Because Earth is tilted at an angle, the amount of sunlight reaching different parts of the world varies throughout the year. When part of Earth is tilted towards the Sun, it is summer there. When it is tilted away from the Sun, it is winter.

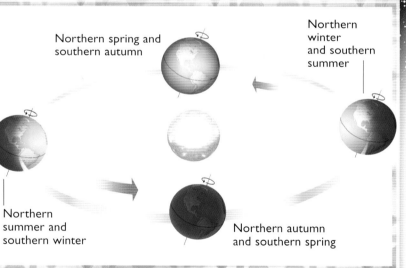

Northern spring and southern autumn

Northern winter and southern summer

Northern summer and southern winter

Northern autumn and southern spring

FIT FOR LIFE

Some planets are surrounded by a layer of gases called an atmosphere. As far as we know, Earth is the only planet in the Solar System with an atmosphere that contains sufficient water and oxygen for life to flourish. Our atmosphere is so thin that if the planet were the size of an apple, the atmosphere would be only as thick as the peel.

Neptune Year: 165 Earth years. Day: 19.2 hours.

Pluto Year: 248 Earth years. Day: 6.4 Earth days.

An Ever-Changing Planet

THE EARTH IS SHAPED like a large ball. Inside are several layers made of different materials. As the Earth formed, heavy minerals such as iron and nickel sank to the centre, while lighter materials rose to the middle and upper levels. At first, the upper levels consisted entirely of hot, liquid rock, but as the Earth cooled, the outside solidified to form a thin, hard crust. This crust broke into several pieces, known as lithospheric plates. These plates float on the liquid, molten rock – or magma – underneath and are constantly moving, although you cannot feel the movement. Energy from the Earth's core creates powerful convection currents that force the plates together and apart. This happens extremely slowly, but over millions of years these movements shape and shift the surface of the Earth, causing earthquakes and volcanic eruptions and forming mountains and islands.

Inner core
Outer core
Lower mantle
Asthenosphere
Lithosphere
Upper mantle
Ocean crust
Continental crust
Convection currents

INSIDE EARTH
Our planet's solid iron inner core is surrounded by an outer core of liquid iron and nickel. Above this is a layer of solid rock called the lower mantle and a wide band of quite soft rock known as the asthenosphere. The Earth's outer layer is called the lithosphere. It consists of the solid rock of the upper mantle, and the crust. Crust under the land (continental crust) is usually thicker than crust under the sea (ocean crust). In the Earth's core, temperatures reach more than 3,000°C (5,400°F). This heat creates strong convection currents that push the crust in different directions.

◆ PROJECTS: *Folding the Crust* ◆

❶ Cut a paper plate in half. These halves represent two of the Earth's lithospheric plates.

❷ Using sticky tape, attach a sheet of paper to the plate halves. The paper represents the Earth's crust.

❸ If you slide one half of the plate under the other, the paper buckles. Similarly, when two of the Earth's plates collide, their crusts fold, forming mountains.

❶ Take a sheet of paper, fold it in half and continue to fold it.

❷ After six folds, it becomes difficult to fold the paper any further. In the same way, the thicker the Earth's crust, the greater the force required to fold it.

Spreading plates

Hot-spot volcanoes

Coastal collisions

Coastal Collisions
When thin, dense ocean crust meets thick continental crust, the thin crust slides under the thicker crust. Magma rises to the surface and forms a line of volcanoes. This process formed Mount St. Helens in the U.S.A.

Hot-Spot Volcanoes
Weaknesses in the middle of plates, known as hot spots, allow magma from the asthenosphere to burst through the crust and form volcanoes. The Hawaiian Islands were created by hot-spot volcanoes.

Spreading Plates
Circulating magma may force plates apart. Where the plates separate, magma rises through the gap, then cools and hardens to form a ridge. Normally this happens under the sea, but it happens on land in Iceland.

WORLD IN MOTION
Convection currents cause the Earth's plates to collide, separate and slide past each other. The effects of these movements are shown in the illustration above and in the photographs on the right.

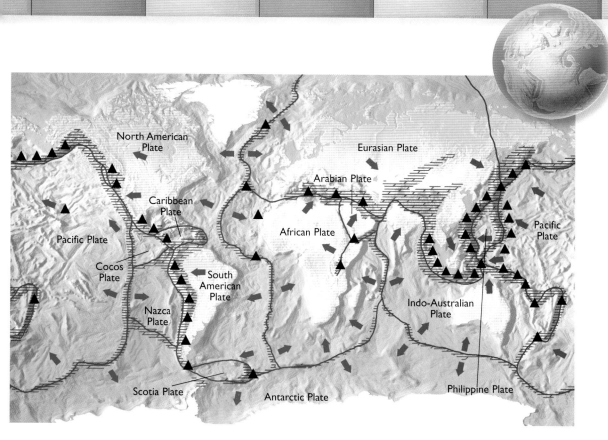

200 million years ago

90 million years ago

Present

60 million years from now

ON THE MOVE

Over millions of years, plate movements have joined and divided the Earth's land masses. Two hundred million years ago, there was a single 'super continent'. It split into two land masses, which then broke up to form the continents we know today. Further changes to these land masses will occur as the Earth's plates continue to drift.

PLATE MOVEMENTS

The Earth's plates fit together like the pieces of a jigsaw puzzle, but the plates are constantly moving. This map shows the direction in which each plate moves. Most volcanoes and earthquakes occur where plates meet. This means that countries in the centre of plates, such as Australia, have few earthquakes and volcanoes, whereas countries at the edges of plates, such as Japan, have many.

 Direction of movement

 Volcanoes

 Earthquake zones

◆ AMAZING FACTS ◆

- When the island volcano of Krakatoa in Indonesia erupted on August 27, 1883, the explosion was heard up to 4,800 kilometres (3,000 mi) away!

- More than 500,000 earthquakes occur every year. Fortunately, most of these are too weak to cause any damage.

Sliding plates

Folding crust

Undersea collisions

Sliding Plates

A fault line forms where two plates slide past each other. The friction between the plates creates earthquakes. These occur regularly along the San Andreas fault in California, U.S.A., as part of the coastline slides northward.

Folding Crust

When two plates with crusts of similar thickness collide, the edge of one plate slides under the other, and the crusts buckle and fold to form mountains. This process created the massive Himalayas mountain range in Asia.

Undersea Collisions

When two plates with ocean crust collide, one may sink beneath the other, forming a deep trench. In places, magma bursts through the crust to form volcanic islands. The islands of Japan formed in this way.

◆ LOOK AGAIN ◆

- What is the Earth's inner core made of?

- What kind of volcanoes formed the Hawaiian Islands?

- Where are earthquakes most likely to occur?

Weather and Climate

OUR WEATHER MAY CHANGE from day to day, but we usually experience the same kind of weather from year to year. The pattern of weather that occurs in a region over a long period is known as the climate. The climate of an area depends on three main factors: how far north or south of the Equator it is (its latitude), how high it is (its altitude), and how close it is to the sea. As a result of the Earth's orbit and its round shape, sunlight warms areas near the Equator more than areas near the poles. Tropical regions are therefore hot all year round, and the poles are always cold. Areas between the tropics and the poles are temperate. This means that they have warm summers and cool winters. Mountains are colder than lowland areas because as you climb higher the atmosphere becomes thinner and retains less heat. In coastal regions, sea breezes and ocean currents also affect the climate. Usually they prevent the weather from becoming too hot or too cold. Where winds blow inland from the sea, they are usually moist and bring high rainfall.

WIND PATTERNS

Because hot air rises and cold air sinks, the Sun's uneven heating of the Earth's surface causes air to circulate as shown in the large diagram below. These patterns of air circulation are deflected by the planet's rotation, and form the major wind systems shown on the globe below right. These winds carry warm or cold, moist or dry air, and are an important influence on the Earth's climates.

Air Circulation

Warm and cold air meet, creating a belt of stormy, wet weather.

Cold easterly winds blow from the poles.

60°N

Air flows poleward from the south-west

30°N

Air flows toward the Equator from the north-east

Equator

WORLD CLIMATES

The world can be divided into eight major climate zones, which are shown on this map and described on these pages. Ocean currents influence many of these climates. For example, north-western Europe has a mild climate as a result of the warm waters of the Gulf Stream.

warm currents   cool currents

Mountain

Mountains are normally colder, wetter and windier than neighbouring regions that lie nearer sea level.

Polar

The polar regions are extremely cold for most of the year. Although snow falls regularly, the poles are relatively dry.

Upper air cools and sinks, creating dry conditions.

Warm, moist air rises at the Equator, clouds form and rain falls.

Cold Temperate

These regions have long, bitterly cold and snowy winters. Their summers are usually mild and damp.

Wind Systems

Polar easterlies ———

Westerlies ———

Trade winds ———

Westerlies ———

Polar easterlies ———

Wet Temperate
Wet temperate regions have four distinct seasons, with cool, wet winters and warm, wet summers.

Dry Temperate
Rainfall is relatively low in these regions. Most areas have mild, wet winters and hot, dry summers.

Desert and Semi-desert
These are dry, barren areas with very low rainfall. They are usually hot by day, but may be cold, or even frosty, at night.

Subtropical
In summer, these regions are hot and wet like tropical areas. In winter, they are dry and mild like deserts.

Tropical
The tropics are hot and wet. In some areas, it rains all year round. In others, most of the rain falls in summer.

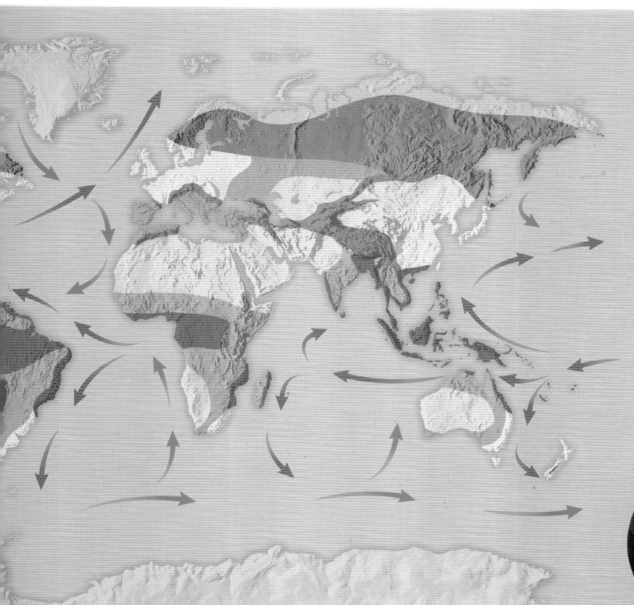

◆AMAZING FACT◆

Thunderstorms are most common in tropical areas, but occur all over the world. At least 20,000 storms occur each day, and at any one time about 2,000 may be taking place. Lightning from these storms strikes the ground as frequently as 100 times every second.

ENERGY FROM THE SUN
Because the Earth is shaped like a ball, the Sun strikes it more directly near the Equator than at the poles. This is why tropical areas are hot and the polar regions are cold.

◆PROJECT: Why the Poles Are Colder Than the Equator◆

❶ In a dark room, shine a torch a few centimetres above, and at right angles to, a flat surface such as a tabletop. Observe the shape and brightness of the patch of light.

❷ Tilt the torch and note how the light changes. When the light strikes the surface from directly overhead, the patch of light is small and intense. When the light strikes the table at an angle, the patch is larger and weaker.

In a similar way, sunlight is most intense at the Equator, where it strikes the ground from directly overhead. At the poles, the light strikes the Earth at an angle and is spread across a wider area, making it much weaker.

The Living World

ALMOST EVERY PART OF OUR PLANET is inhabited by an amazing variety of living things. So far, scientists have named about two million kinds, or species, of plants and animals, but there may be between 10 and 100 million species on Earth! All living things inhabit the biosphere, which is made up of the land, oceans and atmosphere. Within the biosphere, there are many kinds of environment. Over millions of years, plants and animals have gradually altered their bodies and behaviour to suit particular environments. This process is known as adaptation. Together, an environment and its inhabitants are known as an ecosystem. The living things in an ecosystem depend on each other for food and other resources. For example, vegetation provides food for plant-eating animals (herbivores) which may in turn be eaten by meat-eating animals (carnivores). These close relationships mean that damage to one part of an ecosystem is likely to affect every other part of it.

GLOBAL ECOSYSTEMS
Each of the Earth's environments has its own community of plants and animals. This illustration shows how ecosystems change between the tropical rainforests (far left) and the polar ice-caps (far right).

Oceans
The oceans contain a huge variety of species that have adapted to life under water. Marine plants include many kinds of seaweed. Animals include sea mammals such as seals and whales, coral, and thousands of fish species.

Tropical Rainforests
The hot, humid weather of the tropics creates dense forests that are home to more species than any other environment. Monkeys and birds live high in the trees, while jaguars and other mammals prowl the forest floor.

Subtropical Savannahs
With rain falling only in summer, subtropical areas have few trees. The African savannah grasslands support herds of herbivores such as zebras, which are hunted by lions and other carnivores. Vultures and other scavengers eat the leftovers.

Deserts and Semi-deserts
Desert species have adapted to drought. Some plants, such as cacti, store water in their stems. Others have long roots that reach water far underground. In hot deserts, many animals come out only at night, when it is cooler.

WORLD ENVIRONMENTS

Because the weather determines the types of plants that grow, the Earth's environments are closely related to its climate zones.

- Tropical rainforests
- Subtropical savannahs
- Deserts and semi-deserts
- Temperate grasslands and shrub woodlands
- Temperate forests
- Coniferous forests
- Mountains
- Polar ice-caps and tundra

♦ AMAZING FACT ♦

The world's largest flower, the rafflesia, is found in the rainforests of South-east Asia. It can measure up to one metre (3 ft) in diameter. It gives off a smell like rotting flesh which attracts insects.

Mountains

The higher the land, the less vegetation there is and the colder and windier it gets. Thick fur coats keep many mountain animals warm. Some species, such as mountain goats, have special hooves that help them climb rocky slopes.

Polar Ice-caps and Tundra

The ice-caps are bitterly cold and offer little shelter. Some animals have fur and a thick layer of fat to keep them warm. Tundra is treeless land that surrounds the Arctic ice-cap. Its low shrubs feed hares, lemmings and other herbivores.

Temperate Grasslands and Shrub Woodlands

Moderate rainfall creates grasslands and shrub woodlands. Grasslands attract herbivores such as bison and are ideal hunting grounds for birds of prey. There is little shelter, so some animals live in burrows.

Temperate Forests

Trees grow well in wet temperate regions. In areas with cold winters, most of the trees are deciduous, which means that they shed their leaves in autumn. Some animals migrate in winter; others survive on food stored during summer.

Coniferous Forests

Cold temperate regions are covered by forests of evergreen trees called conifers. Shaped so that snow slides off them, these trees are well adapted to the cold winters. Many animals have thick fur, and some hibernate during winter.

♦ LOOK AGAIN ♦

- Name a plant-eating animal that lives on the African savannah.
- Which plants store water in their stems?
- How have animals adapted to mountain environments?

Our Natural Resources

THE EARTH PROVIDES US with everything that we need to live. Its atmosphere, rivers and lakes supply fresh water which, with sunshine and soil, enables plants to grow. In turn, plants produce vital supplies of oxygen and provide us and other animals with food. Animals supply humans with meat, wool and dairy products. Plants also provide timber, fuel and textiles such as cotton. All these resources – water, plants, crops, animals – are renewable. This means that if we manage them carefully they will never run out. Other resources are non-renewable. They do not regrow or replenish themselves and will eventually be used up. They include minerals, precious stones and fossil fuels. Minerals – such as clay, chalk and many metals – and precious stones – such as diamonds and emeralds – have a wide range of uses, particularly in industry. Coal, oil and gas supply most of the energy we need for lighting and heating our homes and for fuelling our cars. They are known as fossil fuels because they are the remains of animals and plants buried deep underground millions of years ago. Some of these non-renewable resources may run out within the next 50 years. Because of this, and because burning fossil fuels creates pollution, scientists are trying to find ways of using renewable resources (Sun, wind and sea) to supply some energy.

ENERGY SUPPLIES

The illustration below shows our principal sources of energy. As the chart on the right indicates, coal, oil and gas still supply most of our fuel. But alternative energy supplies such as wind and solar power are being developed in many parts of the world. As reserves of fossil fuels run out, these sources will become increasingly important.

Energy Use

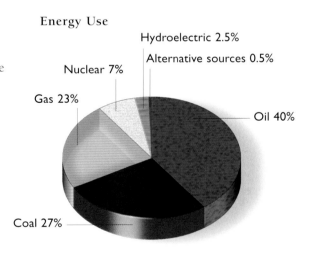

Hydroelectric 2.5%

Alternative sources 0.5%

Nuclear 7%

Gas 23%

Oil 40%

Coal 27%

THE EARTH'S RESOURCES

The map above shows how land is used in different parts of the world, and where major fuel reserves are located.

- Major gas field
- Major coal field
- Major oil field

- Urban areas: towns, cities and industries

- Areas with large farms where people grow crops and raise animals for sale

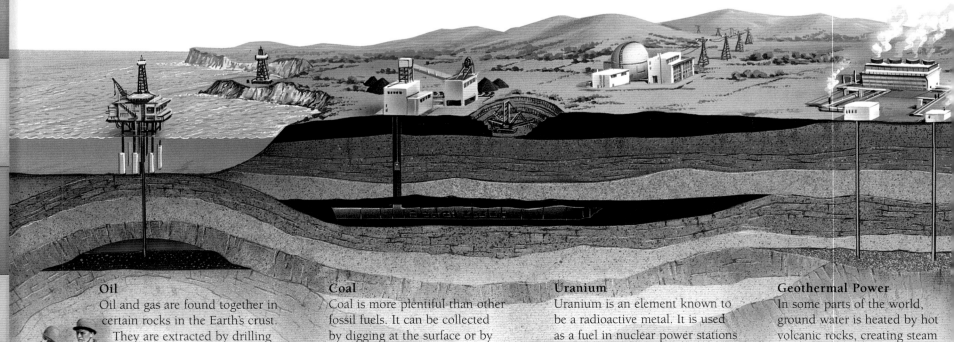

Oil
Oil and gas are found together in certain rocks in the Earth's crust. They are extracted by drilling from sea or land rigs.

Coal
Coal is more plentiful than other fossil fuels. It can be collected by digging at the surface or by mining deep underground.

Uranium
Uranium is an element known to be a radioactive metal. It is used as a fuel in nuclear power stations to produce electricity.

Geothermal Power
In some parts of the world, ground water is heated by hot volcanic rocks, creating steam that is used to generate power.

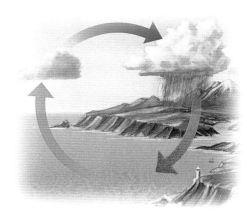

THE WATER CYCLE

A process known as the water cycle provides us with a regular supply of fresh water. Water in oceans, lakes and rivers is constantly evaporating into the air, where it exists as water vapour. The warmer the air, the more water vapour it can hold. When air cools, its ability to hold water decreases, and some of the water vapour turns, or condenses, into tiny water droplets or ice crystals. These droplets or crystals form clouds. If the droplets or crystals combine and become heavy enough, they fall as rain or snow. Water that falls on land drains into rivers, lakes and underground channels. It then flows into the sea, replenishing the oceans and completing the water cycle.

Areas with small farms where people grow crops and raise animals mainly for their own use

Grassland areas used for grazing large numbers of animals

Deserts, dry grasslands and tundra used for grazing small numbers of animals

Forested areas with some farming, hunting and mining

Areas that are too cold or dry for farming, but include some mining and hunting

Major fishing grounds

◆ PROJECT: *Create a Water Cycle* ◆

This simple experiment will show you how the water cycle works.

❶ Cool a long, metal spoon or ladle by placing it in a freezer for a few minutes. Choose a spoon with a wooden handle.

❷ Ask an adult to help you boil some water in a kettle or saucepan.

❸ As the water boils, the warm air above the water rises. As it starts to cool, it condenses and forms clouds of steam.

❹ Hold the cold spoon over the steam, being careful not to burn yourself. The cooling effect of the cold metal causes the water vapour to condense more quickly and form droplets of water on the underside of the spoon.

❺ The droplets grow in size until they become heavy enough to fall, just like rain. Some of the droplets may fall back into the kettle or saucepan, replenishing the water supply.

Hydroelectric Power
Hydroelectric power is created when water is passed through electricity-generating turbines at the bottom of a dam.

Wind Power
Windmills convert the power of the wind into electricity. The wind turns the windmills, which drive electrical generators.

Solar Power
Clusters of mirror-like solar panels reflect the Sun's rays on to a solar furnace, where the intense heat is converted into electricity.

Sea Power
At a tidal dam or barrage, waves pass through narrow tunnels, driving huge turbines that produce power.

The Human Family

OUR PLANET IS HOME to about 6 billion people. This population is not spread evenly over Earth's land masses. Instead, people are concentrated where resources are plentiful, or can be easily obtained by trade. Therefore, few people live in deserts or polar regions, but many live in fertile areas, close to energy sources, and near rivers and coasts. The world's population is now growing more quickly than ever before. In the time it takes you to read this sentence, more than 20 babies will have been born. Since 1950 the number of people on the Earth has more than doubled. This growth is the result of a longer life expectancy due to improved medical services, and a high birth rate in some parts of the world. The most rapid population growth occurs in developing countries – poorer countries with little industry or technology. It is difficult for these countries to feed and take care of their growing populations, so many of them are urging their people to have fewer children.

NATIONAL POPULATIONS
This diagram shows the 10 countries with the world's largest populations. China has by far the biggest population – in fact, one in every five people in the world lives in China!

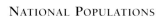

China	India	U.S.A.	Indonesia	Brazil	Russia	Pakistan	Bangladesh	Japan	Nigeria
1.25 billion	1 billion	274 million	216 million	172 million	146 million	138 million	127 million	126 million	114 million

WHERE PEOPLE LIVE
The dots on this map show the world's most densely populated areas.

 Developed countries
Developing countries

CROWDED COUNTRIES
Some countries are densely populated – a large population lives in a small area. Others are sparsely populated – a small population occupies a large area.

The Netherlands:
400 people per square kilometre
(1,000 per sq. mi)

Australia:
2 people per square kilometre
(6 per sq. mi)

GROWING CITIES
As countries develop, people move to cities to look for work in factories and businesses. This comparison of the populations of Paris, France, and Jakarta, Indonesia, shows these cities in developing countries are now growing more rapidly than those in developed countries.

Paris   Jakarta

1970		1990		2010	
8.5 million	3.9 million	9.3 million	9.3 million	9.6 million	19.2 million

Population Growth

Every four days, one million children are born. If the world's population continues to grow at this rate, it will have reached 10 billion by the year 2100. The populations of developing countries are expanding rapidly while those of developed countries are growing slowly or decreasing.

🌐 Developing countries

🌐 Developed countries

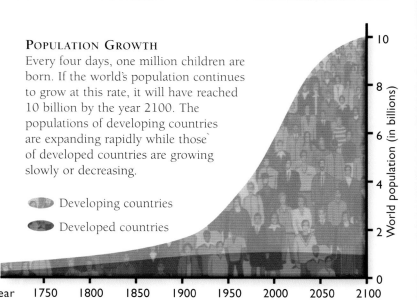

Year 1750 1800 1850 1900 1950 2000 2050 2100

Rich and Poor

Countries with large industries and high levels of technology are described as developed countries. People in these parts of the world are generally wealthy and have many possessions. In countries with little industry and technology, people are poorer and have few possessions. These countries are described as developing countries. Although they are home to far fewer people, developed countries are much richer and use a much larger proportion of the world's resources than developing countries. This map divides the countries into developed and developing countries.

Developed countries:
make up 20% of the world's population
own 80% of the world's wealth
use 70% of the world's energy

Developing countries:
make up 80% of the world's population
own 20% of the world's wealth
use 30% of the world's energy

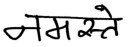

A Shrinking World

IN 1850, THE JOURNEY BETWEEN London and New York took about three weeks. Now the same distance can be travelled in just over three hours. This dramatic difference has altered our view of the world. Countries now seem closer together than ever before – the world seems to be shrinking! Faster means of transportation, along with recently developed technologies, have greatly increased international trade and communication. Aeroplanes can carry goods to the other side of the world within a day. Fresh foods, such as meat, fruit and vegetables, which would previously have spoiled before they reached their destinations, can now be transported over long distances in refrigerated container ships. Modern telecommunications – telephone, fax and electronic mail services – allow businesses to deal directly with customers anywhere in the world. Telecommunications also enable us to increase our understanding of other places and peoples. We can watch television programmes about other countries, speak to people on the other side of the world by telephone, and make friends on computer networks such as the Internet.

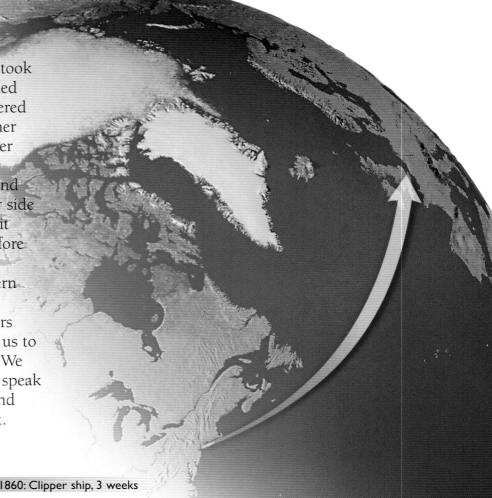

1860: Clipper ship, 3 weeks

1910: *Mauretania* steamship, 5 days

1939: Boeing 314 Clipper seaplane, 24 hours

Today: Concorde supersonic jet, 3½ hours

TRANSATLANTIC TRANSPORTATION

In the mid-19th century, a clipper ship was the fastest means of transportation between New York and London. The exact length of the journey depended on the weather, but the trip usually took about three weeks. By 1910, the steamship *Mauretania* had cut the Atlantic crossing to five days. In 1939, the Boeing 314 Clipper seaplane provided the first passenger aircraft service across the Atlantic, with a flight time of about 24 hours. Today, the Concorde supersonic jet can complete the same trip in three and a half hours.

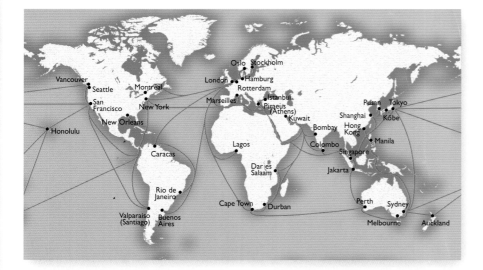

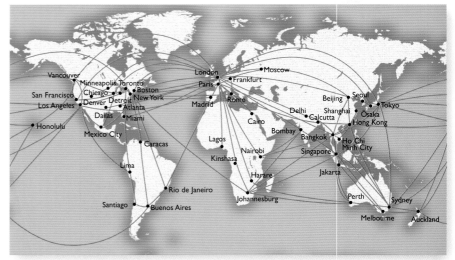

SEA ROUTES

Today, few people travel by sea, but goods of all kinds are transported by container ships and tankers. This map shows the world's most important shipping routes and busiest ports. Rotterdam in the Netherlands handles more cargo than any other seaport.

AIR ROUTES

Flying is now the most popular form of international travel. This map shows the busiest international air routes and airports. Heathrow in London handles more international flights than any other airport, but Chicago's O'Hare Airport is the world's busiest, with more than 2,000 planes landing and taking off each day.

INTERNATIONAL TRADE

The countries of the world exchange a wide variety of goods. Countries that have more raw materials and produce more food and goods than they need export some of those materials to countries that have few resources. Other countries export little because they need all their own resources. In the diagram below, the arrows indicate the direction of trade in three categories of goods: food, raw materials (including minerals, fuels and timber), and manufactured goods (goods that are made in factories, such as cars and electrical equipment). The illustrations show the most important products in each region.

• LOOK AGAIN •

- If it is midday in England, what is the time in eastern Australia?
- Which is New Zealand's busiest port?
- What kinds of manufactured goods does Japan export?

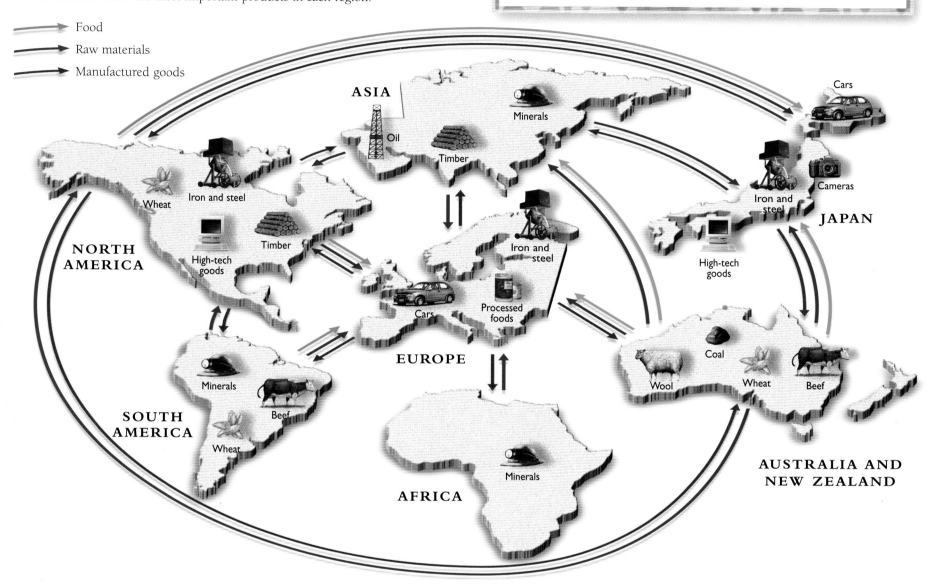

Food

Raw materials

Manufactured goods

ASIA

Oil

Minerals

Timber

Iron and steel

Timber

High-tech goods

NORTH AMERICA

Wheat

Iron and steel

Cars

Processed foods

EUROPE

Minerals

Beef

SOUTH AMERICA

Wheat

AFRICA

Minerals

Cars

Cameras

Iron and steel

JAPAN

High-tech goods

Wool

Coal

Wheat

Beef

AUSTRALIA AND NEW ZEALAND

TIME ZONES

The world is divided into 24 time zones, and time is measured in hours ahead of or behind the time in Greenwich, England. The time is the same throughout each zone and is usually one hour ahead of or behind the neighbouring time zones. The International Date Line marks where one day ends, and another begins.

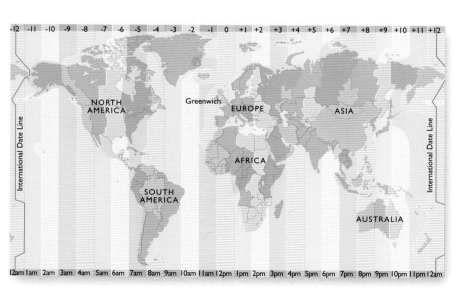

A VIRTUAL WORLD

Computers are changing the ways in which we work, relax and communicate. You can now send electronic mail (e-mail) and other digital information from one computer to another almost anywhere in the world. You can also read magazines, hear music and even shop using information networks such as the Internet. Some networks allow you to speak directly to other people and even see them on your computer screen. This is called video conferencing. In the future, more and more people are likely to use computers for shopping, entertainment and business.

25

Planet in Peril

THE FUTURE OF OUR PLANET is at risk, now more than ever before. In the last 200 years, rapid population growth and the development of industry and technology have magnified the effect of our activities on the environment. Supplies of fossil fuels and other non-renewable resources are running out. We are over-using the soil, forests and fishing grounds, and no longer giving these renewable resources a chance to recover. Waste from our homes and industries is poisoning water supplies, and gases from our cars and factories are polluting the air we breathe. Increasing air pollution may even be changing the climate. Scientists all over the world are trying to find ways to preserve resources and limit the damage we are doing to the Earth. Through simple activities such as recycling, using our cars less and buying environmentally friendly products, we can all play a part in protecting the Earth and preserving its resources for future generations.

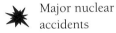

◆ AMAZING FACTS ◆

- A hectare (2.47 acres) of Brazilian rainforest is destroyed every 20 seconds.
- Every day, more than 50 species become extinct. This is mainly the result of human activities such as forestry and hunting.

A Global Crisis
This map shows that environmental problems affect almost every part of the Earth. The most serious problems are described and illustrated on these pages.

- Existing deserts
- Areas at risk of becoming deserts
- Existing rainforest
- Cleared rainforest
- Cities with severe air pollution
- Areas affected by acid rain
- Polluted waterways
- Heavy oil slicks created by shipping
- Light oil slicks created by shipping
- Major nuclear accidents
- Major oil tanker disasters
- Major oil rig explosions

Holding Back the Desert
In dry parts of the world, overgrazing and clearing the land of its natural vegetation can turn fertile areas into desert. To keep deserts from spreading further, we need to manage better the land we farm and replant trees and shrubs.

Saving the Forests
Vast areas of natural forest are being cleared to supply timber, fuel and paper, and to make way for towns and farms. You can help protect the world's forests and reduce the need for more wood by recycling paper. Replanting trees also helps.

Reducing Air Pollution
Cars and factories fill the air with grime and poisonous gases. Industries and car manufacturers are trying to reduce such pollution. You can also help by walking, cycling or using public transport instead of travelling by car.

Oil Spills
Oil and other pollutants spilled by ships are a threat to wildlife. In 1989, oil spilt by the tanker *Exxon Valdez* off the coast of Alaska, in the United States, killed thousands of animals, including 350,000 seabirds.

Nuclear Accidents
Nuclear accidents occur rarely but can be devastating. In 1986, an accident at the Chernobyl nuclear power plant in the Ukraine released a cloud of radioactive gas across Europe, poisoning land, crops and people.

Oil Well Explosions
Accidents on oil and gas rigs can cause major environmental problems. During the Gulf War in Kuwait in 1992, hundreds of oil wells were set on fire, causing serious water and air pollution throughout the region.

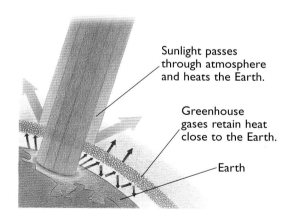

Sunlight passes through atmosphere and heats the Earth.

Greenhouse gases retain heat close to the Earth.

Earth

Eliminating Acid Rain
Air pollution can turn rain into a strong acid. Acid rain kills trees, pollutes rivers and even damages buildings. The only way to stop acid rain is to reduce air pollution.

Saving the Ozone Layer
A layer of ozone in the upper atmosphere filters out harmful radiation from the Sun. This layer is being damaged by chloro-fluorocarbons (CFCs) – chemicals found in some aerosols and refrigerators. Always buy CFC-free products.

Keeping Our Water Clean
The world's rivers and oceans are being poisoned by waste from factories and shipping, and sewage from homes and offices. To help protect water supplies, support local clean-up programmes, and never dispose of rubbish in or near waterways.

GLOBAL WARMING
Gases in the atmosphere, known as greenhouse gases, keep the Earth warm by trapping some of the energy that comes from the Sun. But the burning of fossil fuels is raising the levels of these gases, causing the planet to warm up too much. If this continues, some fertile land may turn into desert, and ice-caps may melt, causing flooding in lowland areas. Most countries are trying to reduce greenhouse gas emissions.

• LOOK AGAIN •

- How can we prevent acid rain?
- Which gases keep the Earth warm?
- How can you help protect the ozone layer?

The Physical World

WE CALL OUR PLANET EARTH, but more than two-thirds of its surface is covered by salt water. Large areas of salt water are called oceans, and smaller areas are known as seas. There are four oceans – the Pacific, Atlantic, Indian and Arctic – and many seas. The Pacific Ocean alone is larger than all of Earth's land masses combined. Land covers only 29 per cent of our planet's surface. Its shape and the kind of soil and vegetation that cover it vary enormously from place to place. Throughout the world there are hills, mountains and areas of flat land called plains. Trees and other plants cover many parts of the Earth, but some places have almost no vegetation. Deserts – very dry areas with sparse vegetation – cover about one-fifth of the world's land. The polar regions and many mountain tops are covered in ice and snow. The seas, too, have their mountains and valleys. Deep trenches are found in most oceans, and mountains on many islands are actually the tops of undersea mountains. For instance, Mauna Kea, on the island of Hawaii in the Pacific Ocean, is 10,205 metres (33,480 ft) high, measured from the sea floor to its highest point. That's far taller than Mount Everest, the highest mountain on land.

PHYSICAL FACTS

Circumference of Earth around the Equator:
40,067 km (24,902 mi)
Area of sea: 362,033,000 sq. km
(139,782,000 sq. mi)
Area of land above sea level: 148,021,000 sq. km
(57,151,000 sq. mi)
Largest ocean: Pacific Ocean, 166,241,700 sq. km
(64,186,300 sq. mi)
Largest land mass: Eurasia (Europe and Asia),
53,698,000 sq. km (20,733,000 sq. mi)
Deepest ocean trench: Mariana Trench, Pacific
Ocean, 10,911 m (35,797 ft)
Largest island: Greenland, 2,175,000 sq. km
(840,000 sq. mi)

◆ AMAZING FACT ◆

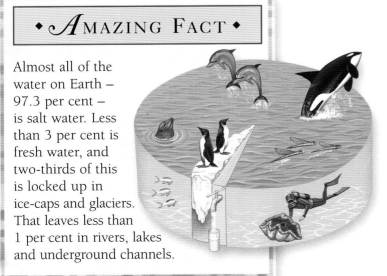

Almost all of the water on Earth – 97.3 per cent – is salt water. Less than 3 per cent is fresh water, and two-thirds of this is locked up in ice-caps and glaciers. That leaves less than 1 per cent in rivers, lakes and underground channels.

ARCTIC OCEAN

Spitsbergen
SVALBARD
FRANZ JOSEF LAND
NOVAYA ZEMLYA
SEVERNAYA ZEMLYA
Laptev Sea
NEW SIBERIAN ISLANDS
East Siberian Sea
Chukchi Sea

Greenland Sea
Barents Sea
Kara Sea
CENTRAL SIBERIAN PLATEAU

Jan Mayen Island
SCANDINAVIA
Dvina
Yenisey
Lena
Bering Strait

Iceland
Norwegian Sea
WESTERN SIBERIAN PLAIN
Bering Sea

FAEROE ISLANDS
North Sea
Ob'
Ob'
SIBERIA
ALEUTIAN ISLANDS
ALEUTIAN TRENCH

RIDGE
Ireland
BRITISH ISLES
EUROPEAN PLAIN
Volga
URAL MOUNTAINS
Irtysh
Yenisey
Angara
EUROPE
ASIA
Lake Baikal
Amur
Sea of Okhotsk

CHANNEL ISLANDS
CARPATHIAN MTS.
Dnieper
KIRGIZ STEPPE
Lake Balkhash
GOBI DESERT
KURIL ISLANDS
KURIL TRENCH

AZORES
ALPS
Danube
Caspian Sea
Aral Sea
TIAN SHAN
Sea of Japan
Hokkaidō
NORTH-WEST PACIFIC BASIN

MADEIRA
Black Sea
KUNLUN MTS.
Huang (Yellow)
Honshū
PACIFIC

ATLAS MTS.
Mediterranean Sea
Tigris
ZAGROS MTS.
HINDU KUSH
PLATEAU OF TIBET
Chang (Yangtze)
East China Sea
MIDWAY ISLANDS
OCEAN

CANARY ISLANDS
Euphrates
HIMALAYAS
Taiwan
Wake Island

VERDE LANDS
SAHARA DESERT
NUBIAN DESERT
Red Sea
ARABIAN PENINSULA
Arabian Sea
DECCAN
Ganges
Bay of Bengal
Mekong
Luzon
PHILIPPINE BASIN
MARIANA ISLANDS
MARIANA TRENCH
MID-PACIFIC MOUNTAINS
Johnston Atoll

Nile
SAHEL
Niger
AFRICA
LACCADIVE ISLANDS
ANDAMAN ISLANDS
South China Sea
Philippine Sea
Guam
PHILIPPINE TRENCH
PHILIPPINE ISLANDS
MICRONESIA
MARSHALL ISLANDS
CENTRAL PACIFIC BASIN

Gulf of Guinea
Uele
Congo
MALDIVES
Sri Lanka
NICOBAR ISLANDS
Palau
CAROLINE ISLANDS

Ascension
Ubangi
CONGO BASIN
Kasai
GREAT RIFT VALLEY
Lake Victoria
SEYCHELLES
MID-INDIAN RIDGE
Sumatra
Borneo
MELANESIA
Nauru
OCEANIA
GILBERT ISLANDS

St. Helena
Zambezi
COMOROS ISLANDS
MID-INDIAN BASIN
NINETY-EAST RIDGE
SUNDA ISLANDS
Java
New Guinea
SOLOMON ISLANDS
Tuvalu
Tokelau

MARTIN VAZ ISLANDS
NAMIB DESERT
Mayote
Madagascar
Mauritius
INDIAN
Christmas Island
JAVA TRENCH
Coral Sea
Vanuatu
SAMOA ISLANDS

MID-ATLANTIC RIDGE
KALAHARI DESERT
Orange
Réunion
OCEAN
COCOS (KEELING) ISLANDS
WHARTON BASIN
GREAT SANDY DESERT
SIMPSON DESERT
New Caledonia
FIJI ISLANDS
Niue
Tonga

Tristan da Cunha
WALVIS RIDGE
CAPE OF GOOD HOPE
AUSTRALIA
GREAT DIVIDING RANGE
Norfolk Island
KERMADEC ISLANDS

Gough Island
GREAT VICTORIAN DESERT
Lake Eyre
Darling
NEW ZEALAND
KERMADEC TRENCH
TONGA TRENCH

Amsterdam Island
SOUTH-WEST INDIAN RIDGE
SOUTH-EAST INDIAN RIDGE
Great Australian Bight
Murray
Tasman Sea
North Island

St. Paul Island
CROZET ISLANDS
Tasmania
South Island
CHATHAM ISLANDS

ATLANTIC-INDIAN RIDGE
PRINCE EDWARD ISLANDS
KERGUÉLEN ISLANDS
RIDGE

Bouvet Island
ATLANTIC-INDIAN BASIN
HEARD AND McDONALD ISLANDS
Macquarie Island
AUCKLAND ISLANDS

SOUTH SANDWICH ISLANDS
SOUTH INDIAN BASIN

ANTARCTICA
Ross Sea

Countries of the World

APART FROM ANTARCTICA, which has no permanent population, all the land on Earth is divided into countries. There are almost 200 countries in the world, and each country has its own government and its own laws. The world's smallest country, the Vatican City, measures about one-half of a square kilometre (0.17 sq. mi). That's about the size of 100 football fields. The largest country in the world, Russia, is 39 million times bigger! The lines that separate countries are called borders. On this world map, the countries are shown in different colours so that you can see the borders clearly. Borders may be straight or curved. Some are formed by rivers or mountain ranges; others cross lakes or seas. The sizes of countries and the shapes of their borders often change. Sometimes a large country divides into smaller countries because groups of people want to form separate countries. Neighbouring countries often disagree about where a border ought to be. Such disputes have led to wars in many parts of the world. In this atlas, disputed borders are shown by a dotted line. Many countries govern areas of land in other parts of the world. These are called territories. On a map, the name of the governing country usually appears in brackets after the name of the territory.

POLITICAL FACTS

Number of countries: around 193
Largest countries:
Russia, 17,075,383 sq. km (6,592,812 sq. mi)
Canada, 9,976,185 sq. km (3,851,809 sq. mi)
China, 9,583,000 sq. km (3,700,000 sq. mi)
Smallest country: Vatican City, 0.44 sq. km (0.17 sq. mi)
Longest border: U.S.-Canada, 6,416 km (3,987 mi)

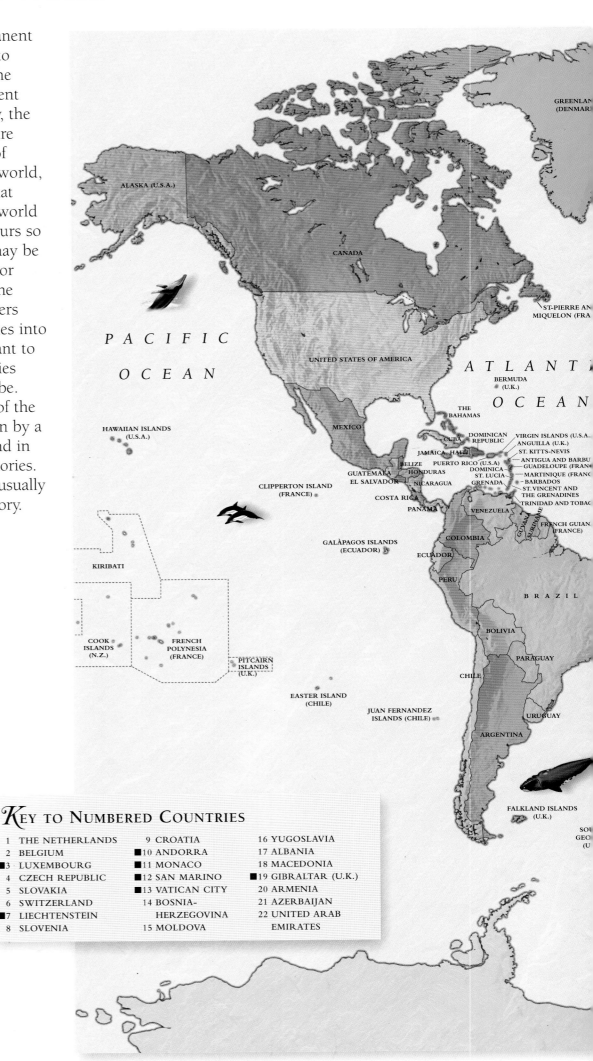

◆ LOOK AGAIN ◆

The following shapes represent countries shown on the world map on the right. Can you find and name them?

KEY TO NUMBERED COUNTRIES

1 THE NETHERLANDS	9 CROATIA	16 YUGOSLAVIA
2 BELGIUM	■10 ANDORRA	17 ALBANIA
■3 LUXEMBOURG	■11 MONACO	18 MACEDONIA
4 CZECH REPUBLIC	■12 SAN MARINO	■19 GIBRALTAR (U.K.)
5 SLOVAKIA	■13 VATICAN CITY	20 ARMENIA
6 SWITZERLAND	14 BOSNIA-	21 AZERBAIJAN
■7 LIECHTENSTEIN	HERZEGOVINA	22 UNITED ARAB
8 SLOVENIA	15 MOLDOVA	EMIRATES

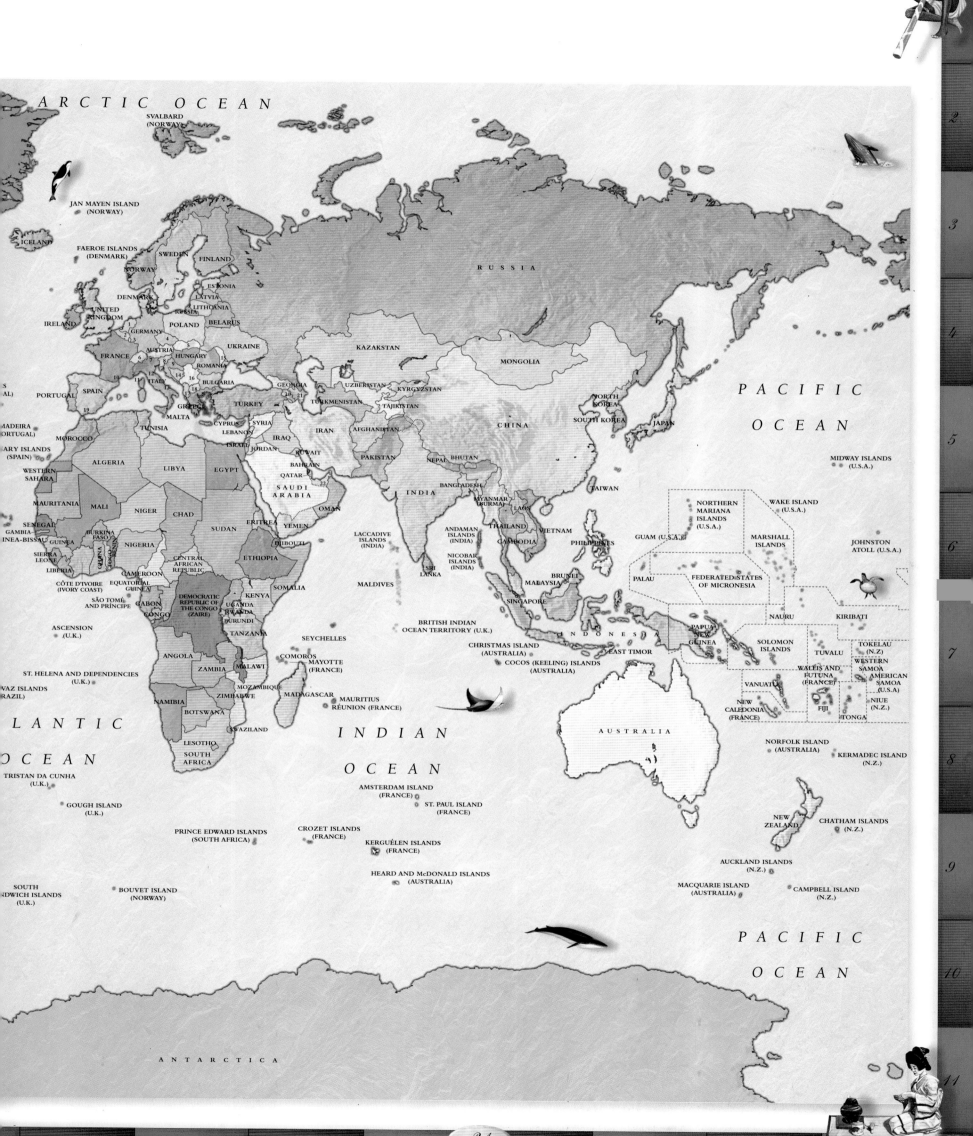

North America

THE CONTINENT OF NORTH AMERICA extends from just south of the North Pole to just north of the Equator. It includes almost every kind of environment, from ice-caps to forests, mountains, deserts and rainforest. In the west, an almost unbroken chain of mountains stretches from Alaska to Costa Rica and includes the Rocky Mountains, one of the world's most famous mountain ranges. The United States of America (U.S.A.) and Canada are the largest of the continent's 23 countries. The U.S.A. is made up of 50 states. Canada is divided into ten provinces and three territories. North America includes some of the world's biggest cities, but also vast areas of wilderness. Most North Americans are descendants of European immigrants, but there are also many people of African and Asian origin, as well as native peoples.

CONTINENT FACTS

Regional land area: 22,078,049 sq. km (8,522,127 sq. mi)
Regional population: 471,868,000
Independent countries: Antigua and Barbuda, The Bahamas, Barbados, Belize, Canada, Costa Rica, Cuba, Dominica, Dominican Republic, El Salvador, Grenada, Guatemala, Haiti, Honduras, Jamaica, Mexico, Nicaragua, Panama, St. Kitts–Nevis, St. Lucia, St. Vincent and the Grenadines, Trinidad and Tobago, United States of America

WORLD RECORDS

WORLD'S LARGEST GORGE
GRAND CANYON, U.S.A., 446 KM (277 MI) LONG, 16 KM (10 MI) WIDE, 1.6 KM (1 MI) DEEP

WORLD'S LARGEST FRESHWATER LAKE
LAKE SUPERIOR, U.S.A.-CANADA, 82,350 SQ. KM (31,800 SQ. MI)

WORLD'S LONGEST CAVE SYSTEM
MAMMOTH CAVES, U.S.A., 565 KM (351 MI)

WORLD'S LARGEST ACTIVE VOLCANO
MAUNA LOA, HAWAII, U.S.A., 4,170 M (13,680 FT) HIGH, 120 KM (75 MI) LONG, 50 KM (31 MI) WIDE

WORLD'S LONGEST BORDER
U.S.-CANADIAN BORDER, 6,416 KM (3,987 MI)

WORLD'S TALLEST ACTIVE GEYSER
STEAMBOAT GEYSER, YELLOWSTONE NATIONAL PARK, U.S.A., 115 M (380 FT)

WORLD'S LARGEST THEME PARK
WALT DISNEY WORLD, U.S.A., 122 SQ. KM (47 SQ. MI)

CONTINENT RECORDS

HIGHEST MOUNTAIN
MOUNT MCKINLEY (DENALI), U.S.A., 6,194 M (20,320 FT)

LOWEST POINT
DEATH VALLEY, U.S.A., 86 M (282 FT) BELOW SEA LEVEL

LONGEST RIVER
MISSISSIPPI-MISSOURI, U.S.A., 6,020 KM (3,740 MI)

LARGEST COUNTRY BY AREA
CANADA, 9,976,185 SQ. KM (3,851,809 SQ. MI)

LARGEST COUNTRY BY POPULATION
UNITED STATES OF AMERICA, POPULATION 274,088,480

LARGEST CITY BY POPULATION
MEXICO CITY, MEXICO, POPULATION 15,048,000

MAJOR MOUNTAINS AND RIVERS

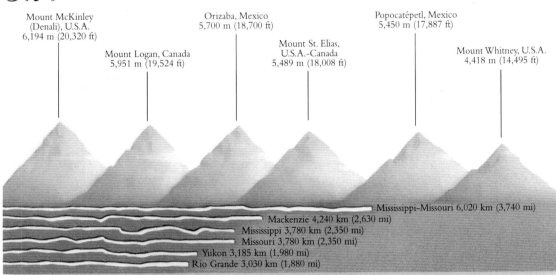

Mount McKinley (Denali), U.S.A. 6,194 m (20,320 ft)

Mount Logan, Canada 5,951 m (19,524 ft)

Orizaba, Mexico 5,700 m (18,700 ft)

Mount St. Elias, U.S.A.-Canada 5,489 m (18,008 ft)

Popocatépetl, Mexico 5,450 m (17,887 ft)

Mount Whitney, U.S.A. 4,418 m (14,495 ft)

Mississippi-Missouri 6,020 km (3,740 mi)
Mackenzie 4,240 km (2,630 mi)
Mississippi 3,780 km (2,350 mi)
Missouri 3,780 km (2,350 mi)
Yukon 3,185 km (1,980 mi)
Rio Grande 3,030 km (1,880 mi)

POLITICAL MAP

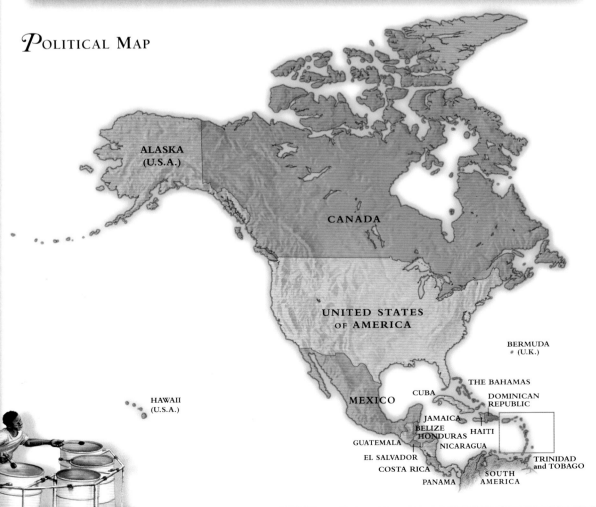

ALASKA (U.S.A.)

CANADA

UNITED STATES of AMERICA

BERMUDA (U.K.)

HAWAII (U.S.A.)

MEXICO

CUBA

THE BAHAMAS

DOMINICAN REPUBLIC

JAMAICA

BELIZE

HONDURAS

HAITI

GUATEMALA

NICARAGUA

EL SALVADOR

COSTA RICA

PANAMA

SOUTH AMERICA

TRINIDAD and TOBAGO

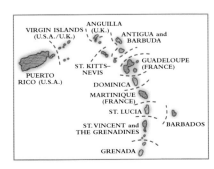

ANGUILLA (U.K.)

VIRGIN ISLANDS (U.S.A./U.K.)

ANTIGUA and BARBUDA

ST. KITTS–NEVIS

GUADELOUPE (FRANCE)

PUERTO RICO (U.S.A.)

DOMINICA

MARTINIQUE (FRANCE)

ST. LUCIA

ST. VINCENT and THE GRENADINES

BARBADOS

GRENADA

PHYSICAL MAP

ASIA

ARCTIC OCEAN

× NORTH POLE

EUROPE

Chukchi Sea

Ellesmere Island

QUEEN ELIZABETH ISLANDS

Greenland

Baffin Bay

Beaufort Sea

Banks Island

Bering Sea

BROOKS RANGE

Yukon

Victoria Island

Baffin Island

ALEUTIAN ISLANDS

Mt. McKinley (Denali) ▲

Mackenzie

Great Bear Lake

Arctic Circle

Labrador Sea

Mt. St. Elias ▲ ▲ Mt. Logan

Gulf of Alaska

Great Slave Lake

CANADIAN

Hudson Bay

LABRADOR

ATLANTIC OCEAN

ROCKY MOUNTAINS

COAST MTS.

GREAT

SHIELD

Newfoundland

QUEEN CHARLOTTE ISLANDS

Vancouver Island

Lake Winnipeg

Lake Nipigon

Missouri

Lake Superior

Lake Huron

St. Lawrence

PACIFIC OCEAN

COAST RANGES

Great Salt Lake

GREAT BASIN

PLAINS

Mississippi

Lake Michigan

Lake Ontario

APPALACHIAN MOUNTAINS

WAIIAN LANDS

Mt. Whitney ▲

Colorado

Lake Erie

Ohio

Bermuda

SIERRA MADRE OCCIDENTAL

SIERRA MADRE ORIENTAL

Missouri

Mississippi

Gulf of California

Rio Grande

THE BAHAMAS

LESSER ANTILLES

Tropic of Cancer

Gulf of Mexico

GREATER ANTILLES

Bay of Campeche

Caribbean Sea

Popocatépetl ▲

▲ Orizaba

SOUTH AMERICA

Lake Nicaragua

Equator

GALÁPAGOS ISLANDS

Western Canada and Alaska

CANADA, THE WORLD'S SECOND-LARGEST country, covers more than half of North America. Northern Canada is a vast, chilly wilderness where bears fish icy rivers for salmon and wolves hunt caribou across snow-covered plains. The new Arctic territory of Nunavut, occupying the eastern mainland of the Northwest Territories and most of the Arctic islands, came into existence in 1999. Nunavut means 'our land' in the language of its Inuit inhabitants. Few people live in this cold environment. Eighty per cent of Canada's residents live within 300 kilometres (185 miles) of the southern border, where the climate is milder and the land is more fertile. The prairie grassland that covers

parts of Alberta, Manitoba and Saskatchewan is one of the world's most productive farming regions. These provinces also supply most of Canada's oil and gas. West of the towering Rocky Mountains is the Pacific coastline, a maze of islands and narrow waterways. In the Gulf of Alaska, glaciers creep down the mountains toward the shore, while seals and whales swim in the bays. Alaska is not part of Canada. It is the biggest state in the U.S.A. but it is separated from the rest of the country by Canada. More than half of Alaska's lands are wildlife refuges, and the state contains some of North America's largest oil fields.

ALASKA (U.S.A.)
POPULATION: 614,100 ∗ CAPITAL: JUNEAU

ALBERTA
POPULATION: 2,546,000 ∗ CAPITAL: EDMONTON

BRITISH COLUMBIA
POPULATION: 3,282,000 ∗ CAPITAL: VICTORIA

MANITOBA
POPULATION: 1,092,000 ∗ CAPITAL: WINNIPEG

NORTHWEST TERRITORIES
POPULATION: 39,700 ∗ CAPITAL: YELLOWKNIFE

NUNAVUT
POPULATION: 24,730 ∗ CAPITAL: IQALUIT

SASKATCHEWAN
POPULATION: 989,000 ∗ CAPITAL: REGINA

YUKON TERRITORY
POPULATION: 31,200 ∗ CAPITAL: WHITEHORSE

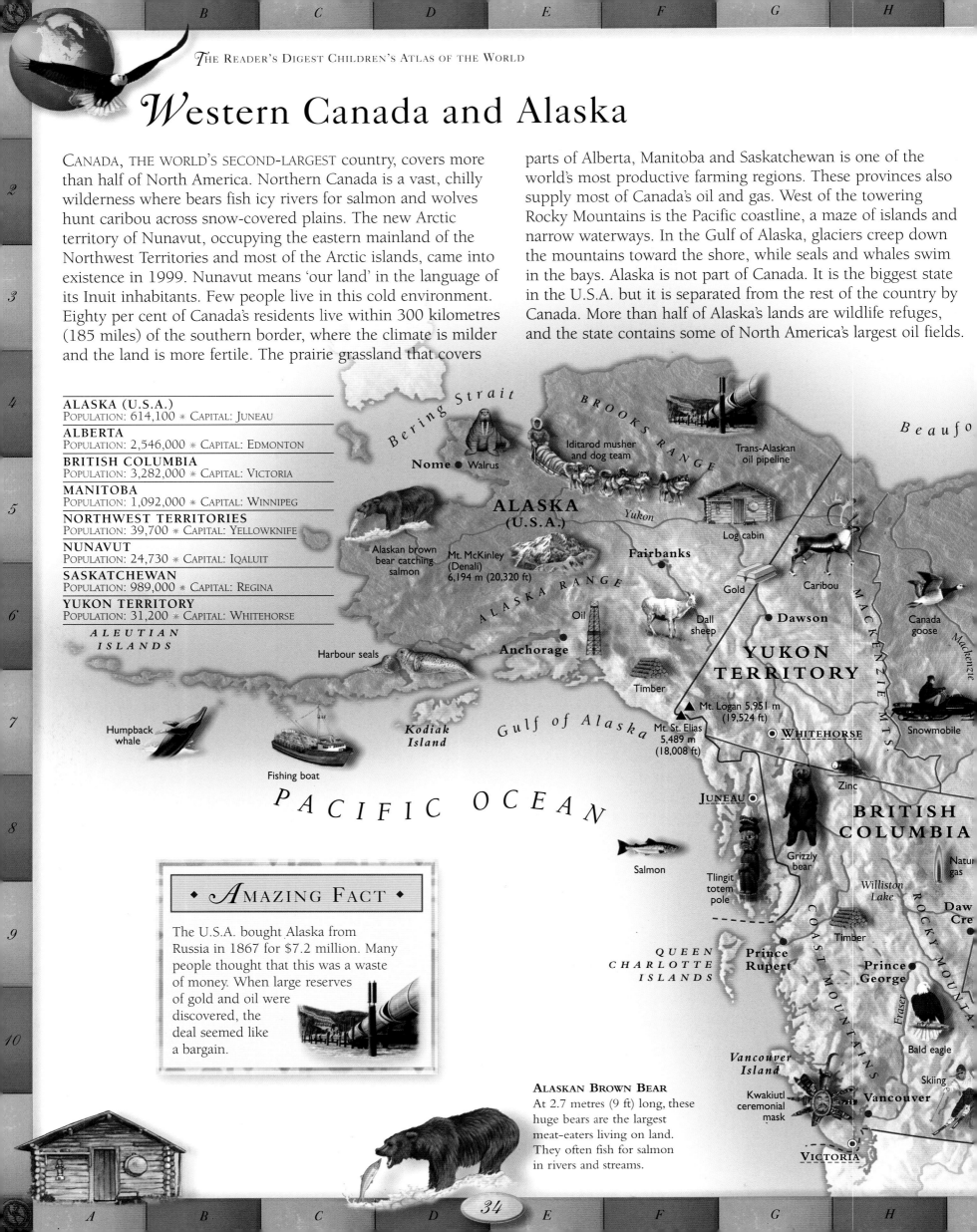

◆ AMAZING FACT ◆

The U.S.A. bought Alaska from Russia in 1867 for $7.2 million. Many people thought that this was a waste of money. When large reserves of gold and oil were discovered, the deal seemed like a bargain.

ALASKAN BROWN BEAR
At 2.7 metres (9 ft) long, these huge bears are the largest meat-eaters living on land. They often fish for salmon in rivers and streams.

ARCTIC OCEAN

Narwhal

Ellesmere Island

Musk ox

QUEEN ELIZABETH ISLANDS

Polar bears

Arctic fox

PARRY ISLANDS

Banks Island

Snow goose

Arctic hare

Victoria Island

Traditional church

Somerset Island

Prince of Wales Island

Inuit building igloo

Baffin Bay

GREENLAND

Davis Strait

Baffin Island

Prince Charles Island

Kittiwake

Harp seals

Innuit fishing through ice

NUNAVUT

⊙ **IQALUIT**

Southampton Island

Hudson Strait

reat Bear Lake

Silver

Wolf

Igloo-shaped houses

Seaplane

ORTHWEST TERRITORIES

YELLOWKNIFE ◉

Great Slave Lake

Gold

Grey jay

Moose

ANADA

Slave

Hudson Bay

QUÉBEC

Ⓔ Beluga whale

Belcher Islands

Zinc and lead

Lake Athabasca

Uranium

Reindeer Lake

LBERTA

Edmontonia dinosaur fossils

Mountie

Beaver

Nelson

Nickel and copper

MANITOBA

ONTARIO

EDMONTON ◉

Oil   Natural gas

SASKATCHEWAN

Wheat

Saskatchewan

Gold

Lake Winnipeg

● **Calgary**

Churchill

● **Churchill**

● **Saskatoon**

⊙ **REGINA**

Grain stores

⊙ **WINNIPEG**

Calgary Stampede

Legislative Building

UNITED STATES OF AMERICA

◆ PROJECT: *Inuit Finger Masks* ◆

In ceremonies and rituals, the Inuit use tiny finger masks to represent their spirit ancestors. The masks are often carved from wood or stone, but you can make some out of cardboard.

❶ Cut out a circle about 10 centimetres (4 in) in diameter. Cut two small holes at the bottom of the circle large enough for your fingers to poke through.

❷ Draw a face in the centre of the circle and colour it. Cut a fringe in the cardboard, or glue feathers or beads around the face.

❸ To perform with the mask, move your hand slowly from side to side to the beat of a drum.

LOCATION

N

W — **E**

S

SCALE

MILES

0   100   200   300

0   100   200   300   400   500

KILOMETRES

ROYAL CANADIAN MOUNTED POLICE (MOUNTIES)
Canada's national police force was founded in 1873 to prevent disputes between native tribes and European traders.

Eastern Canada

ABOUT 60 PER CENT OF THE POPULATION of Canada live along the shores of the St. Lawrence River and the Great Lakes, an area that occupies only 2 per cent of the country's land area. From the early 17th century onwards, European immigrants settled here because the land was fertile and the waterways provided transportation routes. Today, the region is home to many of Canada's biggest cities, including the two largest, Toronto and Montréal. Canada has two main languages – English and French. The majority of French speakers live in the province of Québec, which was once a French territory. The forests, lakes and rivers that cover most of Québec and Ontario provide a wealth of resources. Québec's forestry industry produces about 12 per cent of the world's pulp and paper. Hydroelectric power stations create so much electricity that Québec and Ontario can export energy. The climate of eastern Canada ranges from temperate in the south to arctic in the north. For nine months of the year, Hudson Bay is frozen, allowing polar bears to prowl the pack-ice in search of food. Off Newfoundland's north shore float huge icebergs measuring up to 45 metres (150 ft) high. Further south, enormous tides surge in and out of the bays. In the Bay of Fundy, the sea can rise 15 metres (50 ft) at high tide – high enough to cover a four-storey building!

NEW BRUNSWICK
POPULATION: 723,900 ✳ CAPITAL: FREDERICTON

NEWFOUNDLAND
POPULATION: 568,500 ✳ CAPITAL: ST. JOHN'S

NOVA SCOTIA
POPULATION: 900,000 ✳ CAPITAL: HALIFAX

ONTARIO
POPULATION: 10,085,000 ✳ CAPITAL: TORONTO

PRINCE EDWARD ISLAND
POPULATION: 129,800 ✳ CAPITAL: CHARLOTTETOWN

QUÉBEC
POPULATION: 6,896,000 ✳ CAPITAL: QUÉBEC

◆ LOOK AGAIN ◆

- Which city is Canada's national capital?
- Which endangered sea mammal swims off the east coast of Newfoundland?
- What kind of mineral is mined in Newfoundland?

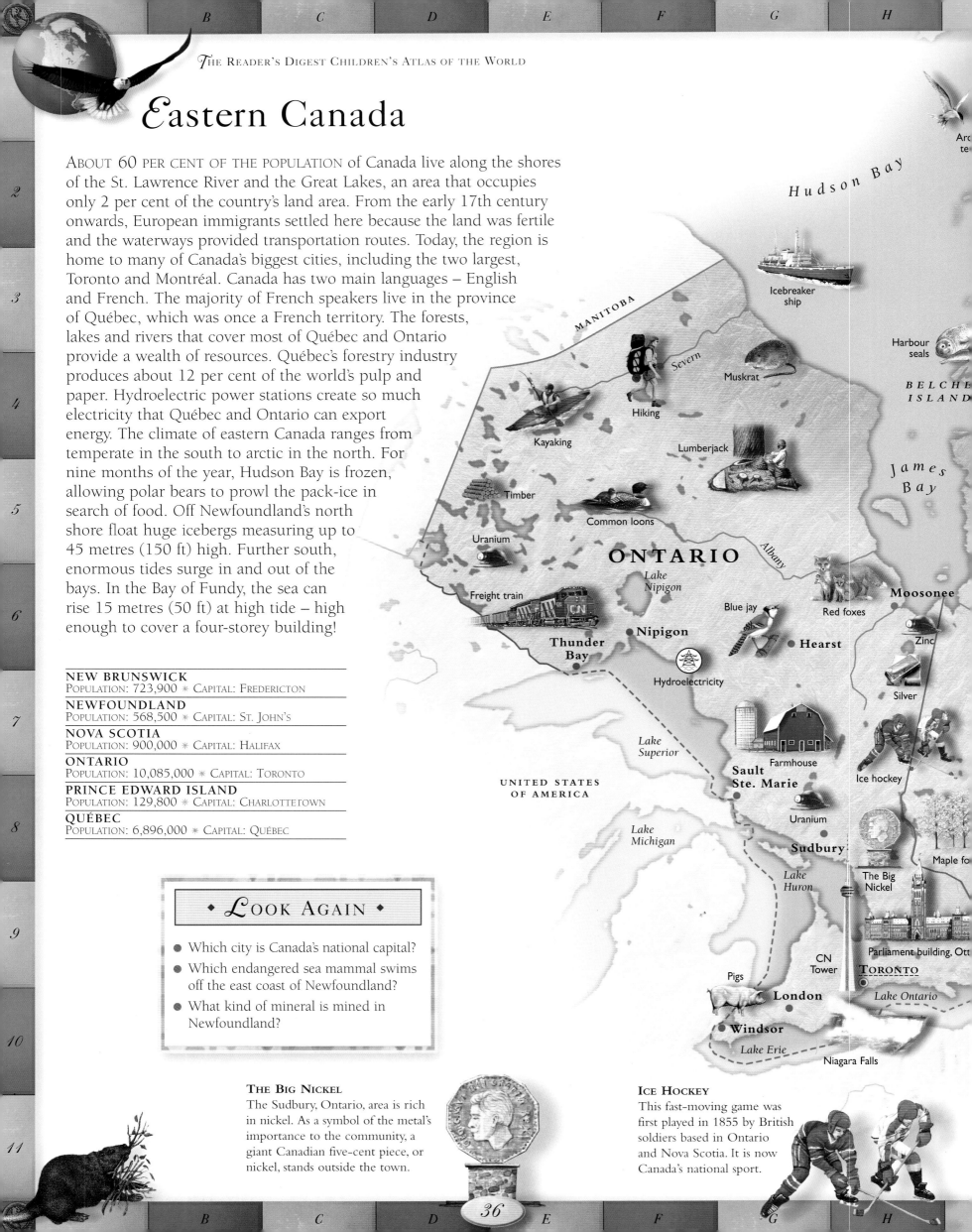

Hudson Bay

MANITOBA

Icebreaker ship

Harbour seals

BELCHER ISLAND

James Bay

Severn

Muskrat

Hiking

Kayaking

Timber

Lumberjack

Common loons

Uranium

ONTARIO

Lake Nipigon

Albany

Red foxes

Moosonee

Blue jay

Zinc

Freight train

Nipigon

Hearst

Silver

Thunder Bay

Hydroelectricity

Lake Superior

UNITED STATES OF AMERICA

Farmhouse

Ice hockey

Sault Ste. Marie

Uranium

Lake Michigan

Sudbury

The Big Nickel

Maple fo

Lake Huron

CN Tower

Parliament building, Ott

Pigs

London

TORONTO

Lake Ontario

Windsor

Lake Erie

Niagara Falls

THE BIG NICKEL
The Sudbury, Ontario, area is rich in nickel. As a symbol of the metal's importance to the community, a giant Canadian five-cent piece, or nickel, stands outside the town.

ICE HOCKEY
This fast-moving game was first played in 1855 by British soldiers based in Ontario and Nova Scotia. It is now Canada's national sport.

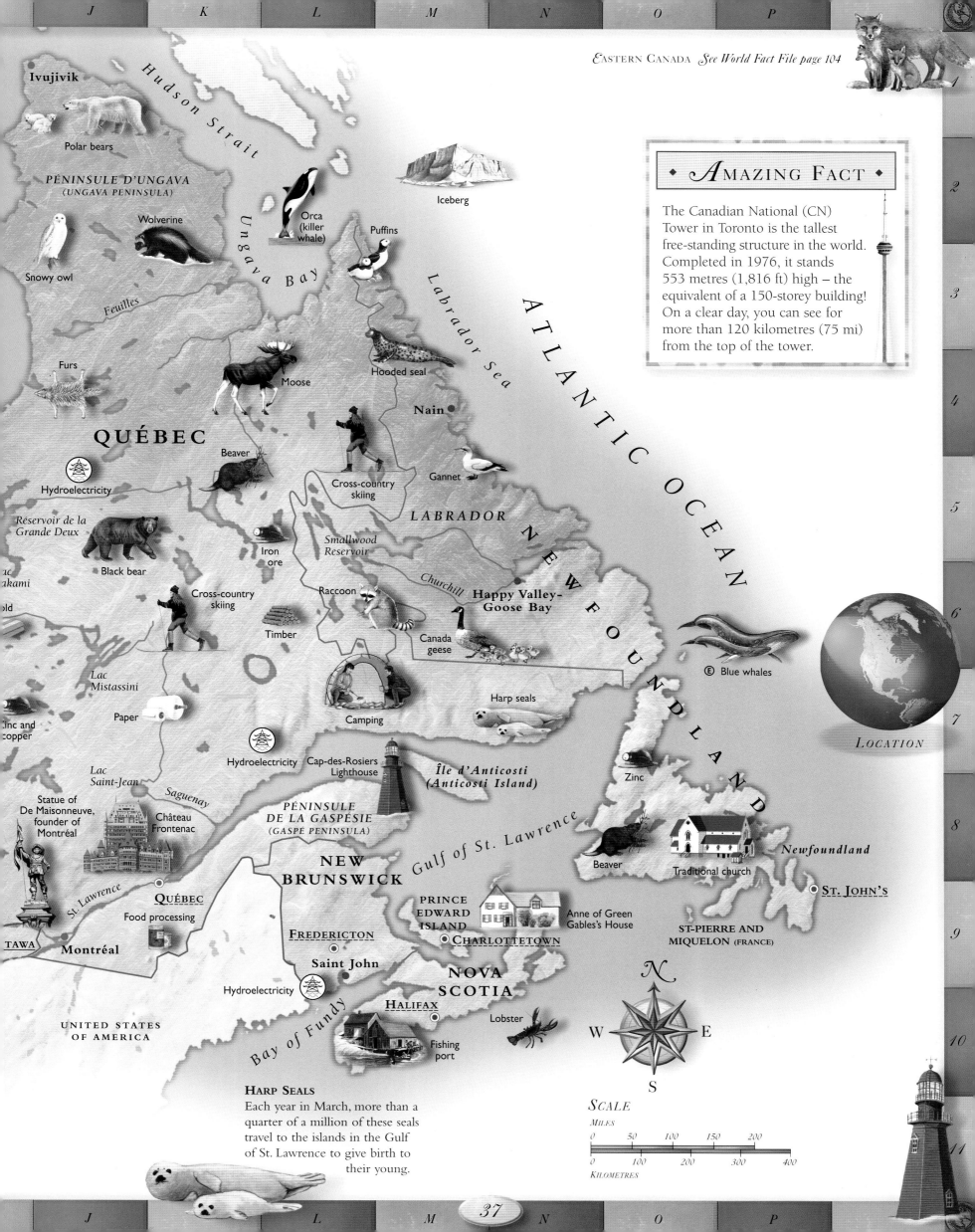

Map border letters (top): J K L M N O P

Ivujivik

Hudson Strait

Polar bears

PÉNINSULE D'UNGAVA
(UNGAVA PENINSULA)

Wolverine

Snowy owl

Ungava Bay

Orca (killer whale)

Puffins

Iceberg

Feuilles

Furs

Moose

Hooded seal

Labrador Sea

ATLANTIC OCEAN

Nain

QUÉBEC

Beaver

Cross-country skiing

Gannet

LABRADOR

Hydroelectricity

Réservoir de la Grande Deux

Iron ore

Smallwood Reservoir

Churchill

Happy Valley-Goose Bay

NEWFOUNDLAND

Black bear

ac akami

Cross-country skiing

Raccoon

Timber

Canada geese

old

Blue whales ⒺLac Mistassini

Paper

Camping

Harp seals

inc and copper

Hydroelectricity

Lac Saint-Jean

Cap-des-Rosiers Lighthouse

Île d'Anticosti (Anticosti Island)

Zinc

Statue of De Maisonneuve, founder of Montréal

Saguenay

Château Frontenac

PÉNINSULE DE LA GASPÉSIE (GASPÉ PENINSULA)

Gulf of St. Lawrence

Newfoundland

St. LAWRENCE

NEW BRUNSWICK

Beaver

Traditional church

ST. JOHN'S

TAWA

Québec

Food processing

PRINCE EDWARD ISLAND

Anne of Green Gables's House

ST-PIERRE AND MIQUELON (FRANCE)

Montréal

FREDERICTON

CHARLOTTETOWN

Saint John

NOVA SCOTIA

Hydroelectricity

UNITED STATES OF AMERICA

Bay of Fundy

HALIFAX

Lobster

N
W   E
S

Fishing port

HARP SEALS
Each year in March, more than a quarter of a million of these seals travel to the islands in the Gulf of St. Lawrence to give birth to their young.

AMAZING FACT

The Canadian National (CN) Tower in Toronto is the tallest free-standing structure in the world. Completed in 1976, it stands 553 metres (1,816 ft) high – the equivalent of a 150-storey building! On a clear day, you can see for more than 120 kilometres (75 mi) from the top of the tower.

LOCATION

SCALE
MILES
0   50   100   150   200

0   100   200   300   400
KILOMETRES

Map border letters (bottom): J K L M N O P

North-eastern United States

THE NORTH-EAST U.S.A. is home to 70 million people – more than one-quarter of the population of the U.S.A. From Boston in the north to Washington, D.C. in the south, a line of great cities stretches for over 640 kilometres (400 mi) along the Atlantic shore. Including its suburbs, New York City is home to almost 20 million people. It is the largest city in the U.S.A. and the third largest in the world. New York is one of the world's leading centres of trade, industry and culture. The heart of the city is the island of Manhattan, where giant skyscrapers, including some of the world's tallest, tower over long, straight streets packed with people and traffic.

The Appalachian Mountains separate the cities of the coast from the Great Lakes and the plains of the interior. They stretch for more than 2,600 kilometres (600 mi) from northern Alabama, in the southern U.S.A., to northern Maine. In the south, these mountains are rich in minerals – Kentucky produces more coal than any other state. Farms occupy many Appalachian valleys, but large areas of the mountains are covered by deciduous forests, where black bears forage for blueberries and otters swim in the streams. In autumn, these forests provide spectacular displays of colour, as their leaves change from green to brilliant shades of orange, red and gold.

CONNECTICUT
POPULATION: 3,274,000 * CAPITAL: HARTFORD

DELAWARE
POPULATION: 743,600 * CAPITAL: DOVER

DISTRICT OF COLUMBIA
POPULATION: 523,100 * CAPITAL: WASHINGTON, D.C.

KENTUCKY
POPULATION: 3,937,000 * CAPITAL: FRANKFORT

MAINE
POPULATION: 1,244,000 * CAPITAL: AUGUSTA

MARYLAND
POPULATION: 5,135,000 * CAPITAL: ANNAPOLIS

MASSACHUSETTS
POPULATION: 6,147,000 * CAPITAL: BOSTON

NEW HAMPSHIRE
POPULATION: 1,185,000 * CAPITAL: CONCORD

NEW JERSEY
POPULATION: 8,115,000 * CAPITAL: TRENTON

NEW YORK
POPULATION: 18,175,000 * CAPITAL: ALBANY

PENNSYLVANIA
POPULATION: 12,002,000 * CAPITAL: HARRISBURG

RHODE ISLAND
POPULATION: 988,500 * CAPITAL: PROVIDENCE

VERMONT
POPULATION: 590,900 * CAPITAL: MONTPELIER

VIRGINIA
POPULATION: 6,791,000 * CAPITAL: RICHMOND

WEST VIRGINIA
POPULATION: 1,811,000 * CAPITAL: CHARLESTON

◆ PROJECT: *Iroquois Beads* ◆

According to the custom of the native Iroquois people, a person saying something important must give the listener a gift to confirm the truth of the statement. This gift is often a string of white and purple shell beads known as wampum. Try making your own Iroquois friendship beads. Thread some coloured beads onto pieces of string and attach the strings to a length of yarn. Remember to explain the meaning of your gift to the receiver.

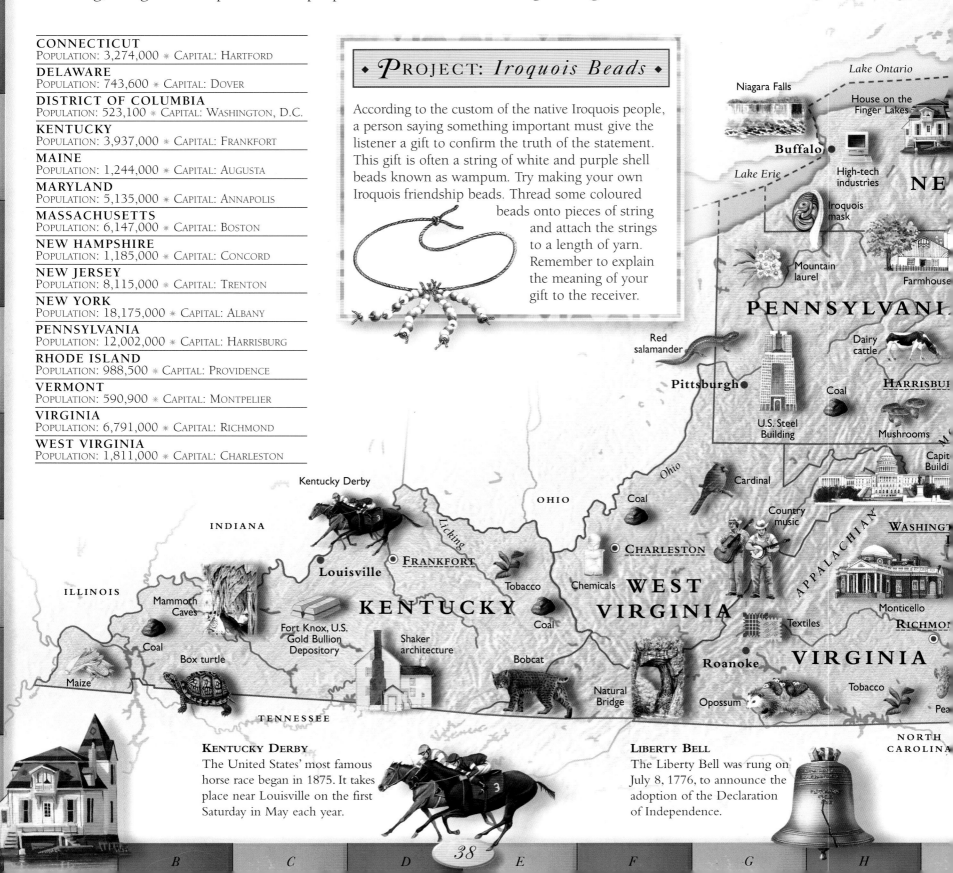

KENTUCKY DERBY
The United States' most famous horse race began in 1875. It takes place near Louisville on the first Saturday in May each year.

LIBERTY BELL
The Liberty Bell was rung on July 8, 1776, to announce the adoption of the Declaration of Independence.

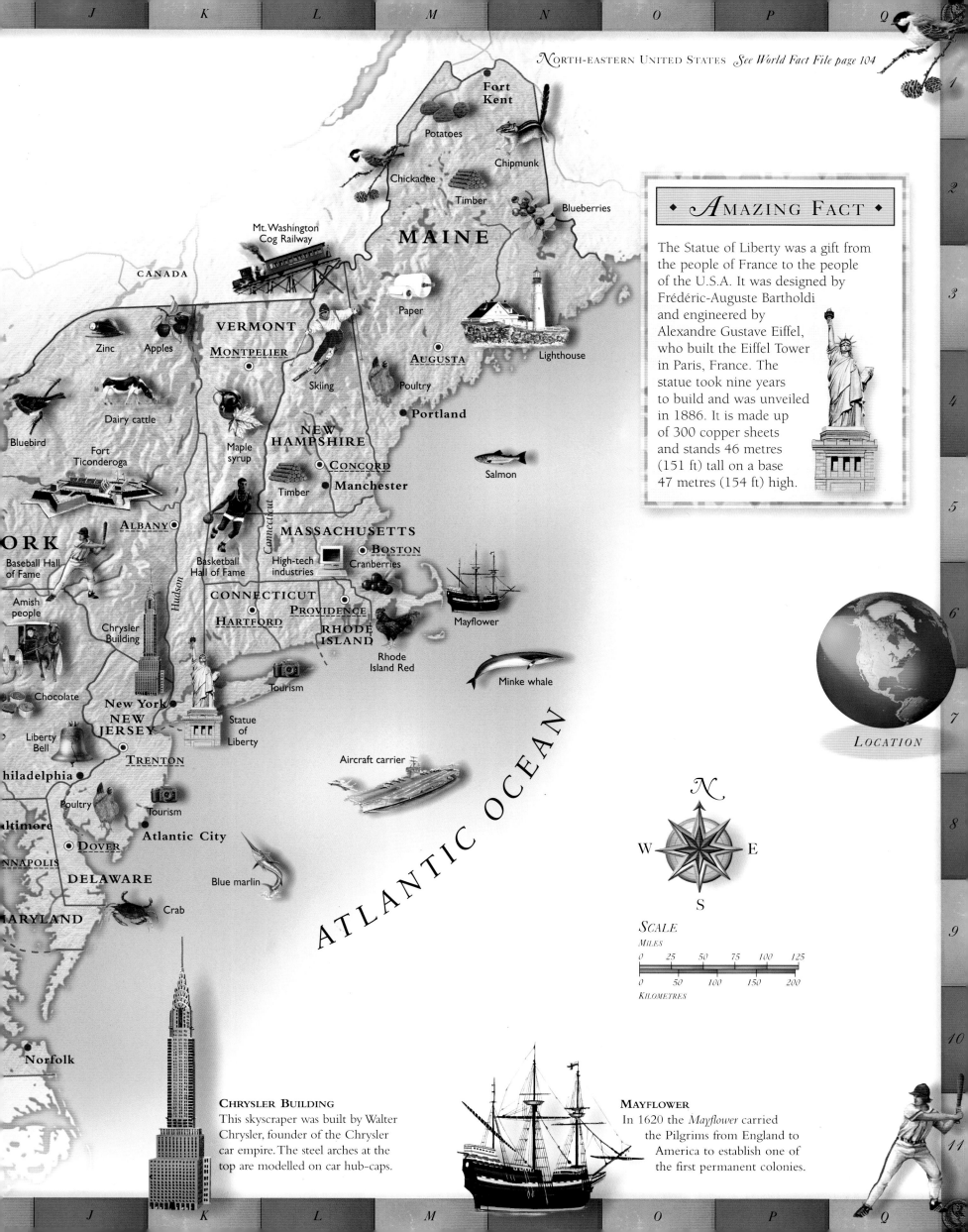

MAINE

Fort Kent

Potatoes

Chipmunk

Chickadee

Timber

Blueberries

Mt. Washington Cog Railway

CANADA

Paper

Lighthouse

VERMONT

Zinc

Apples

MONTPELIER

Skiing

AUGUSTA

Poultry

Dairy cattle

Bluebird

Fort Ticonderoga

Maple syrup

NEW HAMPSHIRE

Portland

Salmon

CONCORD

Manchester

Timber

ALBANY

YORK

Baseball Hall of Fame

Basketball Hall of Fame

MASSACHUSETTS

High-tech industries

BOSTON

Cranberries

Amish people

Chrysler Building

CONNECTICUT

HARTFORD

PROVIDENCE

Mayflower

Chocolate

Statue of Liberty

New York

RHODE ISLAND

NEW JERSEY

Rhode Island Red

Minke whale

Liberty Bell

Tourism

Philadelphia

TRENTON

Poultry

Aircraft carrier

ltimore

Tourism

DOVER

Atlantic City

NNAPOLIS

DELAWARE

Blue marlin

MARYLAND

Crab

ATLANTIC OCEAN

Norfolk

AMAZING FACT

The Statue of Liberty was a gift from the people of France to the people of the U.S.A. It was designed by Frédéric-Auguste Bartholdi and engineered by Alexandre Gustave Eiffel, who built the Eiffel Tower in Paris, France. The statue took nine years to build and was unveiled in 1886. It is made up of 300 copper sheets and stands 46 metres (151 ft) tall on a base 47 metres (154 ft) high.

LOCATION

N
W   E
S

SCALE

MILES

0   25   50   75   100   125

0   50   100   150   200

KILOMETRES

CHRYSLER BUILDING
This skyscraper was built by Walter Chrysler, founder of the Chrysler car empire. The steel arches at the top are modelled on car hub-caps.

MAYFLOWER
In 1620 the *Mayflower* carried the Pilgrims from England to America to establish one of the first permanent colonies.

Southern United States

THE SOUTHERN U.S.A. is a warm, humid region of plains, rivers, swamps and coastal lagoons. From southern Texas, a broad belt of lowland stretches around the Gulf of Mexico, across Florida and along the shores of the Atlantic Ocean. In the north-east, the coastal plains rise to plateaux and mountain ranges, including the Appalachian Mountains, which formed about 400 million years ago and are North America's oldest mountains. Mixed crop and livestock farms cover the fertile eastern and southern plains. In the west, on the dry Texas grasslands, ranch hands tend huge herds of cattle. Texas is the second biggest American state after Alaska, and its beef industry and large oil reserves have made it one of the richest parts of the country. Numerous rivers cross the southern U.S.A., including the Mississippi, one of North America's longest rivers and busiest inland waterways. Along the coast of the Gulf of Mexico and in northern Florida, these rivers have formed shallow lakes, muddy deltas and steamy swamps that are home to snakes, turtles and alligators. Florida's sunny climate and sandy beaches make it a popular holiday destination. The Walt Disney World theme park near Orlando is the world's number one tourist attraction, with more than 25 million visitors each year.

Many of the first Europeans to settle in this region came from France and Spain in the 17th century, and their descendants are called Creoles. Other French-speakers known as Cajuns arrived soon afterwards from Canada. Florida's large Spanish-speaking population includes immigrants from the island of Cuba, which lies just 217 kilometres (135 mi) south of Key West, the southernmost tip of Florida and the U.S.A.

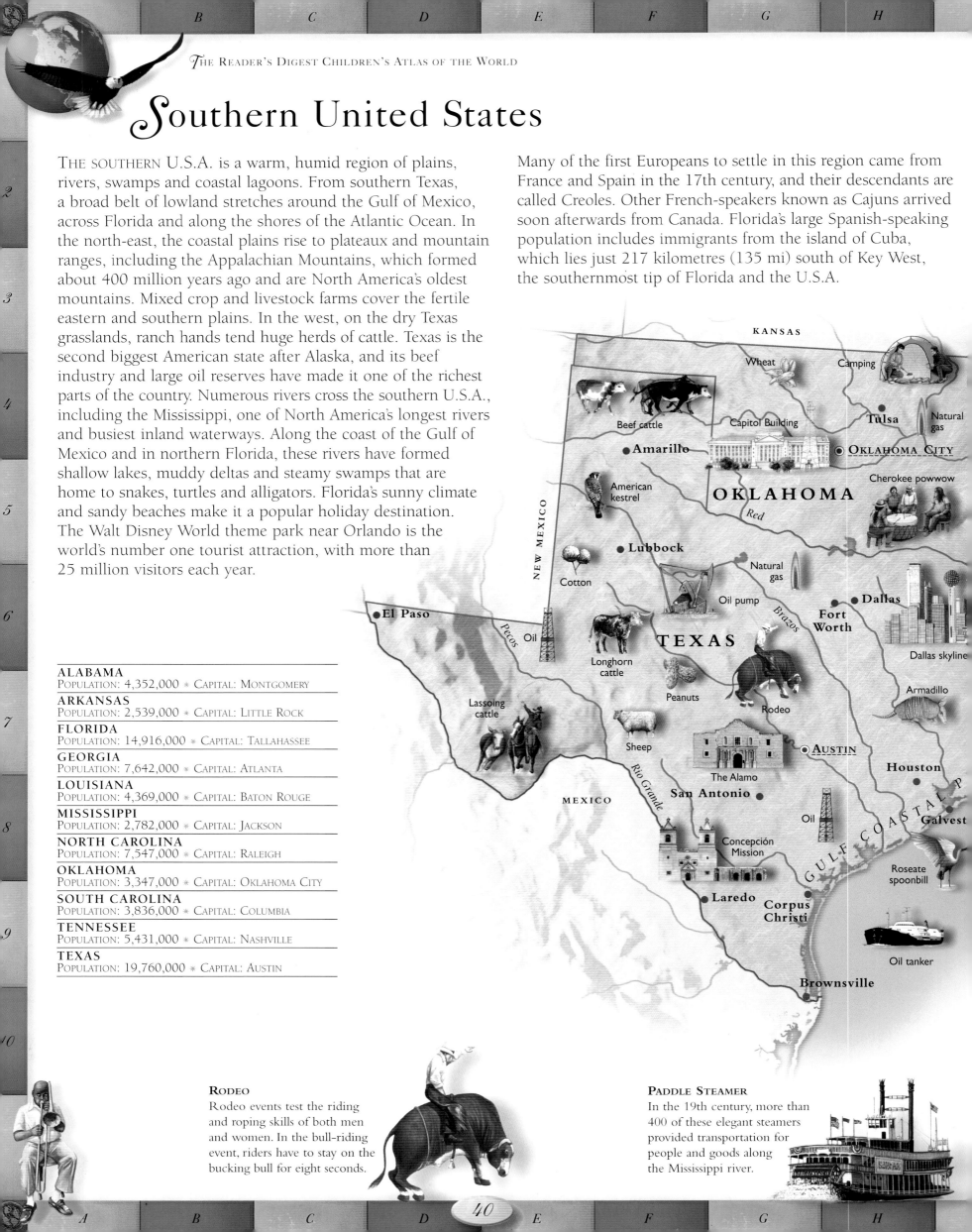

ALABAMA
POPULATION: 4,352,000 ∗ CAPITAL: MONTGOMERY

ARKANSAS
POPULATION: 2,539,000 ∗ CAPITAL: LITTLE ROCK

FLORIDA
POPULATION: 14,916,000 ∗ CAPITAL: TALLAHASSEE

GEORGIA
POPULATION: 7,642,000 ∗ CAPITAL: ATLANTA

LOUISIANA
POPULATION: 4,369,000 ∗ CAPITAL: BATON ROUGE

MISSISSIPPI
POPULATION: 2,782,000 ∗ CAPITAL: JACKSON

NORTH CAROLINA
POPULATION: 7,547,000 ∗ CAPITAL: RALEIGH

OKLAHOMA
POPULATION: 3,347,000 ∗ CAPITAL: OKLAHOMA CITY

SOUTH CAROLINA
POPULATION: 3,836,000 ∗ CAPITAL: COLUMBIA

TENNESSEE
POPULATION: 5,431,000 ∗ CAPITAL: NASHVILLE

TEXAS
POPULATION: 19,760,000 ∗ CAPITAL: AUSTIN

RODEO
Rodeo events test the riding and roping skills of both men and women. In the bull-riding event, riders have to stay on the bucking bull for eight seconds.

PADDLE STEAMER
In the 19th century, more than 400 of these elegant steamers provided transportation for people and goods along the Mississippi river.

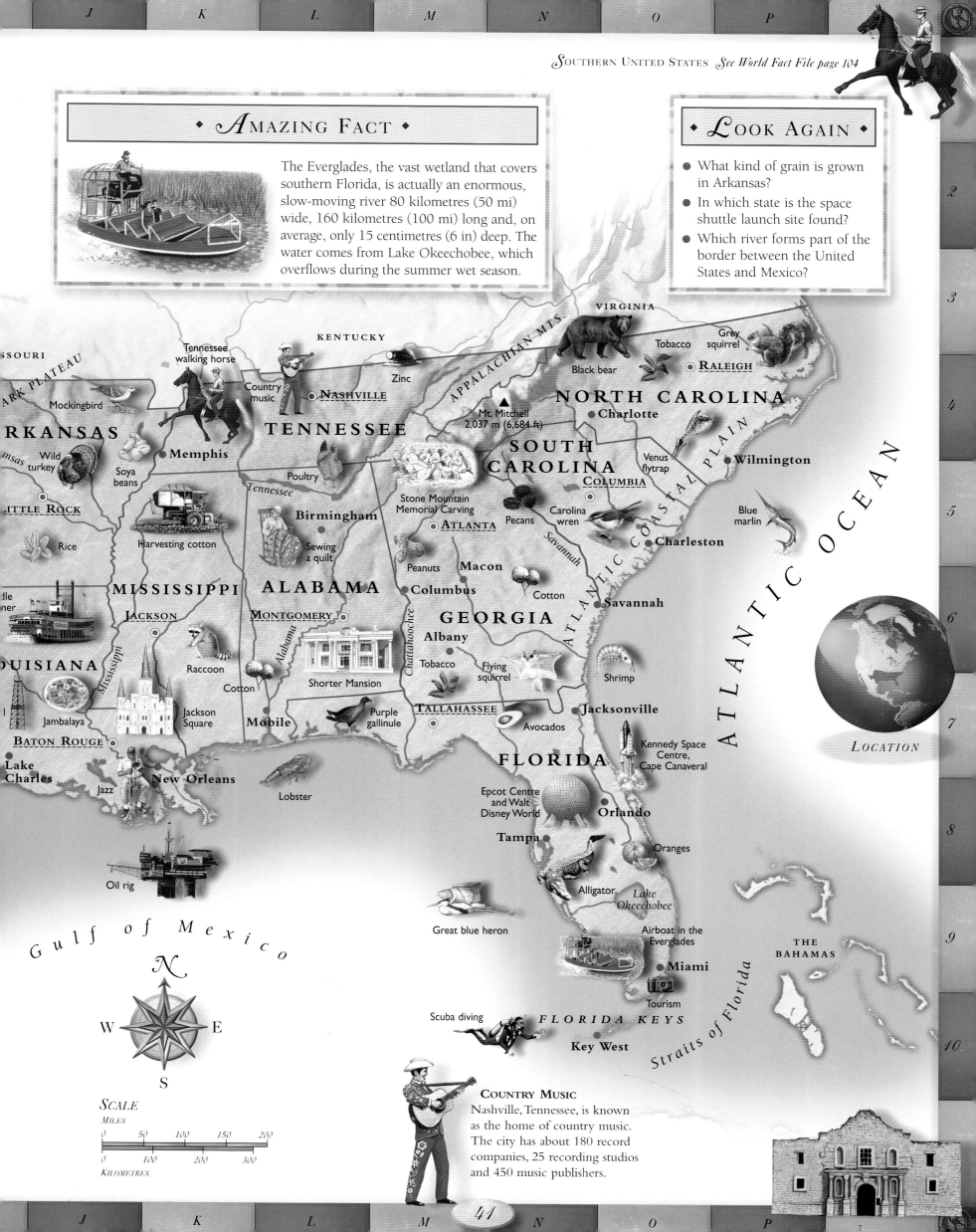

✦ AMAZING FACT ✦

The Everglades, the vast wetland that covers southern Florida, is actually an enormous, slow-moving river 80 kilometres (50 mi) wide, 160 kilometres (100 mi) long and, on average, only 15 centimetres (6 in) deep. The water comes from Lake Okeechobee, which overflows during the summer wet season.

✦ LOOK AGAIN ✦

- What kind of grain is grown in Arkansas?
- In which state is the space shuttle launch site found?
- Which river forms part of the border between the United States and Mexico?

VIRGINIA

KENTUCKY

MISSOURI

ARK PLATEAU

Mockingbird

Tennessee walking horse

Country music

Zinc

APPALACHIAN MTS.

Black bear

Tobacco

Grey squirrel

● RALEIGH

● NASHVILLE

NORTH CAROLINA

Mt. Mitchell 2,037 m (6,684 ft)

● Charlotte

ARKANSAS

Wild turkey

Soya beans

TENNESSEE

Memphis

Poultry

SOUTH CAROLINA

Venus flytrap

● Wilmington

Tennessee

LITTLE ROCK

Rice

Harvesting cotton

Birmingham

Stone Mountain Memorial Carving

ATLANTA

Pecans

Carolina wren

COLUMBIA

Blue marlin

● Charleston

ATLANTIC COASTAL PLAIN

Savannah

ATLANTIC OCEAN

MISSISSIPPI

ALABAMA

Sewing a quilt

Peanuts

Macon

Cotton

Savannah

le ler

JACKSON

Raccoon

MONTGOMERY

Columbus

GEORGIA

LOUISIANA

Jambalaya

Mississippi

Cotton

Jackson Square

Shorter Mansion

Albany

Tobacco

Flying squirrel

Shrimp

Alabama

Mobile

TALLAHASSEE

Avocados

● Jacksonville

BATON ROUGE

Lake Charles

Jazz

New Orleans

Lobster

Purple gallinule

FLORIDA

Kennedy Space Centre, Cape Canaveral

Epcot Centre and Walt Disney World

● Orlando

LOCATION

Oil rig

● Tampa

Oranges

Alligator

Lake Okeechobee

Gulf of Mexico

Airboat in the Everglades

THE BAHAMAS

N

Great blue heron

● Miami

Tourism

Scuba diving

FLORIDA KEYS

Straits of Florida

W   E

S

Key West

SCALE

MILES

0   50   100   150   200

0   100   200   300

KILOMETRES

COUNTRY MUSIC

Nashville, Tennessee, is known as the home of country music. The city has about 180 record companies, 25 recording studios and 450 music publishers.

Central United States

THE CENTRAL U.S.A. consists of a vast area of lowland known as the Midwest or prairies. In the north-eastern part of this region lie the Great Lakes, the largest group of freshwater lakes in the world. Rivers and canals connect the lakes to the Atlantic Ocean and the Gulf of Mexico, forming a major transportation network. This network and the area's many natural resources, including coal and iron ore, have helped to turn the Great Lakes region into the industrial heart of the U.S.A. Factories now line the southern shores of Lake Michigan and Lake Erie, and these supply most of the country's iron, steel and cars. Unfortunately, these industries create a great deal of waste, and the Great Lakes are now badly polluted. The area south and west of the lakes was once an enormous natural grassland, roamed by millions of bison and deer, and home to Native American tribes such as the Sioux and the Comanche. Now it is one of the world's most important farming regions. Iowa lies at the centre of an area known as the Corn Belt because it produces half of the world's corn, or maize. Almost all of this maize is used to fatten the region's pigs and cattle, which provide most of the U.S.A.'s meat. Further west, on the Great Plains, is a wheat belt. Here, immense fields of wheat stretch as far as the eye can see.

State	Population	Capital
ILLINOIS	12,045,000	Springfield
INDIANA	5,899,000	Indianapolis
IOWA	2,862,000	Des Moines
KANSAS	2,629,000	Topeka
MICHIGAN	9,817,000	Lansing
MINNESOTA	4,725,000	St. Paul
MISSOURI	5,439,000	Jefferson City
NEBRASKA	1,663,000	Lincoln
NORTH DAKOTA	638,300	Bismarck
OHIO	11,210,000	Columbus
SOUTH DAKOTA	738,200	Pierre
WISCONSIN	5,224,000	Madison

CANADA
MONTANA
WYOMING
COLORADO
OKLAHOMA
NORTH DAKOTA
SOUTH DAKOTA
NEBRASKA
KANSAS
GREAT PLAINS
Oil
Mallard duck
Hiking
Hay
Sugar beets
Minot
Grand Forks
Red
Red foxes
Bald eagle
Coal
Bismarck
Fargo
Moorhead
Missouri
Food processing
Wheat
White-tailed deer
Dairy cattle
Prairie dogs
James
Hay
Corn
Gold
Pierre
Rapid City
Sioux head-dress
Food processing
Sioux Falls
Mount Rushmore
Beef cattle
Badlands National Park
Sioux City
Missouri
Windmill
Lassoing cattle
Chimney Rock
Bison
Food processing
Omaha
North Platte
Platte
Grand Island
Lincoln
Council Bluffs
Maize
Buffalo Bill's ranch house
Turkeys
Oil
Sunflowers
Harvesting wheat
Salina
Beef cattle
Wheat
Arkansas
Wichita
Monument Rocks
Dodge City
Natural gas
Aircraft manufacturing

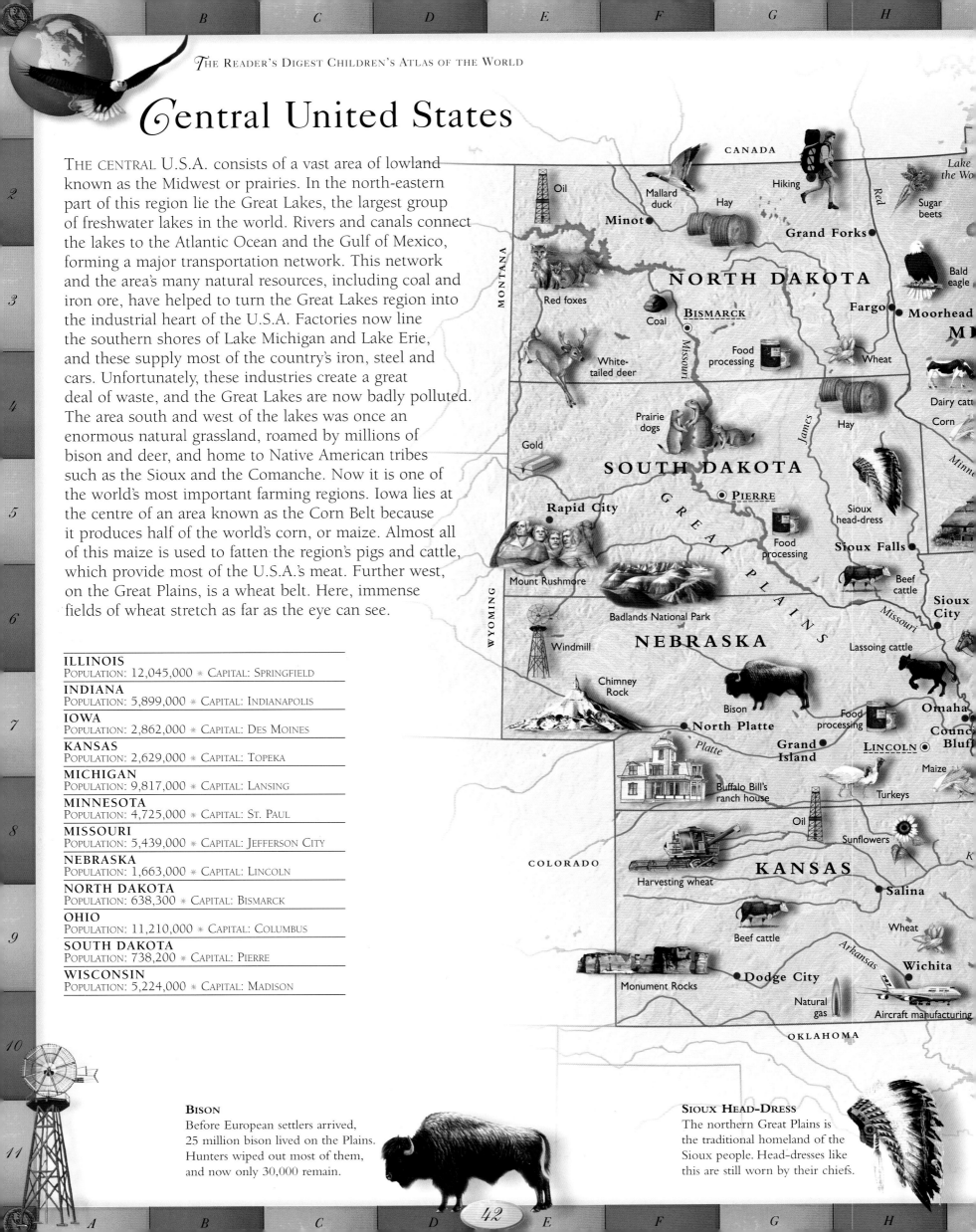

Bison
Before European settlers arrived, 25 million bison lived on the Plains. Hunters wiped out most of them, and now only 30,000 remain.

Sioux Head-Dress
The northern Great Plains is the traditional homeland of the Sioux people. Head-dresses like this are still worn by their chiefs.

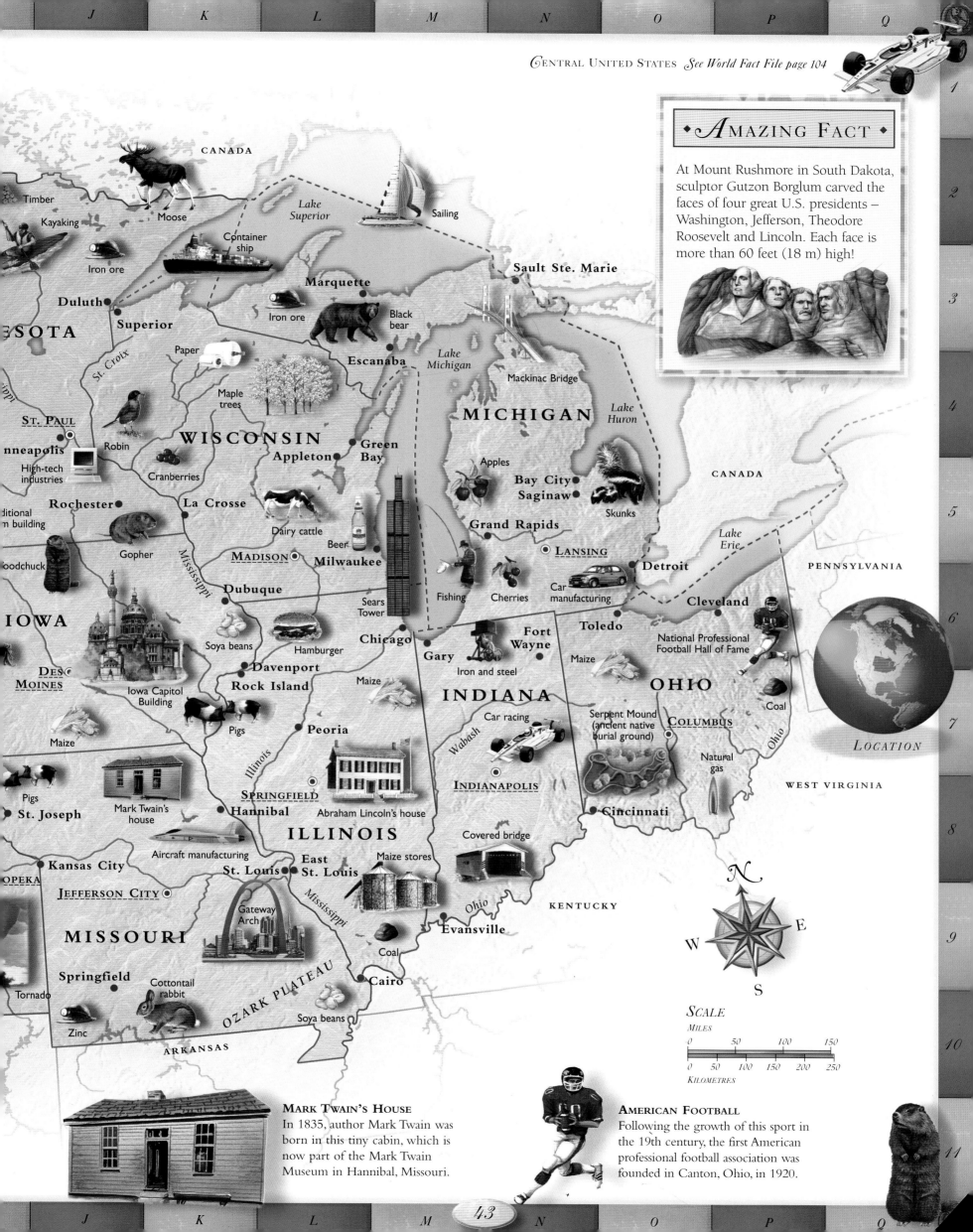

J K L M N O P Q

CANADA

Timber

Kayaking

Moose

Lake Superior

Sailing

Container ship

Iron ore

Duluth

Superior

Marquette

Iron ore

Black bear

Escanaba

Lake Michigan

Mackinac Bridge

Sault Ste. Marie

◆ AMAZING FACT ◆

At Mount Rushmore in South Dakota, sculptor Gutzon Borglum carved the faces of four great U.S. presidents – Washington, Jefferson, Theodore Roosevelt and Lincoln. Each face is more than 60 feet (18 m) high!

ESOTA

Paper

St. Croix

ST. PAUL

Robin

nneapolis

High-tech industries

Rochester

ditional building

oodchuck

Maple trees

WISCONSIN

Appleton

Green Bay

Cranberries

La Crosse

Dairy cattle

Gopher

Beer

MADISON

Milwaukee

Mississippi

Dubuque

Sears Tower

MICHIGAN

Apples

Bay City

Saginaw

Grand Rapids

Skunks

Lake Huron

LANSING

Fishing

Cherries

Car manufacturing

Detroit

Lake Erie

CANADA

PENNSYLVANIA

Cleveland

National Professional Football Hall of Fame

OHIO

Coal

Serpent Mound (ancient native burial ground)

COLUMBUS

Ohio

Natural gas

WEST VIRGINIA

LOCATION

IOWA

Pigs

Maize

DES MOINES

Iowa Capitol Building

Soya beans

Hamburger

Chicago

Davenport

Rock Island

Gary

Iron and steel

Maize

Peoria

Illinois

Fort Wayne

INDIANA

Car racing

Wabash

INDIANAPOLIS

Maize

Toledo

SPRINGFIELD

Pigs

St. Joseph

Mark Twain's house

Hannibal

Abraham Lincoln's house

Covered bridge

Cincinnati

ILLINOIS

Aircraft manufacturing

Kansas City

East St. Louis

St. Louis

Maize stores

OPEKA

JEFFERSON CITY

Gateway Arch

Mississippi

Ohio

KENTUCKY

MISSOURI

Springfield

Cottontail rabbit

Evansville

Coal

Cairo

OZARK PLATEAU

N

W E

S

Tornado

Zinc

Soya beans

ARKANSAS

SCALE

MILES

0 50 100 150

0 50 100 150 200 250

KILOMETRES

MARK TWAIN'S HOUSE

In 1835, author Mark Twain was born in this tiny cabin, which is now part of the Mark Twain Museum in Hannibal, Missouri.

AMERICAN FOOTBALL

Following the growth of this sport in the 19th century, the first American professional football association was founded in Canton, Ohio, in 1920.

J K L M N O P Q

Western United States

THE COLOSSAL ROCKY MOUNTAINS separate the western U.S.A. from the plains of the Midwest. Among the valleys and peaks of this spectacular range, mountain goats bound up steep rock faces and moose feed beside fast-flowing streams. There is little agriculture here, but herds of cattle graze the mountain meadows. West of the Rockies lies a series of dry plateaux, valleys and ranges. The Colorado Plateau has some of the continent's most spectacular scenery, including the world's largest gorge, the Grand Canyon. The states of Washington, Oregon and Idaho are known as the Pacific Northwest. The wet, densely forested western part of this area provides 40 per cent of the U.S.A.'s timber. The largest state in the region, California, is home to more people than any other American state. Most of the population lives in or near the coastal cities of Los Angeles and San Francisco. Inland, between the mountains of the Coast Ranges and the Sierra Nevada, farms form a patchwork of fields across the fertile, irrigated Central Valley. The most westerly state, Hawaii, lies 4,000 kilometres (2,500 mi) off the coast, in the middle of the Pacific Ocean. Hawaii consists of 132 islands, which were formed by undersea volcanoes. Several Hawaiian volcanoes still erupt, including Mauna Loa, the largest active volcano in the world.

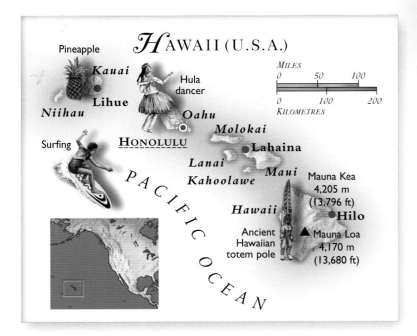

HAWAII (U.S.A.)

Pineapple
Kauai
Hula dancer
Lihue
Niihau
Oahu
Molokai
Surfing
HONOLULU
Lahaina
Lanai
Maui
Kahoolawe
Hawaii
Hilo
Ancient Hawaiian totem pole
Mauna Kea 4,205 m (13,796 ft)
Mauna Loa 4,170 m (13,680 ft)

MILES
0   50   100
0   100   200
KILOMETRES

PACIFIC OCEAN

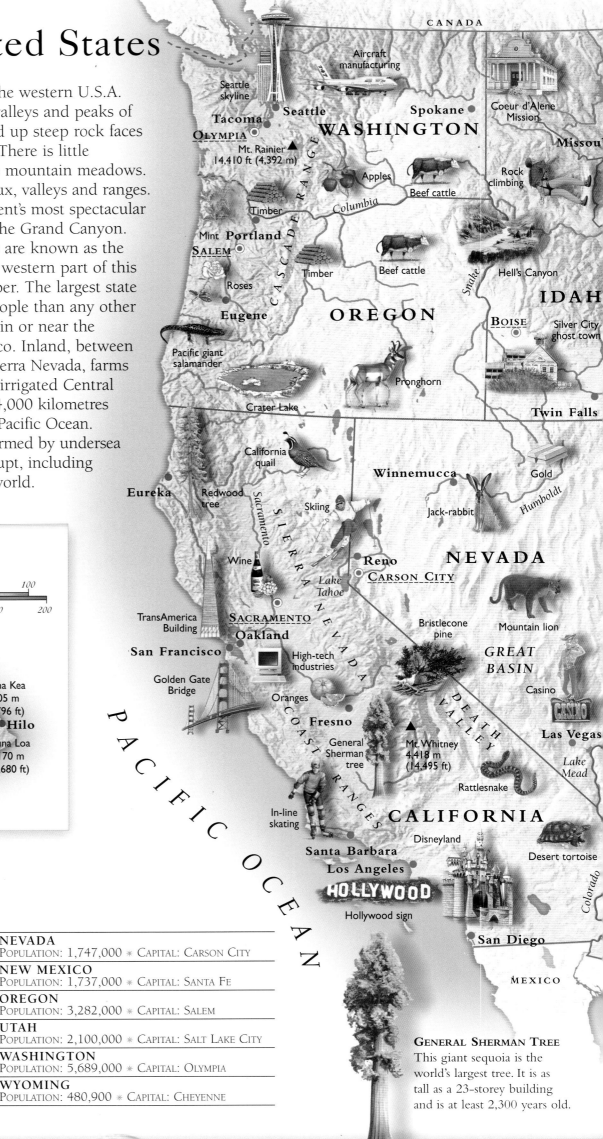

CANADA

Aircraft manufacturing
Seattle skyline
Tacoma   Seattle   Spokane   Coeur d'Alene Mission
OLYMPIA   WASHINGTON   Missou
Mt. Rainier 14,410 ft (4,392 m)
Apples   Rock climbing
Timber   Columbia   Beef cattle
Mint   Portland   Timber   Beef cattle   Hell's Canyon   IDAHO
SALEM   Roses   BOISE   Silver City ghost town
Eugene   OREGON   Snake
Pronghorn
Pacific giant salamander
Crater Lake   Twin Falls

California quail
Winnemucca   Gold
Eureka   Redwood tree   Humboldt
Skiing   Jack-rabbit
Wine   Reno   NEVADA
CARSON CITY
TransAmerica Building   SACRAMENTO   Bristlecone pine   Mountain lion
Oakland   Lake Tahoe
San Francisco   High-tech industries   GREAT BASIN
Golden Gate Bridge   Casino
Oranges   Fresno   Las Vegas
General Sherman tree   Mt. Whitney 4418 m (14,495 ft)   Lake Mead
In-line skating   Rattlesnake
CALIFORNIA
Santa Barbara   Disneyland   Desert tortoise
Los Angeles
HOLLYWOOD
Hollywood sign
San Diego
MEXICO
Colorado

PACIFIC OCEAN

ARIZONA	NEVADA
POPULATION: 4,669,000 * CAPITAL: PHOENIX	POPULATION: 1,747,000 * CAPITAL: CARSON CITY
CALIFORNIA	NEW MEXICO
POPULATION: 32,667,000 * CAPITAL: SACRAMENTO	POPULATION: 1,737,000 * CAPITAL: SANTA FE
COLORADO	OREGON
POPULATION: 3,971,000 * CAPITAL: DENVER	POPULATION: 3,282,000 * CAPITAL: SALEM
HAWAII	UTAH
POPULATION: 1,193,000 * CAPITAL: HONOLULU	POPULATION: 2,100,000 * CAPITAL: SALT LAKE CITY
IDAHO	WASHINGTON
POPULATION: 1,229,000 * CAPITAL: BOISE	POPULATION: 5,689,000 * CAPITAL: OLYMPIA
MONTANA	WYOMING
POPULATION: 880,500 * CAPITAL: HELENA	POPULATION: 480,900 * CAPITAL: CHEYENNE

GENERAL SHERMAN TREE
This giant sequoia is the world's largest tree. It is as tall as a 23-storey building and is at least 2,300 years old.

Wheat

Whitewater rafting

Oil

Natural gas

NORTH DAKOTA

Missouri

Great Falls

HELENA

MONTANA

Yellowstone

Grizzly bear

Bighorn sheep

Billings

SOUTH DAKOTA

Bighorn Canyon

Coal

Devil's Tower

Idaho Falls

Old Faithful geyser

WYOMING

Uranium

Beef cattle

Potatoes

Casper

American kestrel

Great Salt Lake

Rock Springs

Coyote

CHEYENNE

NEBRASKA

Ogden

Green

SALT LAKE CITY

Provo

Stegosaur skeleton

KANSAS

mon Temple

Boulder

Skiing

DENVER

UTAH

Arches National Park

COLORADO

Grand Junction

Colorado Springs **Pueblo**

OLORADO PLATEAU

Lake Powell

Arkansas

edar City

Monument Valley

Mountain goat

Cumbres and Toltec Scenic Railway

Appaloosa horses

Plains Indian dancer

Natural gas

Taos Pueblo (native village)

Grand Canyon

SANTA FE

Uranium

Flagstaff

Albuquerque

Pueblo pottery

Navajo woman weaving

NEW MEXICO

TEXAS

guaro ctus

ARIZONA

Zuni jewelry

Rio Grande

Roswell

PHOENIX

Gila

High-tech industries

Copper

Oil

National Astronomy Observatory

Tucson

TEXAS

San Xavier de Bac Mission

Roadrunner

Western United States *See World Fact File page 104*

◆ PROJECT: *Sand-Art Jars* ◆

The Navajo and Pueblo people of the south-western U.S.A. make ceremonial paintings with coloured sand. After the ceremony, the paintings are erased. You can make your own coloured-sand painting in a jar.

❶ First sift the sand to make sure it is clean and fine. Divide the sand into small piles, adding a few drops of food colouring to each to make different-coloured sands. Stir the sand every few hours to dry it.

❷ When the sand is dry, slowly pour some into a clean glass jar. Then pour a layer of another colour. Keep pouring layers of different colours until the jar is full.

❸ Now make patterns by pushing a length of wire, or the end of a thin paintbrush, down the inside of the glass, between the sand and the jar. Be careful not to stir the sand! As the wire goes up and down, different colours will slide into the spaces and create designs.

❹ Finally, top off the jar with more of the coloured sand and put on the lid.

◆ AMAZING FACT ◆

Carved out by the Colorado river, the Grand Canyon is about 350 kilometres (220 mi) long and 1.6 kilometres (1 mi) deep. The rocks at its bottom are more than two billion years old!

LOCATION

N
W   E
S

SCALE

MILES
0   50   100   150   200

0   100   200   300
KILOMETRES

ROADRUNNER

Roadrunners seldom fly, preferring to race along on their powerful legs. They can reach speeds of 32 kilometres per hour (20 mph).

PLAINS INDIAN DANCER

By dressing as buffalo (bison), dancers appeal to the sacred spirits of these animals to bring them health and good fortune.

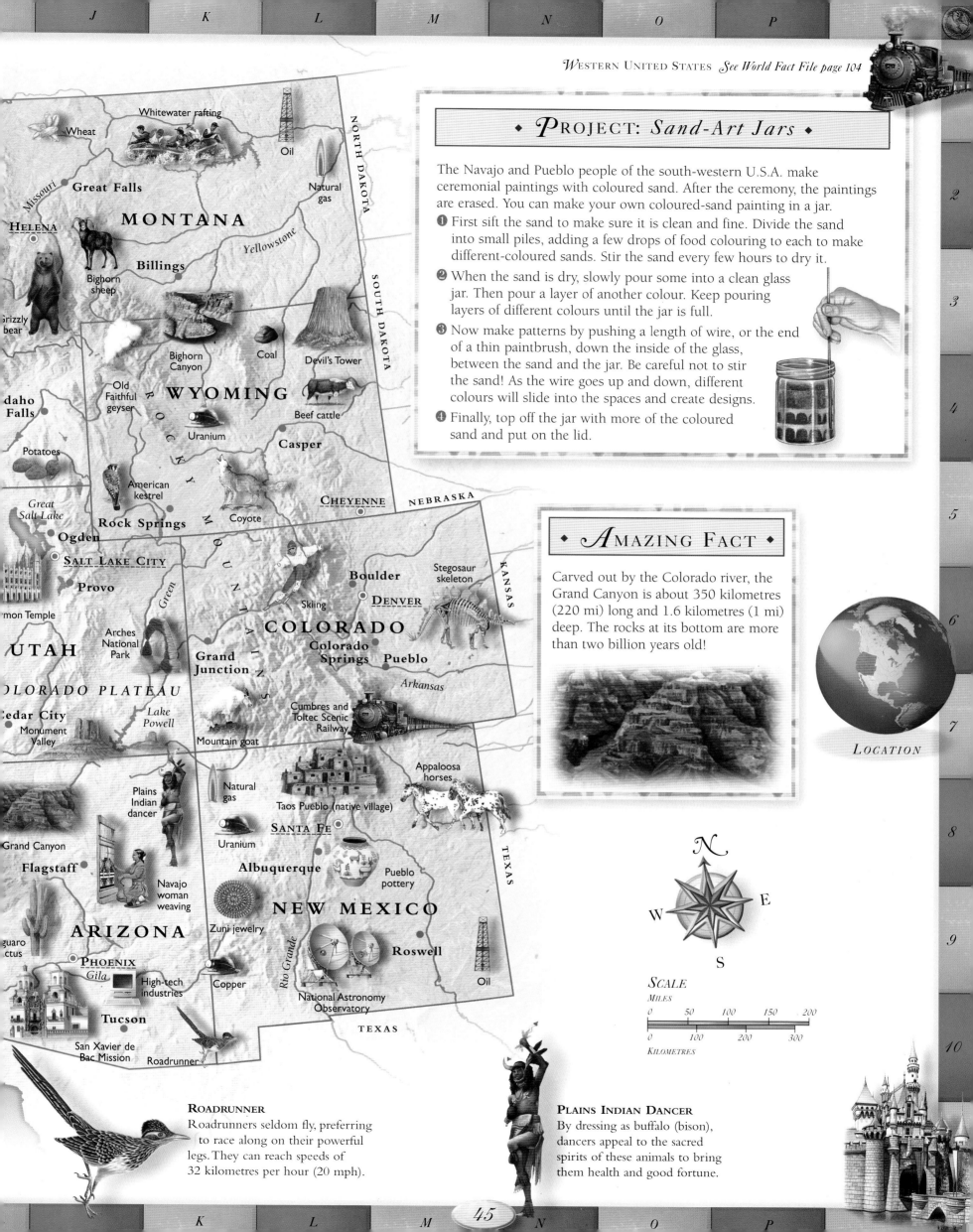

Mexico, Central America and the Caribbean

MEXICO AND CENTRAL AMERICA form a land bridge between the United States and South America. At its narrowest point, this strip of land is only 80 kilometres (50 mi) wide and is split by the Panama Canal, an artificial waterway that links the Atlantic and Pacific Oceans. Mexico is more than twice the size of the seven Central American countries combined. It is dominated by a large dry plateau, and only 18 per cent of the land can be farmed. The narrow plains on the east coast are warm and humid, and contain large oil reserves. Three-quarters of Mexicans live in cities and towns, and Mexico City is

one of the largest and fastest-growing cities in the world. Most of Central America is mountainous, and much of the land is covered in rainforests, where colourful parrots shriek from the tree-tops and chattering monkeys swing among branches. Although only a small proportion of Central America can be farmed, about half of the people live in rural areas and many grow their own food on small plots of land. To the east lie the Caribbean Islands, most of which are covered by tropical forests and surrounded by sandy beaches. Spain ruled much of Mexico, Central America and the Caribbean for centuries, and today most of the people speak Spanish. Their ancestors may be settlers from Europe, Native American peoples or Africans who were first brought to the region as slaves.

ANTIGUA AND BARBUDA
POPULATION: 64,300 * CAPITAL: ST. JOHN'S

THE BAHAMAS
POPULATION: 284,800 * CAPITAL: NASSAU

BARBADOS
POPULATION: 259,200 * CAPITAL: BRIDGETOWN

BELIZE
POPULATION: 235,800 * CAPITAL: BELMOPAN

COSTA RICA
POPULATION: 3,675,000 * CAPITAL: SAN JOSÉ

CUBA
POPULATION: 11,097,000 * CAPITAL: HAVANA

DOMINICA
POPULATION: 64,900 * CAPITAL: ROSEAU

DOMINICAN REPUBLIC
POPULATION: 8,130,000 * CAPITAL: SANTO DOMINGO

EL SALVADOR
POPULATION: 5,840,000 * CAPITAL: SAN SALVADOR

GRENADA
POPULATION: 97,100 * CAPITAL: ST. GEORGE'S

GUATEMALA
POPULATION: 12,336,000 * CAPITAL: GUATEMALA

HAITI
POPULATION: 6,885,000 * CAPITAL: PORT-AU-PRINCE

HONDURAS
POPULATION: 5,998,000 * CAPITAL: TEGUCIGALPA

JAMAICA
POPULATION: 2,653,000 * CAPITAL: KINGSTON

MEXICO
POPULATION: 100,295,000 * CAPITAL: MEXICO CITY

NICARAGUA
POPULATION: 4,718,000 * CAPITAL: MANAGUA

PANAMA
POPULATION: 2,779,000 * CAPITAL: PANAMA

ST. KITTS–NEVIS
POPULATION: 42,900 * CAPITAL: BASSETERRE

ST. LUCIA
POPULATION: 154,100 * CAPITAL: CASTRIES

ST. VINCENT AND THE GRENADINES
POPULATION: 120,600 * CAPITAL: KINGSTOWN

TRINIDAD AND TOBAGO
POPULATION: 1,103,000 * CAPITAL: PORT-OF-SPAIN

Tijuana
Mexicali
Gila monster
Tourism
Ciudad Juárez
Saguaro cactus
Beef cattle
Mexican cowboy
UNITED STATES OF AMERICA
Great white shark
BAJA CALIFORNIA
Gulf of California
Hermosillo
Vampire bat
Chihuahua
Silver
Singing grasshopper mouse
Natural gas
Rio Grande
Leatherback turtle
Gulf of Mexico
Elephant seals
SIERRA MADRE OCCIDENTAL
Monarch butterfly
Culiacán
Monarch butterfly
Monterrey
Cotton
Matamoros
La Paz
Gold
Torreón
Iron ore
Ancient Toltec stone statue
Mariachi musicians
Snapper
Lobster
El Castillo, Chichen Itza, Maya city ruins
Folk dancer
MEXICO
Tampico
YUCATÁ PENINSU
Common dolphins
Guadalajara
Maize
Metropolitan Cathedral
Oil
Bay of Campeche
Oil
Aztec snake carving
MEXICO CITY
Orizaba 5,700 m (18,700 ft)
Veracruz
Jagu
Soccer
Olmec stone carving
Great Plaza, Tikal
BELMOPAN
Tourism
Scarlet macaw
Acapulco
Thatched corncrib
Folk costume
GUATEMAL
PACIFIC OCEAN
Eagle ray
GUATEMALA
SAN SALVADOR
EL SALVAD

SINGING GRASSHOPPER MOUSE
This mouse is named for its habit of squeaking or 'singing' to warn off rivals. Grasshoppers are its favourite food.

◆ Amazing Fact ◆

The saguaro cactus is found only in the deserts of north-western Mexico and the south-western United States. It grows incredibly slowly, taking 25 years to reach a height of 30 centimetres (12 in). But it can live for 200 years and grow as high as a four-storey house. Like other cacti, the saguaro survives on water stored in its stem. A fully grown saguaro may contain enough water to fill 100 bathtubs!

◆ Project: *Make a Mexican Piñata* ◆

A piñata is a pot made from papier mâché often shaped like a star or animal and filled with toys and sweets. It is a popular part of many celebrations and festivals in Mexico and Central America. Children hang the piñata from the ceiling or a tree branch and take turns trying to break it open. You can make a Mexican piñata for your next party.

❶ Cover a large balloon with strips of newspaper dipped in flour-and-water paste or white glue. Wait for this papier mâché to dry and then repeat with at least two more layers of newspaper.

❷ When the papier mâché is completely dry, cut a small hole in the top and fill the piñata with all sorts of goodies. Re-cover the hole with more papier mâché.

❸ Make star points out of cardboard as shown. Tape them to the ball using the tabs. Decorate the star with paint and coloured tissue paper.

Step 3A   Step 3B

❹ Make two small holes next to each other at the top of the piñata. Thread curved wire through one hole and out the other. Hang up the piñata and ask guests to take turns hitting it with a stick to open it.

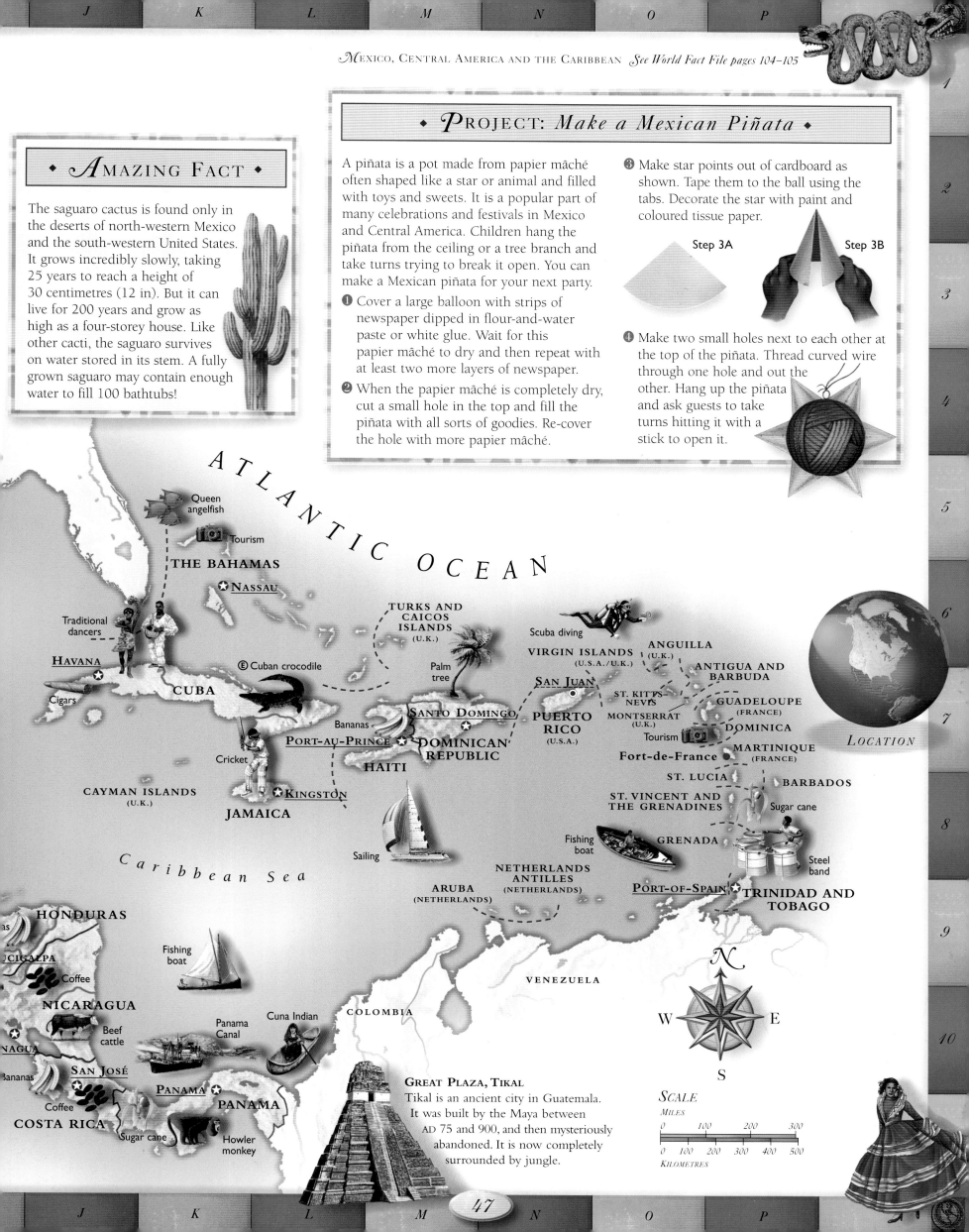

ATLANTIC OCEAN

Queen angelfish

Tourism

THE BAHAMAS

★ **Nassau**

Traditional dancers

TURKS AND CAICOS ISLANDS (U.K.)

Scuba diving

Palm tree

VIRGIN ISLANDS (U.S.A./U.K.)

ANGUILLA (U.K.)

ANTIGUA AND BARBUDA

Havana

Ⓔ Cuban crocodile

CUBA

Cigars

Bananas

SAN JUAN

Santo Domingo

PUERTO RICO (U.S.A.)

ST. KITTS– NEVIS

MONTSERRAT (U.K.)

GUADELOUPE (FRANCE)

DOMINICA

Tourism

MARTINIQUE (FRANCE)

Port-au-Prince

DOMINICAN REPUBLIC

HAITI

Fort-de-France

ST. LUCIA

LOCATION

Cricket

CAYMAN ISLANDS (U.K.)

★ **Kingston**

JAMAICA

Sailing

ST. VINCENT AND THE GRENADINES

BARBADOS

Sugar cane

Caribbean Sea

Fishing boat

GRENADA

Steel band

NETHERLANDS ANTILLES (NETHERLANDS)

ARUBA (NETHERLANDS)

Port-of-Spain

TRINIDAD AND TOBAGO

HONDURAS

Fishing boat

UCIGALPA

Coffee

VENEZUELA

NICARAGUA

Beef cattle

Cuna Indian

COLOMBIA

AGUA

Bananas

San José

Panama Canal

PANAMA ★

PANAMA

Coffee

COSTA RICA

Sugar cane

Howler monkey

N

W E

S

GREAT PLAZA, TIKAL
Tikal is an ancient city in Guatemala. It was built by the Maya between AD 75 and 900, and then mysteriously abandoned. It is now completely surrounded by jungle.

SCALE

MILES
0   100   200   300

0   100   200   300   400   500
KILOMETRES

South America

FROM ITS TROPICAL NORTHERN SHORE, South America stretches 7,240 kilometres (4,500 mi) southwards to the chilly, storm-battered peninsula of Cape Horn, just 1,000 kilometres (600 mi) from Antarctica. The Andes run the entire length of the continent's west coast, forming the longest mountain chain in the world. In the north, the Amazon River (the world's second-longest river) snakes eastwards from the Andes to the Atlantic Ocean, through vast rainforests that once covered more than one-third of the continent. To the south, the forests give way to the grasslands of the Gran Chaco and the Pampas. The southern tip of South America is a dry, windswept plateau known as Patagonia. South America's inhabitants include people of European, native American and African origin. Most people speak Spanish, but Portuguese is the official language in Brazil.

Major Mountains and Rivers

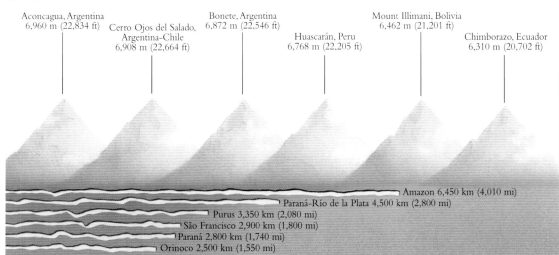

Aconcagua, Argentina 6,960 m (22,834 ft)
Cerro Ojos del Salado, Argentina-Chile 6,908 m (22,664 ft)
Bonete, Argentina 6,872 m (22,546 ft)
Huascarán, Peru 6,768 m (22,205 ft)
Mount Illimani, Bolivia 6,462 m (21,201 ft)
Chimborazo, Ecuador 6,310 m (20,702 ft)

Amazon 6,450 km (4,010 mi)
Paraná-Río de la Plata 4,500 km (2,800 mi)
Purus 3,350 km (2,080 mi)
São Francisco 2,900 km (1,800 mi)
Paraná 2,800 km (1,740 mi)
Orinoco 2,500 km (1,550 mi)

Political Map

VENEZUELA
GUYANA
SURINAME
FRENCH GUIANA (FRANCE)
COLOMBIA
GALÁPAGOS ISLANDS (ECUADOR)
ECUADOR
BRAZIL
PERU
BOLIVIA
MARTIN VAZ ISLANDS (BRAZIL)
PARAGUAY
EASTER ISLAND (CHILE)
CHILE
JUAN FERNANDEZ ISLANDS (CHILE)
URUGUAY
ARGENTINA
FALKLAND ISLANDS (U.K.)
SOUTH GEORGIA (U.K.)

Continent Facts

Regional land area: 6,877,943 sq. miles (17,818,505 sq. km)
Regional population: 343,131,400
Independent countries: Argentina, Bolivia, Brazil, Chile, Colombia, Ecuador, Guyana, Paraguay, Peru, Suriname, Uruguay, Venezuela

World Records

WORLD'S LONGEST MOUNTAIN CHAIN
ANDES, WESTERN SOUTH AMERICA 7,600 KM (4,700 MI)

WORLD'S DRIEST PLACE
ATACAMA DESERT, CHILE, AVERAGE ANNUAL RAINFALL LESS THAN 0.1 MM (1/250 IN)

WORLD'S HIGHEST WATERFALL
ANGEL FALLS, VENEZUELA, 979 M (3,212 FT)

WORLD'S HIGHEST CAPITAL CITY
LA PAZ, BOLIVIA, 3,631 M (11,913 FT)

WORLD'S HIGHEST NAVIGABLE LAKE
LAKE TITICACA, PERU-BOLIVIA, 3,810 M (12,500 FT)

WORLD'S LARGEST RIVER BY VOLUME
AMAZON, PERU-BRAZIL, DISCHARGES 200,000 CUBIC M (7,100,000 CUBIC FT) PER SECOND INTO ATLANTIC OCEAN

WORLD'S LARGEST RIVER BASIN
AMAZON BASIN, NORTHERN SOUTH AMERICA, 7,045,000 SQ. KM (2,720,000 SQ. MI)

WORLD'S LARGEST LAGOON
LAGOA DOS PATOS, BRAZIL, 9,850 SQ. KM (3,803 SQ. MI)

Continent Records

HIGHEST MOUNTAIN
ACONCAGUA, ARGENTINA, 6,960 M (22,834 FT)

LOWEST POINT
VALDÉS PENINSULA, ARGENTINA, 40 M (131 FT) BELOW SEA LEVEL

LARGEST LAKE
LAKE TITICACA, PERU-BOLIVIA, 8,288 SQ. KM (3,200 SQ. MI)

LONGEST RIVER
AMAZON RIVER, PERU-BRAZIL, 6,450 KM (4,010 MI)

LARGEST COUNTRY BY AREA
BRAZIL, 8,506,663 SQ. KM (3,284,426 SQ. MI)

LARGEST COUNTRY BY POPULATION
BRAZIL, POPULATION 171,854,000

LARGEST CITY BY POPULATION
SÃO PAULO, BRAZIL, POPULATION 16,800,000

• AMAZING FACT •

The Atacama Desert in northern Chile is the driest place in the world. Rain showers occur only once or twice a century, and in some parts of the desert rain has never been recorded.

PHYSICAL MAP

NORTH AMERICA

AFRICA

Tropic of Cancer

Caribbean Sea

Lake Maracaibo

Orinoco

GUIANA HIGHLANDS

Amazon Delta

Gulf of Panama

LLANOS

Rio Negro

Rio Branco

ATLANTIC OCEAN

GALÁPAGOS ISLANDS

Chimborazo

AMAZON BASIN

Amazon

Equator

Gulf of Guayaquil

Marañón

SELVAS

Tapajós

Xingu

A N D E S

Purus

PACIFIC OCEAN

Huascarán

Madeira

Tocantins

São Francisco

MATO GROSSO PLATEAU

BRAZILIAN HIGHLANDS

Lake Titicaca

Mt. Illimani

Lake Poopó

GRAN CHACO

Parana

Tropic of Capricorn

ATACAMA DESERT

A N D E S

Paraguay

SERRA DO MAR

Cerro Ojos del Salado

Uruguay

Lagoa dos Patos

Bonete

Easter Island

Aconcagua

PAMPAS

Rio de la Plata

Colorado

Blanca Bay

PATAGONIA

San Matías Gulf

VALDÉS PENINSULA

San Jorge Gulf

FALKLAND ISLANDS

Tierra del Fuego

South Georgia

CAPE HORN

Drake Passage

Antarctic Circle

ANTARCTICA

Northern South America

MOST OF NORTHERN SOUTH AMERICA is drained by the world's second longest river, the Amazon, and its more than 200 tributaries. These waterways flow through lush tropical rainforests that are home to a tenth of all the plants and animals on Earth. Sadly, the rainforests are rapidly disappearing as a growing population clears the land for farming. Every minute, an area of forest the size of five football pitches is cut down. More than a quarter of the world's rainforests lie within Brazil, the largest country in South America. Brazil has many resources, including iron ore, oil and gold. It is the continent's most industrialized country and the world's leading producer of coffee, bananas and sugar cane. North-west of Brazil lies Venezuela, a sparsely populated country that is South America's top oil producer. From Venezuela, the Andes curve southwards through Colombia, Ecuador and Peru. At the northern end of this mountain range, the climate is wet, and large coffee and banana plantations cover the hillsides. Further south, little rain falls and crops can be grown only by using water from mountain streams. On the upper slopes of the Peruvian Andes, farmers grow potatoes and wheat and raise animals, including llamas and alpacas. One thousand kilometres (600 mi) off the coast of Ecuador lie the Galápagos Islands. These volcanic islands are famous for their unusual wildlife, which includes marine iguanas and giant tortoises.

BRAZIL
POPULATION: 171,854,000 * CAPITAL: BRASÍLIA

COLOMBIA
POPULATION: 39,310,000 * CAPITAL: BOGOTÁ

ECUADOR
POPULATION: 12,563,000 * CAPITAL: QUITO

GUYANA
POPULATION: 705,200 * CAPITAL: GEORGETOWN

PERU
POPULATION: 26,625,000 * CAPITAL: LIMA

SURINAME
POPULATION: 431,200 * CAPITAL: PARAMARIBO

VENEZUELA
POPULATION: 23,204,000 * CAPITAL: CARACAS

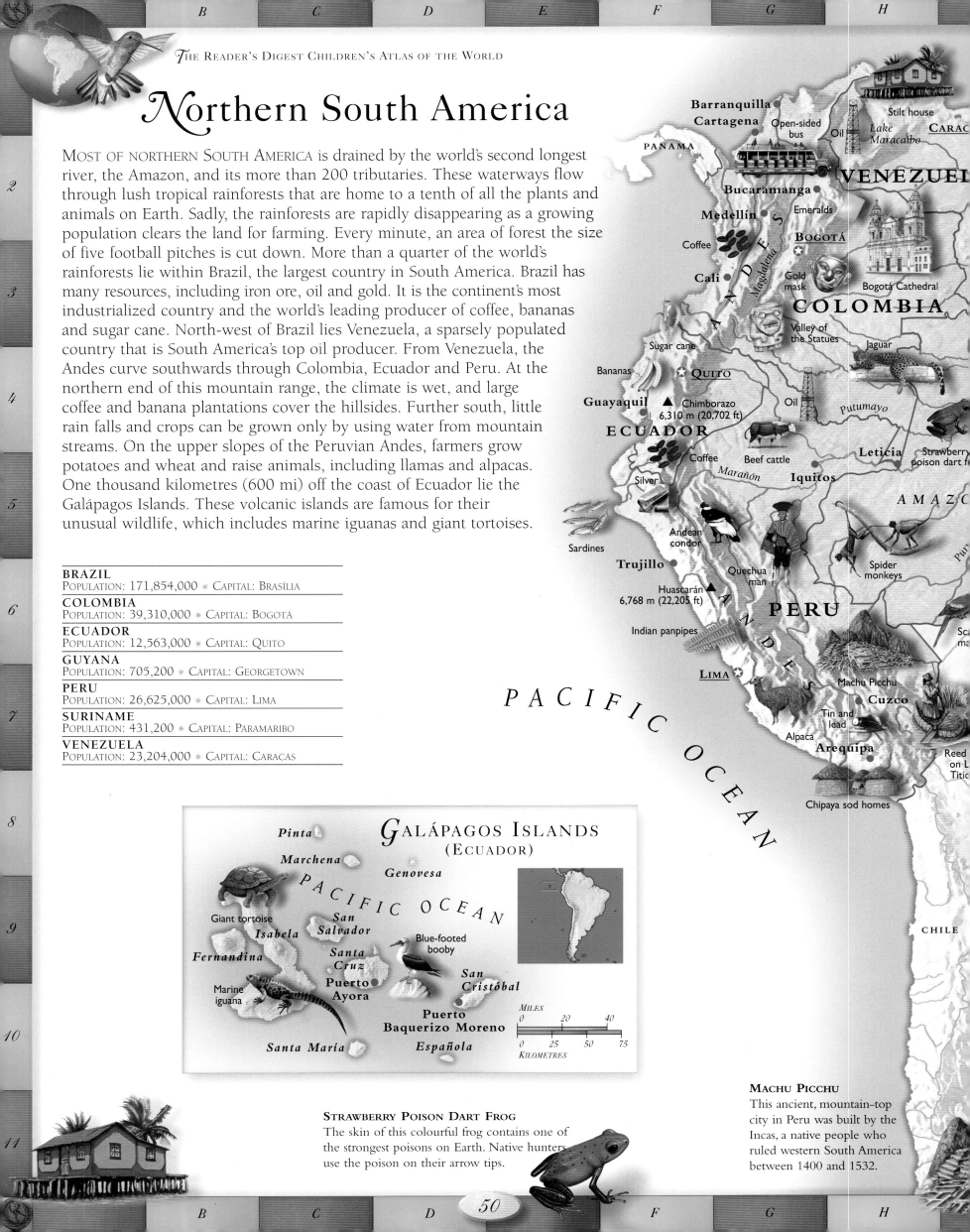

GALÁPAGOS ISLANDS
(ECUADOR)

Pinta
Marchena
Genovesa
PACIFIC OCEAN
Giant tortoise
Isabela
San Salvador
Fernandina
Santa Cruz
Blue-footed booby
Marine iguana
Puerto Ayora
San Cristóbal
Puerto Baquerizo Moreno
Santa María
Española

MILES
0   20   40

0   25   50   75
KILOMETRES

STRAWBERRY POISON DART FROG
The skin of this colourful frog contains one of the strongest poisons on Earth. Native hunters use the poison on their arrow tips.

MACHU PICCHU
This ancient, mountain-top city in Peru was built by the Incas, a native people who ruled western South America between 1400 and 1532.

Barranquilla
Cartagena
PANAMA
Open-sided bus
Oil
Lake Maracaibo
Stilt house
CARAC
VENEZUELA
Bucaramanga
Emeralds
Medellín
Coffee
BOGOTÁ
Gold mask
Bogotá Cathedral
Cali
COLOMBIA
Valley of the Statues
Sugar cane
Jaguar
Bananas
QUITO
Guayaquil
Chimborazo 6,310 m (20,702 ft)
Oil
Putumayo
ECUADOR
Coffee
Beef cattle
Leticia
Strawberry poison dart f
Silver
Marañón
Iquitos
AMAZO
Sardines
Andean condor
Spider monkeys
Trujillo
Quechua man
Huascarán 6,768 m (22,205 ft)
PERU
Indian panpipes
Sc ma
Machu Picchu
LIMA
Cuzco
Tin and lead
Alpaca
Arequipa
Reed on L Titic
Chipaya sod homes
CHILE

PACIFIC OCEAN

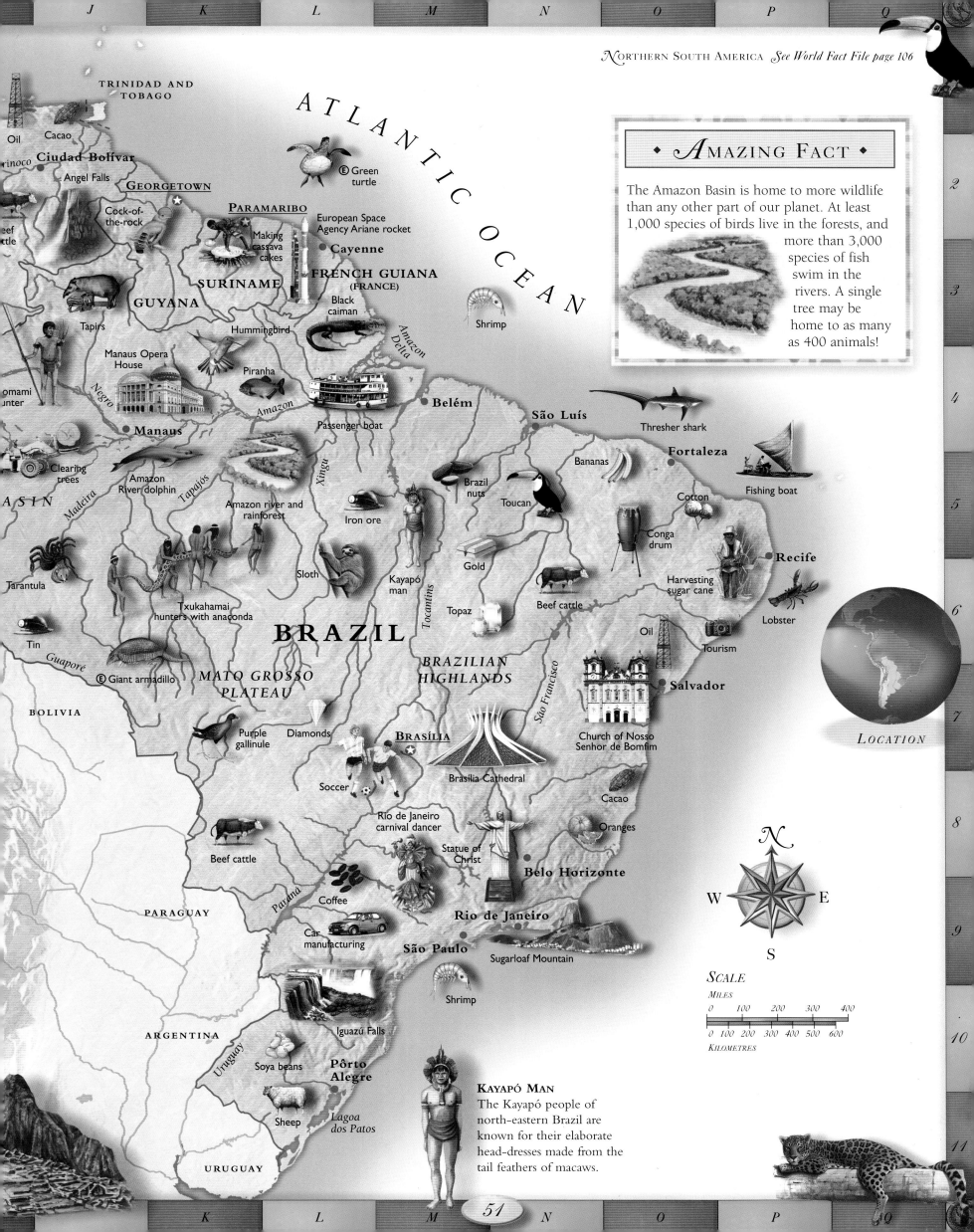

ATLANTIC OCEAN

TRINIDAD AND TOBAGO

Oil
Cacao
Ciudad Bolívar
Orinoco
Angel Falls
Beef cattle
GEORGETOWN
Cock-of-the-rock
GUYANA
Tapirs
Yanomami hunter
Manaus Opera House
Negro
Manaus
Clearing trees
Amazon River dolphin
Madeira
BASIN
Tarantula
Tin
Guaporé
Ⓔ Giant armadillo

PARAMARIBO
Making cassava cakes
SURINAME
Green turtle
European Space Agency Ariane rocket
Cayenne
FRENCH GUIANA (FRANCE)
Black caiman
Hummingbird
Amazon Delta
Piranha
Passenger boat
Amazon
Xingu
Tapajós
Amazon river and rainforest
Iron ore
Sloth
Txukahamai hunters with anaconda
Kayapó man
Purple gallinule
Diamonds
Soccer

Shrimp

Belém
São Luís
Thresher shark
Bananas
Fortaleza
Brazil nuts
Toucan
Cotton
Conga drum
Fishing boat
Gold
Harvesting sugar cane
Recife
Topaz
Beef cattle
Lobster
Oil
Tourism

BRAZIL
MATO GROSSO PLATEAU
BRAZILIAN HIGHLANDS
Tocantins
São Francisco
Salvador
Church of Nosso Senhor de Bomfim
BRASÍLIA
Brasília Cathedral
Rio de Janeiro carnival dancer
Statue of Christ
Cacao
Oranges
Belo Horizonte
Rio de Janeiro
Sugarloaf Mountain

BOLIVIA
Beef cattle
Coffee
Car manufacturing
São Paulo
Paraná
PARAGUAY
Shrimp

Iguazú Falls
Uruguay
Soya beans
Pôrto Alegre
Sheep
Lagoa dos Patos
ARGENTINA
URUGUAY

LOCATION

N
W E
S

♦ AMAZING FACT ♦

The Amazon Basin is home to more wildlife than any other part of our planet. At least 1,000 species of birds live in the forests, and more than 3,000 species of fish swim in the rivers. A single tree may be home to as many as 400 animals!

KAYAPÓ MAN
The Kayapó people of north-eastern Brazil are known for their elaborate head-dresses made from the tail feathers of macaws.

SCALE
MILES
0 100 200 300 400
0 100 200 300 400 500 600
KILOMETRES

THE READER'S DIGEST CHILDREN'S ATLAS OF THE WORLD

Southern South America

SOUTHERN SOUTH AMERICA IS SHAPED like a long, narrow triangle that tapers to a point on the southern island of Tierra del Fuego. The Andes run down the western side of the region, separating the country of Chile from its neighbours. Twenty times as long as it is wide, Chile has a variety of climates and landscapes. In the cold, wet, sparsely populated south, mountains rise steeply from the ocean, and glaciers snake through valleys. Central Chile has milder weather and many farms, vineyards and orchards. The north is very arid and includes the driest place in the world, the Atacama Desert. East of the Atacama, the Andes spread into Bolivia, one of the poorest countries in South America. From eastern Bolivia, wide plains stretch southwards through Paraguay, Uruguay and northern Argentina. Enormous herds of cattle and sheep roam the eastern and southern parts of these plains, tended by gauchos, South America's ranch hands. Argentina has more than 50 million cattle, and beef production is one of its most important industries. The country's most fertile grasslands, the Pampas, surround the capital, Buenos Aires. This city is home to one-third of the Argentinian population. In the south of the continent is a cold, barren plateau known as Patagonia. Few people live here, but the area is rich in minerals. The seas around Tierra del Fuego in the far south are often stormy. Hundreds of ships have been wrecked around Cape Horn and the Strait of Magellan.

ARGENTINA
POPULATION: 36,738,000 * CAPITAL: BUENOS AIRES

BOLIVIA
POPULATION: 7,983,000 * CAPITALS: LA PAZ, SUCRE

CHILE
POPULATION: 14,974,000 * CAPITAL: SANTIAGO

PARAGUAY
POPULATION: 5,435,000 * CAPITAL: ASUNCION

URUGUAY
POPULATION: 3,309,000 * CAPITAL: MONTEVIDEO

◆ PROJECT: *Easter Island Moai* ◆

Easter Island is covered with huge statues called moai. Some are more than 9 metres (30 ft) high. The early inhabitants of Easter Island may have built the statues to honour their ancestors. You can make an Easter Island statue, too.

1 Mix equal parts of plaster and vermiculite (both available at model shops). Stir as you add enough water to make a thick plaster. Pour the mixture into an old shoe box.

2 When the mixture hardens, tear away the cardboard. Carve the stone using tools such as a plastic knife or an ice lolly stick.

3 Alternatively, make your carving out of a block of modelling clay, plaster of Paris or any other modelling material.

LLAMA
A common domestic animal in South America, the llama is a relative of the camel. It is kept for its wool and is also used for carrying goods through mountainous terrain.

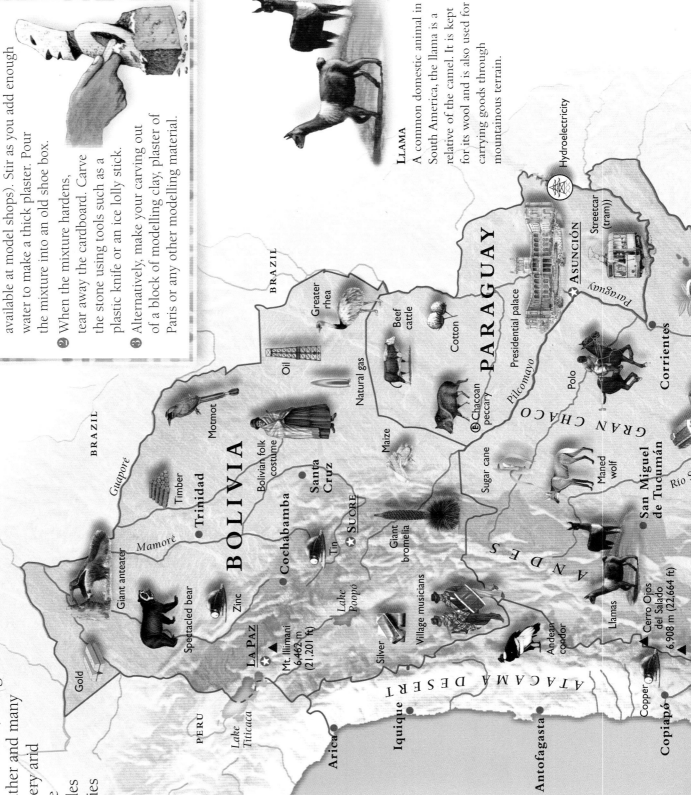

PERU

BRAZIL

BOLIVIA

PARAGUAY

GRAN CHACO

ANDES

ATACAMA DESERT

Lake Titicaca

LA PAZ — Mt. Illimani 6,462 m (21,201 ft)

Trinidad

Cochabamba

Santa Cruz

SUCRE

Lake Poopó

Arica

Iquique

Antofagasta

Copiapó

Cerro Ojos del Salado 6,908 m (22,664 ft)

Bonete 6,872 m (22,546 ft)

ASUNCIÓN — Presidential palace, Streetcar (tram)

San Miguel de Tucumán

Corrientes

Río Salado

Guaporé

Mamoré

Pilcomayo

Paraguay

Gold, Spectacled bear, Giant anteater, Timber, Motmot, Zinc, Tin, Silver, Giant bromelia, Village musicians, Andean condor, Llamas, Copper, Bolivian folk costume, Maize, Sugar cane, Maned wolf, Polo, Cotton, Beef cattle, Greater rhea, Chacoan peccary, Natural gas, Oil, Maté (tea), Hydroelectricity

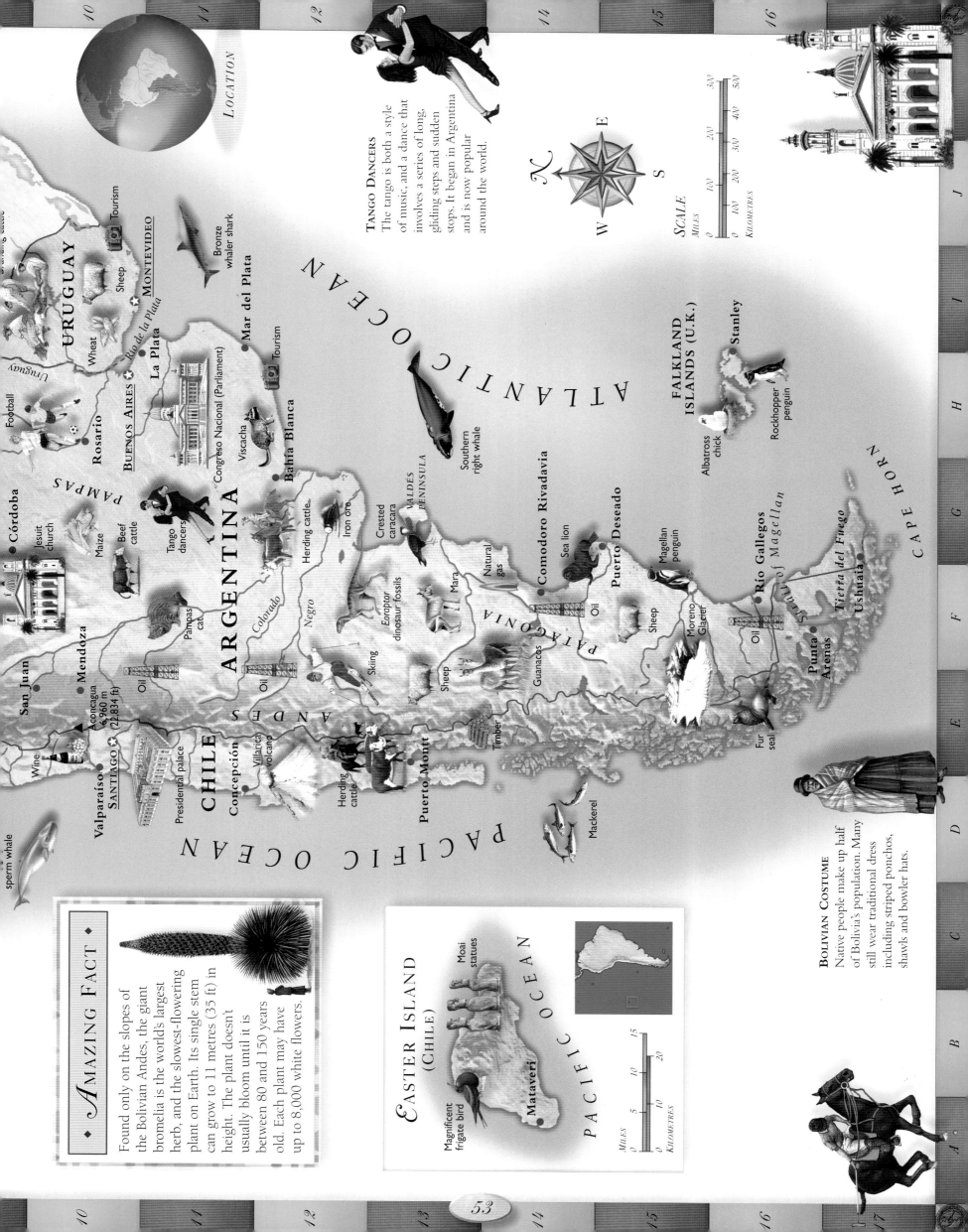

Location

Tango Dancers
The tango is both a style of music, and a dance that involves a series of long, gliding steps and sudden stops. It began in Argentina and is now popular around the world.

Scale
MILES
KILOMETRES

Bolivian Costume
Native people make up half of Bolivia's population. Many still wear traditional dress including striped ponchos, shawls and bowler hats.

◆ **Amazing Fact** ◆
Found only on the slopes of the Bolivian Andes, the giant bromelia is the world's largest herb, and the slowest-flowering plant on Earth. Its single stem can grow to 11 metres (35 ft) in height. The plant doesn't usually bloom until it is between 80 and 150 years old. Each plant may have up to 8,000 white flowers.

Easter Island (CHILE)
Moai statues
Magnificent frigate bird
Mataveri
PACIFIC OCEAN
MILES
KILOMETRES

URUGUAY
Uruguay
Sheep
Tourism
MONTEVIDEO
Wheat
Río de la Plata
La Plata
Bronze whaler shark
Mar del Plata
Tourism

Córdoba
Jesuit church
Maize
Beef cattle
Rosario
BUENOS AIRES
Congreso Nacional (Parliament)
Football
PAMPAS
Tango dancers
Viscacha
Bahía Blanca
ARGENTINA
Pampas cat
Iron ore
Herding cattle
Crested caracara
VALDÉS PENINSULA
Southern right whale
ATLANTIC OCEAN

San Juan
Mendoza
Aconcagua 6,960 m (22,834 ft)
Oil
Colorado
Negro
Eoraptor dinosaur fossils
Mara
Natural gas
Comodoro Rivadavia
Sea lion
FALKLAND ISLANDS (U.K.)
Stanley
Albatross chick
Rockhopper penguin

Wine
Valparaíso
SANTIAGO
CHILE
Concepción
Presidential palace
Villarrica volcano
ANDES
Skiing
Sheep
Herding cattle
Puerto Montt
Timber
Guanacos
Oil
Sheep
PATAGONIA
Puerto Deseado
Magellan penguin
Moreno Glacier
Río Gallegos
Strait of Magellan
Oil
Punta Arenas
Tierra del Fuego
Ushuaia
CAPE HORN

PACIFIC OCEAN
Mackerel
sperm whale

N E S W

Europe

EUROPE IS A SMALL, DENSELY POPULATED CONTINENT made up of many countries, each of which has its own culture and, in most cases, its own language. It is bounded by the Arctic and Atlantic Oceans in the north and west, and the Mediterranean Sea in the south. In the east, Russia's Ural Mountains separate Europe from Asia. A series of mountain ranges, including the Pyrenees, the Alps and the Carpathian Mountains, crosses Europe from east to west. South of these ranges, the land is rugged and the climate is warm and dry in summer, and mild and wet in winter. To the north, a broad band of flat land, known as the Northern European Plain, extends from the Atlantic coast to western Russia. North-western Europe has a mild, wet climate, but in the east and far north winters can be bitterly cold. Once, most of Europe was covered in forest, but over many years the trees were cleared to make way for cities, farms and industry.

Major Mountains and Rivers

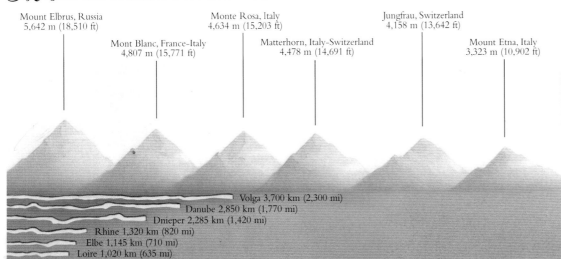

Mount Elbrus, Russia
5,642 m (18,510 ft)

Monte Rosa, Italy
4,634 m (15,203 ft)

Jungfrau, Switzerland
4,158 m (13,642 ft)

Mont Blanc, France-Italy
4,807 m (15,771 ft)

Matterhorn, Italy-Switzerland
4,478 m (14,691 ft)

Mount Etna, Italy
3,323 m (10,902 ft)

Volga 3,700 km (2,300 mi)
Danube 2,850 km (1,770 mi)
Dnieper 2,285 km (1,420 mi)
Rhine 1,320 km (820 mi)
Elbe 1,145 km (710 mi)
Loire 1,020 km (635 mi)

Continent Facts

Regional land area: 10,354,636 sq. km (3,997,929 sq. mi) (including European Russia)
Regional population: 698,727,000 (including European Russia)
Independent countries: Albania, Andorra, Austria, Belarus, Belgium, Bosnia and Herzegovina, Bulgaria, Croatia, Czech Republic, Denmark, Estonia, Finland, France, Germany, Greece, Hungary, Iceland, Ireland, Italy, Latvia, Liechtenstein, Lithuania, Luxembourg, Macedonia, Malta, Moldova, Monaco, The Netherlands, Norway, Poland, Portugal, Romania, Russia, San Marino, Slovakia, Slovenia, Spain, Sweden, Switzerland, Ukraine, United Kingdom, Vatican City, Yugoslavia

World Records

WORLD'S SMALLEST COUNTRY
VATICAN CITY, 0.44 SQ. KM (0.17 SQ. MI)

WORLD'S TALLEST STALAGMITE
KRÁSNOHORSKÁ CAVE, SLOVAKIA, 32 M (105 FT)

Continent Records

HIGHEST MOUNTAIN
MOUNT ELBRUS, RUSSIA, 5,642 M (18,510 FT)

LOWEST POINT
VOLGA RIVER DELTA, 28 M (92 FT) BELOW SEA LEVEL

LARGEST LAKE
LAKE LADOGA, RUSSIA, 17,703 SQ. KM (6,835 SQ. MI)

LONGEST RIVER
VOLGA RIVER, RUSSIA, 3,700 KM (2,300 MI)

LARGEST COUNTRY BY AREA
EUROPEAN RUSSIA, 603,701 SQ. KM (233,089 SQ. MI)

LARGEST COUNTRY BY POPULATION
EUROPEAN RUSSIA, POPULATION 117,115,000

LARGEST CITY BY POPULATION
PARIS, FRANCE, POPULATION 9,775,000

Political Map

ICELAND

FAEROE ISLANDS
(DENMARK)

SWEDEN

FINLAND

NORWAY

ESTONIA

UNITED
KINGDOM

LATVIA

RUSSIA

DENMARK

KALININGRAD
OBLAST
(RUSSIA) LITHUANIA

IRELAND

THE
NETHERLANDS

BELARUS

GERMANY

POLAND

BELGIUM

LUXEMBOURG

CZECH
REPUBLIC

SLOVAKIA

UKRAINE

FRANCE

AUSTRIA

1

SWITZERLAND

HUNGARY

MOLDOVA

SLOVENIA

ROMANIA

CROATIA

3

YUGOSLAVIA

BOSNIA and
HERZEGOVINA

4

BULGARIA

2

5

ALBANIA MACEDONIA

SPAIN

ITALY

PORTUGAL

GREECE

MALTA

Key to Numbered Countries

- ■ 1 LIECHTENSTEIN
- ■ 2 ANDORRA
- ■ 3 MONACO
- ■ 4 SAN MARINO
- ■ 5 VATICAN CITY

EUROPE

PHYSICAL MAP

ARCTIC OCEAN

× NORTH POLE

NORTH AMERICA

Greenland

Norwegian Sea

Barents Sea

FAEROE ISLANDS

Iceland

Arctic Circle

ATLANTIC OCEAN

URAL MOUNTAINS

ASIA

SCANDINAVIA

Lake Onega

Gulf of Bothnia

Lake Ladoga

Lake Vänern

North Sea

Baltic Sea

Volga

Ireland

NORTHERN EUROPEAN PLAIN

Great Britain

English Channel

Seine

Rhine

Elbe

CARPATHIAN MTS.

Dnieper

Don

Bay of Biscay

Loire

Jungfrau

A L P S

Matterhorn

Mont Blanc ▲ ▲ ▲

Monte Rosa

Danube

Mt. Elbrus ▲

Caspian Sea

CAUCASUS MTS.

PYRENEES

IBERIAN PENINSULA

Corsica

Adriatic Sea

Black Sea

BALKAN PENINSULA

BALEARIC IS.

APENNINES

Strait of Gibraltar

Sardinia

Sicily

Mediterranean Sea

Ionian Sea

Aegean Sea

▲ Mt. Etna

Crete

Tropic of Cancer

AFRICA

Equator

The United Kingdom and the Republic of Ireland

THE UNITED KINGDOM AND THE REPUBLIC OF IRELAND occupy islands known as the British Isles. The United Kingdom (U.K.) is made up of the countries of England, Wales, Scotland and Northern Ireland, which are ruled by one government based in London but have their own cultures and regional assemblies. Scotland has its own legal and educational systems, churches and bank notes. England is a crowded country with many large cities. Almost eight million people live in London, the capital city. London is one of the world's most important centres of trade and finance and is famous for its many historic buildings. Southern and eastern England are fairly flat and fertile and their farms provide most of the U.K.'s crops. The country's most important industries are located in central England, an area known as the Midlands, and around the coalfields of the Pennine hills. To the west and north, the countryside is wet and mountainous and is used mainly for grazing animals. In the rugged, sparsely populated Scottish Highlands, red deer and sheep roam the hills and eagles soar overhead.

The Republic of Ireland occupies about 85 per cent of the island of Ireland. It is a land of green plains surrounded by coastal mountains. Most of the country's industries are located in the capital, Dublin, and the southern city of Cork.

IRELAND
POPULATION: 3,633,000 ✷ CAPITAL: DUBLIN

UNITED KINGDOM
POPULATION: 59,114,000 ✷ CAPITAL: LONDON

ENGLAND
POPULATION: 49,089,000 ✷ CAPITAL: LONDON

NORTHERN IRELAND
POPULATION: 1,663,000 ✷ CAPITAL: BELFAST

SCOTLAND
POPULATION: 5,128,000 ✷ CAPITAL: EDINBURGH

WALES
POPULATION: 2,921,000 ✷ CAPITAL: CARDIFF

◆ AMAZING FACT ◆

In the 19th century, as a hoax, the name of the Welsh village Llanfairpwllgwyngyll was lengthened to the tongue-twisting Llanfairpwllgwyngyllgogerychwyrndrobwllllantysiliogogogoch. The name means 'St. Mary's church by the pool of white hazel trees, near the rapid whirlpool, by the red cave of the Church of St. Tysilio'. In 1988 the village officially returned to using the shorter name. However, the railway station is still called by the 58-letter version.

LLANFAIRPWLLGWYNGYLLGOGERYCHWYNDROBWLLLLANTYSILIOGOGOGOCH

◆ LOOK AGAIN ◆

● Which famous railway bridge is located near the capital of Scotland?
● Name a sport that is played in Ireland.
● What is the name of the group of islands near Lands End?

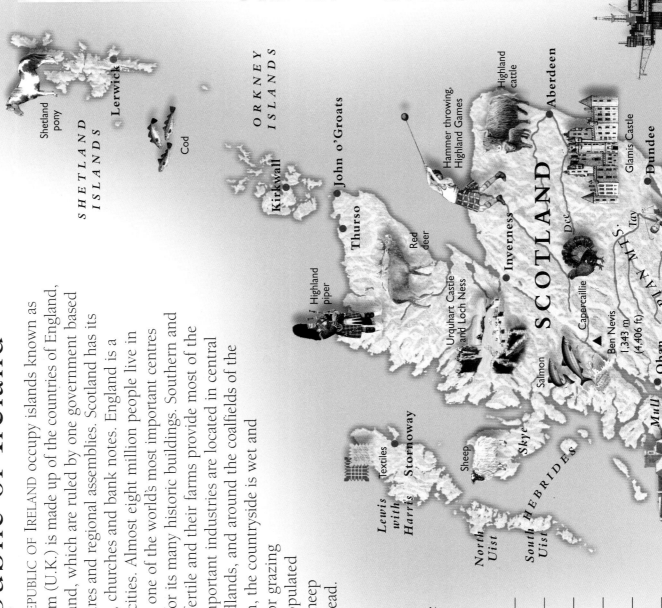

Shetland pony
Lerwick
SHETLAND ISLANDS
Cod
ORKNEY ISLANDS
Kirkwall
John o'Groats
Thurso
Red deer
Highland cattle
Hammer throwing, Highland Games
Aberdeen
Glamis Castle
Highland piper
Urquhart Castle and Loch Ness
Inverness
SCOTLAND
Capercaillie
Dee
Dundee
Tay
Salmon
Ben Nevis 1,343 m (4,406 ft)
Oban
Otter
Mull
Golf
GRAMPIAN MTS.
Forth
Coal
Forth Railway Bridge
Coal
EDINBURGH
Tweed
Beef cattle
Hadrian's Wall
Clyde
Glasgow
Skye
Sheep
Textiles
Stornoway
Lewis with Harris
HEBRIDES
North Uist
South Uist
Iona Abbey
Islay
Arran
Giant's Causeway rock formation
Oil rig
Haddock
N o r t
N o r t h

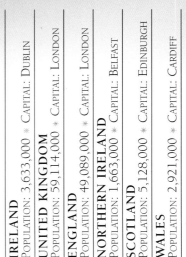

Fishing trawler

STONEHENGE
This prehistoric stone monument, or megalith, was a religious and ceremonial site for thousands of years.

BLARNEY CASTLE
It is said that if you kiss the Blarney Stone in the tower of this castle you will become a clever and persuasive talker.

Spain and Portugal

SPAIN AND PORTUGAL OCCUPY the Iberian Peninsula, a square-shaped piece of land in south-western Europe. This peninsula is separated from the rest of the continent by the Pyrenees, a mountain range that contains the tiny country of Andorra. Most of the Iberian Peninsula consists of a huge plateau known as the Meseta, which is covered with dry grasslands, olive groves and forested hills. At the centre of the Meseta, 646 metres (2,120 ft) above sea level, lies Madrid – the largest city in Spain and the highest capital city in Europe. Spain's second-largest city, Barcelona, lies on the narrow plains of the east coast. This coastline and the nearby Balearic Islands are warm and sunny for much of the year, and in summer, crowds of holiday-makers from all over Europe sunbathe on the sandy beaches. The southern tip of Spain lies only 15 kilometres (9 mi) from Africa. Between AD 711 and the 12th century, most of Spain was ruled by the Moors, an Arabic people from North Africa, and towns such as Granada and Seville have many ornate Moorish buildings. West of Spain lies Portugal. Once the heart of a vast, worldwide empire, Portugal is now one of the poorest countries in western Europe. Olive groves and cork oak forests cover the dry, southern plains. In the many river valleys that cross the country, farmers grow grapes for wine-making. Among the best-known Portuguese wines is port, which is named after the country's second-largest city, Porto.

ANDORRA
POPULATION: 66,000 * CAPITAL: ANDORRA

PORTUGAL
POPULATION: 9,919,000 * CAPITAL: LISBON

SPAIN
POPULATION: 39,168,000 * CAPITAL: MADRID

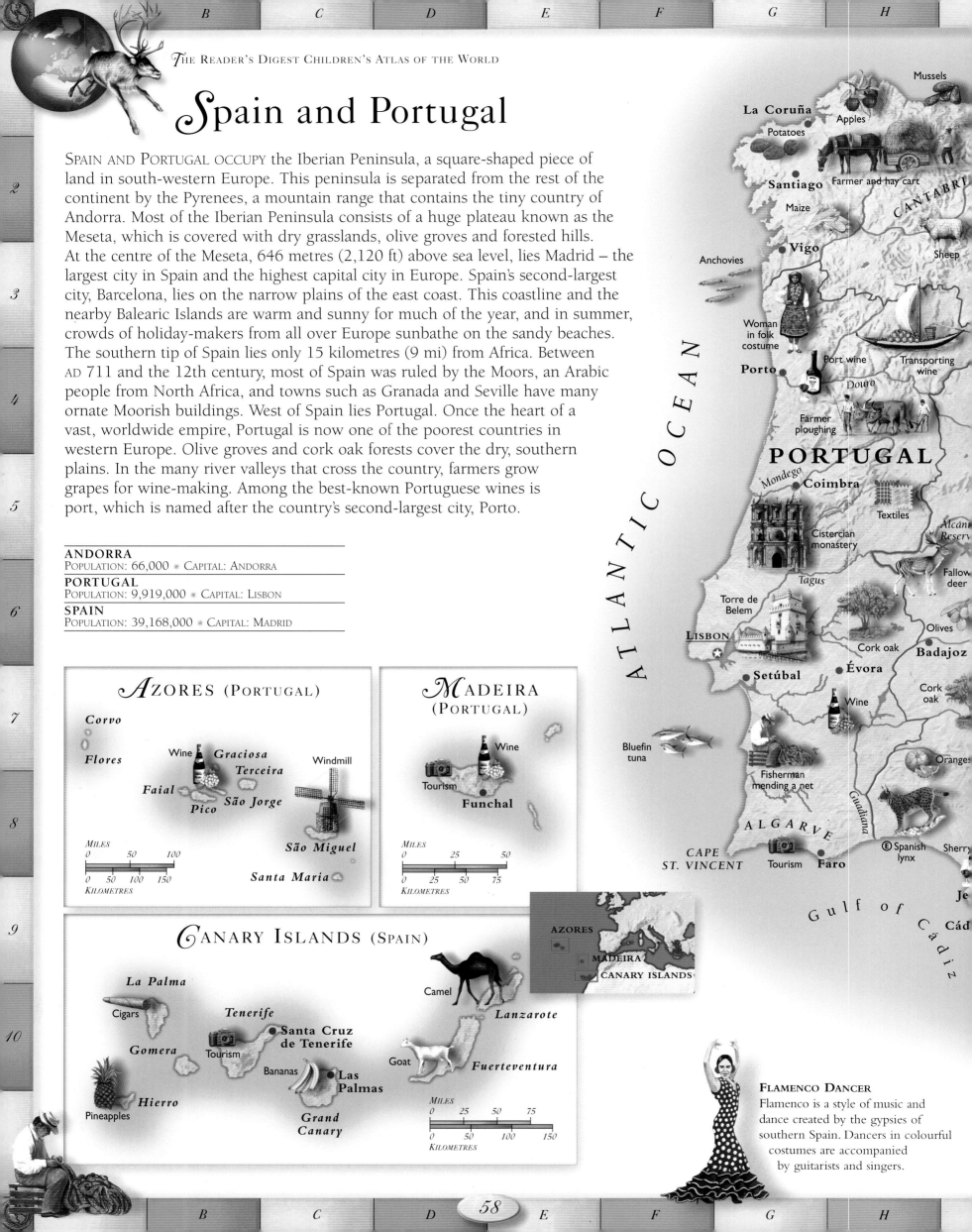

AZORES (PORTUGAL)

Corvo
Flores
Wine
Graciosa
Terceira
Faial
Windmill
Pico
São Jorge
São Miguel
Santa Maria

MILES
0   50   100
0 50 100 150
KILOMETRES

MADEIRA (PORTUGAL)

Wine
Tourism
Funchal

MILES
0   25   50
0   25 50 75
KILOMETRES

CANARY ISLANDS (SPAIN)

La Palma
Cigars
Tenerife
Camel
Lanzarote
Gomera
Santa Cruz
de Tenerife
Tourism
Bananas
Goat
Fuerteventura
Hierro
Las
Palmas
Pineapples
Grand
Canary

MILES
0   25   50   75
0   50   100   150
KILOMETRES

AZORES
MADEIRA
CANARY ISLANDS

Map of Portugal

Mussels
La Coruña
Apples
Potatoes
Santiago
Farmer and hay cart
CANTABRI
Maize
Vigo
Sheep
Anchovies
Woman in folk costume
Porto
Port wine
Transporting wine
Douro
Farmer ploughing
PORTUGAL
Mondego
Coimbra
Textiles
Alcán Reserv
Tagus
Fallow deer
Torre de Belem
Cork oak
Badajoz
LISBON
Setúbal
Évora
Cork oak
Bluefin tuna
Wine
Fisherman mending a net
Oranges
Guadiana
ALGARVE
Spanish lynx
Sherry
CAPE ST. VINCENT
Tourism
Faro
Je
Gulf of
Cádiz
Cád
ATLANTIC OCEAN

FLAMENCO DANCER
Flamenco is a style of music and dance created by the gypsies of southern Spain. Dancers in colourful costumes are accompanied by guitarists and singers.

Bay of Biscay

Gijón

Oviedo

OUNTAINS

Brown bear

Altamira cave paintings

Wheat

Potatoes

FRANCE

Basque folk dancer

Bilbao

Donostia-San Sebastián

P Y R E N E E S

Bearded vulture

Pamplona

Running of the bulls

Iron and steel

Beef cattle

Barley

Pico de Aneto
3,404 m (11,168 ft)

ANDORRA

ANDORRA

Holiday-maker

Textiles

COSTA BRAVA

Valladolid

Douro

Saragossa

Torre de Aragón

Barcelona

Sagrada Familia church

Holy Week procession

Segovia

Alcazar

Wild boars

Spanish guitarist

Wine

Salamanca

heat

High-tech industries

El Escorial

MADRID

Statue of Don Quixote and Sancho Panza

Olives

Oil

BALEARIC ISLANDS

Minorca

Mahón

Toledo

M E S E T A

Tagus

Bullfighting

SPAIN

Oranges

Paella

Sardines

Jara Gate

Palma

Olives

Majorca

Car manufacturing

Valencia

Ibiza

Tourism

Farmhouse

Windmills of La Mancha

Collecting saffron

Tourism

Ibiza

Mediterranean Sea

LOCATION

Guadiana

Mezquita Mosque

Wine

Sunflowers

Alicante

ERRA MORENA

Guadalquivir

Córdoba

Olives

Citrus fruit

Murcia

Fishing boat

eville

Flamenco dancer

Alhambra Palace

Cartagena

Granada

Mulhacén 3,477 m
(11,407 ft)

Málaga

Almería

Tajo Bridge

Andalucian ranch hand

Tourism

COSTA DEL SOL

Sailing

GIBRALTAR (U.K.)

Sardines

Algeciras

Ceuta (SPAIN)

MOROCCO

Melilla (SPAIN)

ALGERIA

N

W   E

S

SAGRADA FAMILIA CHURCH
The spires of this Barcelona church are covered in shells and ceramics, and rise 110 metres (350 ft). The building was begun in 1884. More than 100 years later, it is still not finished.

SCALE

MILES

0   25   50   75   100

0   50   100   150

KILOMETRES

France

FRANCE, THE LARGEST COUNTRY in western Europe, has a varied climate and landscape. In the north, the weather is mild and wet, and much of the land is flat. As you travel south, the climate becomes warmer and the land more mountainous. Three-quarters of the population live in towns and cities, but most of the country is farmland, and France is Europe's leading farming country. The northern plains are covered in fields of wheat and sugar beet, and in central and southern France vineyards dot the hillsides – more wine is produced in France than in any other country except Italy. The area around Paris, the capital, is the most densely populated region. It is home to one-fifth of the country's population and most of its industries. Several great rivers, including the Seine and the Loire, cross France's northern and western plains. These waterways were once the country's main transport routes, and their banks are lined with historic villages and magnificent castles known as châteaux. In the south, the mountains of the Pyrenees and the Alps separate France from Spain and Italy. Among their snow-capped peaks lie popular ski resorts, and national parks that are home to eagles, marmots and goat-like antelopes called chamois. Along the Mediterranean coast there are many busy beach resorts. Near the Italian border lies Monaco, the second-smallest country in the world. Monaco is famous for its casinos and its annual Grand Prix motor race.

FRANCE
POPULATION: 58,979,000 * CAPITAL: PARIS
MONACO
POPULATION: 32,200 * CAPITAL: MONACO

◆ AMAZING FACT ◆

France is now connected to Great Britain by an undersea rail link known as the Channel Tunnel. The tunnel took seven years to build and includes two rail tracks. Trains take 35 minutes to pass through the tunnel. People can travel from London to Paris in about three hours.

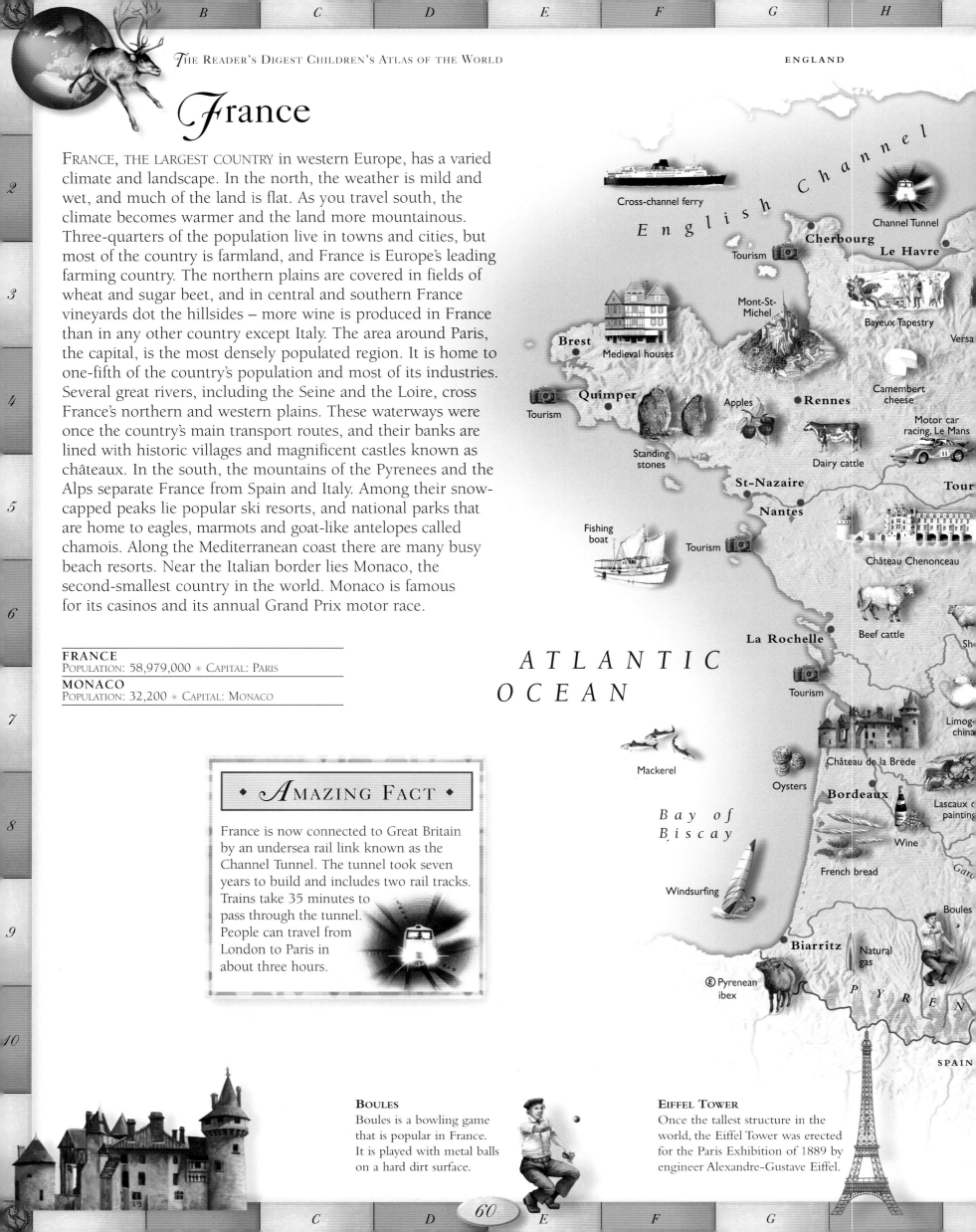

English Channel

Cross-channel ferry

Channel Tunnel

Tourism   **Cherbourg**   **Le Havre**

Mont-St-Michel

Bayeux Tapestry

Versa

Brest   Medieval houses

Camembert cheese

Quimper   Apples   **Rennes**

Tourism   Motor car racing, Le Mans

Standing stones   Dairy cattle

St-Nazaire   **Tour**

Nantes

Fishing boat   Tourism   Château Chenonceau

La Rochelle   Beef cattle

Sh

ATLANTIC OCEAN

Tourism

Limog china

Mackerel

Château de la Brède

Oysters   **Bordeaux**

Bay of Biscay   Lascaux painting

Wine

French bread   Gar

Windsurfing   Boules

Biarritz   Natural gas

Ⓔ Pyrenean ibex   P Y R E N

SPAIN

BOULES
Boules is a bowling game that is popular in France. It is played with metal balls on a hard dirt surface.

EIFFEL TOWER
Once the tallest structure in the world, the Eiffel Tower was erected for the Paris Exhibition of 1889 by engineer Alexandre-Gustave Eiffel.

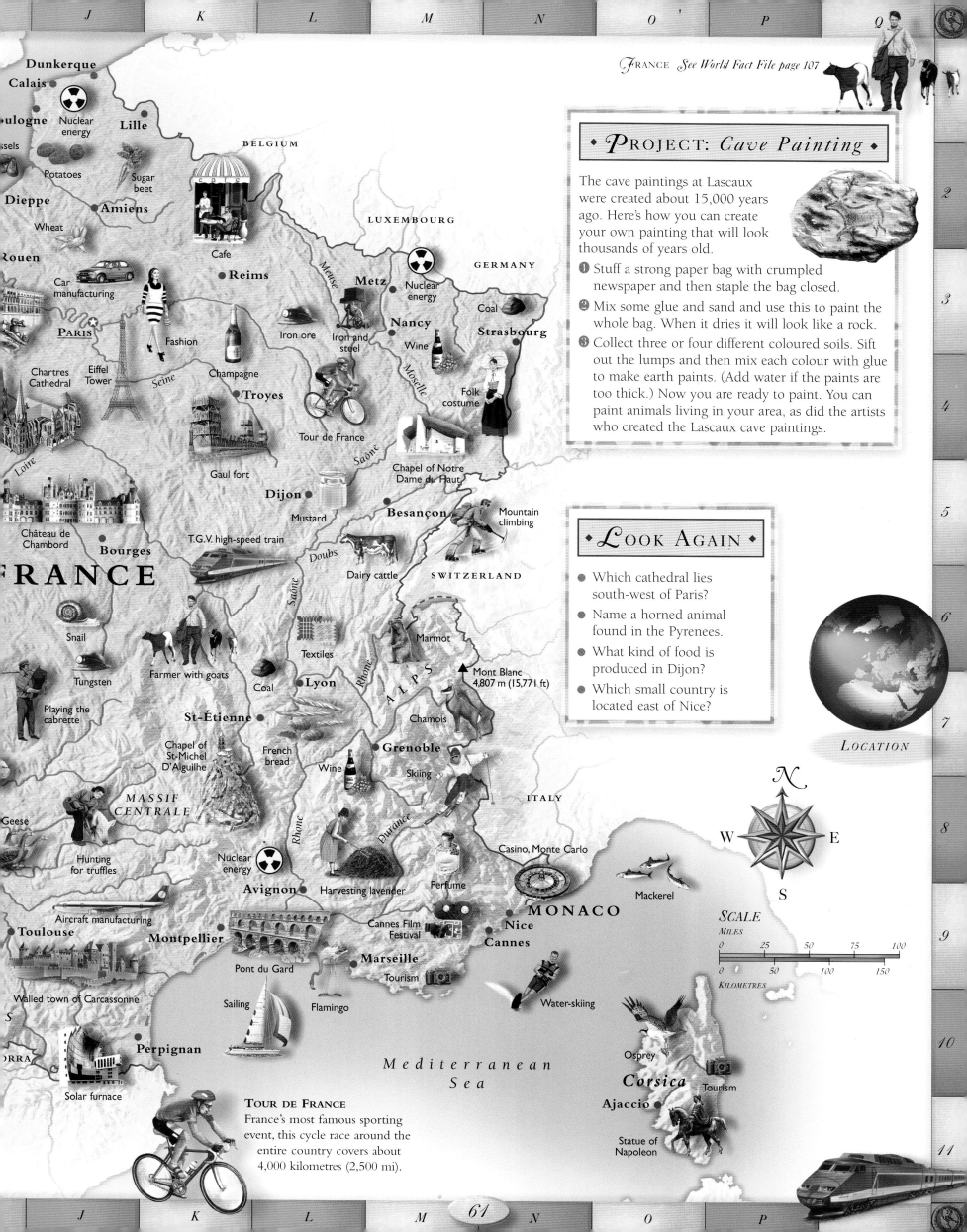

France See World Fact File page 107

Dunkerque
Calais
...ulogne — Nuclear energy
Lille
...sels
Potatoes
Sugar beet
Dieppe
Amiens
Wheat
...ouen
Car manufacturing
PARIS
Fashion
Chartres Cathedral
Eiffel Tower
Seine
FRANCE

BELGIUM
LUXEMBOURG
GERMANY

Cafe
Reims
Metz
Nuclear energy
Coal
Nancy
Iron ore
Iron and steel
Wine
Strasbourg
Champagne
Troyes
Tour de France
Folk costume
Gaul fort
Meuse
Moselle
Saône

◆ PROJECT: *Cave Painting* ◆

The cave paintings at Lascaux were created about 15,000 years ago. Here's how you can create your own painting that will look thousands of years old.

❶ Stuff a strong paper bag with crumpled newspaper and then staple the bag closed.

❷ Mix some glue and sand and use this to paint the whole bag. When it dries it will look like a rock.

❸ Collect three or four different coloured soils. Sift out the lumps and then mix each colour with glue to make earth paints. (Add water if the paints are too thick.) Now you are ready to paint. You can paint animals living in your area, as did the artists who created the Lascaux cave paintings.

Château de Chambord
Bourges
Snail
Tungsten
Playing the cabrette
T.G.V. high-speed train
Dijon
Mustard
Chapel of Notre Dame du Haut
Besançon
Mountain climbing
Dairy cattle
Doubs
Saône

SWITZERLAND

◆ LOOK AGAIN ◆

● Which cathedral lies south-west of Paris?

● Name a horned animal found in the Pyrenees.

● What kind of food is produced in Dijon?

● Which small country is located east of Nice?

Farmer with goats
Coal
Lyon
Textiles
Marmot
Rhône
ALPS
Mont Blanc 4,807 m (15,771 ft)
St-Étienne
Chamois
Chapel of St-Michel D'Aiguilhe
French bread
Wine
Grenoble
Skiing

LOCATION

MASSIF CENTRALE
Geese
Hunting for truffles
Nuclear energy
Avignon
Aircraft manufacturing
Toulouse
Montpellier
Harvesting lavender
Perfume
Casino, Monte Carlo
MONACO
Mackerel
Durance
Rhône

ITALY

N
W — E
S

SCALE
MILES
0   25   50   75   100
0   50   100   150
KILOMETRES

Pont du Gard
Cannes Film Festival
Nice
Cannes
Marseille
Tourism
Water-skiing
Sailing
Flamingo

Walled town of Carcassonne
Perpignan
Solar furnace
...RRA

Mediterranean Sea

Osprey
Corsica
Tourism
Ajaccio
Statue of Napoleon

TOUR DE FRANCE
France's most famous sporting event, this cycle race around the entire country covers about 4,000 kilometres (2,500 mi).

The Low Countries

THE DENSELY POPULATED COUNTRIES of the Netherlands (also called Holland), Belgium and Luxembourg are known as the Low Countries because they have no high mountains and few hills. Much of the land, including one-third of the Netherlands, actually lies below sea level. Over the centuries, local people have built large barriers known as dikes to keep the sea out, pumped water out of the marshes behind the dikes to create areas of new land called polders, and constructed thousands of kilometres of canals. Throughout the region, barges chug along these waterways, past windmills, dairy farms and colourful fields of tulips – both Belgium and the Netherlands export flowers and bulbs all over the world. The capital of the Netherlands, Amsterdam, has more than 150 canals, many of which are lined with tall, narrow, 17th-century buildings. In Belgium, canals link the country's ports to the historic cities of Bruges and Ghent, and to Brussels, the capital. Brussels is often referred to as the capital of Europe because it is the headquarters of the European Union (E.U.). South-east of Brussels lies the only high part of the Low Countries, the Ardennes. This range of forest-covered hills spreads across the northern half of Luxembourg, one of Europe's smallest countries but also one of its most important financial centres.

BELGIUM
POPULATION: 10,183,000 * CAPITAL: BRUSSELS

LUXEMBOURG
POPULATION: 429,100 * CAPITAL: LUXEMBOURG

THE NETHERLANDS
POPULATION: 15,808,000 * CAPITALS: AMSTERDAM, THE HAGUE

◆ AMAZING FACT ◆

The Low Countries have more than 8,000 kilometres (5,000 mi) of canals, which are used to transport people and goods and to drain the land. Because much of the region lies below sea level, water has to be pumped into canals built high above ground level. You could be standing in a field in the Low Countries and see a ship pass by above your head!

THE NETHERLANDS

Wheat
Natural gas
Groningen
Prehistoric hunebed (burial tomb)
Dairy cattle
Sheep
Pigs
Folk dancers
Beef cattle
Cycling
Apeldoorn
Poultry
Leeuwarden
Clogs
Beef cattle
Windmill
Zuider Zee folk costume
Dairy cattle
Arnhem
Potatoes
Tourism
Ameland
Football
Harbour seals
Dom (cathedral) tower
Terschelling
Tourism
Eurasian spoonbill
Amsterdam
Utrecht
Flowers
AMSTERDAM
Vlieland
Diamond cutting
Tulips
Alkmaar
Iron and steel
Texel
Alkmaar cheese market
Herring
Haarlem
THE HAGUE
Mackerel
Peace Palace
Rotterdam
Container ship

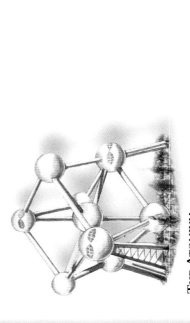

THE ATOMIUM
The Atomium represents an iron molecule and is one of the rare remains of the World Exhibition held in Brussels in 1958.

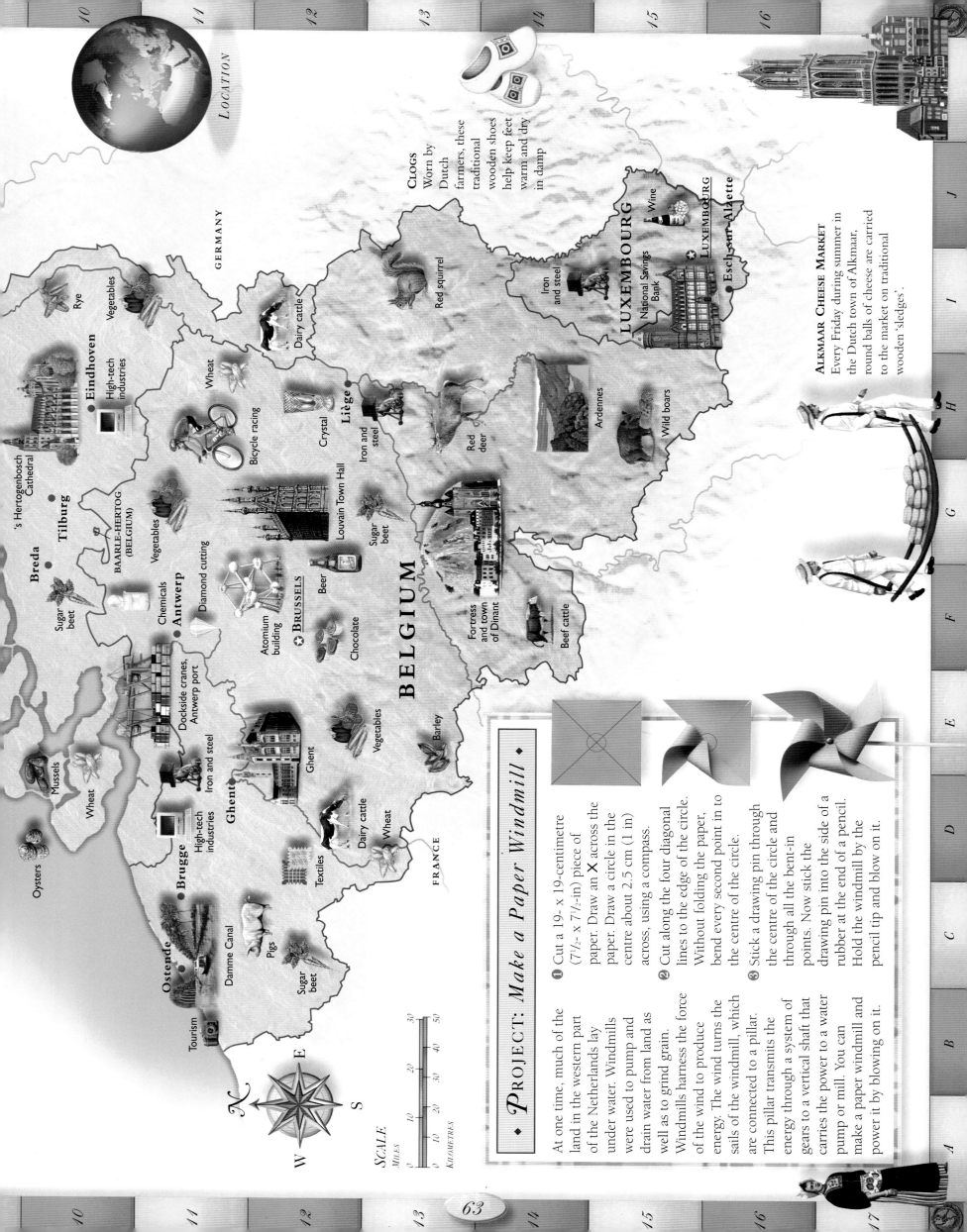

LOCATION

GERMANY

CLOGS
Worn by Dutch farmers, these traditional wooden shoes help keep feet warm and dry in damp

Rye

Vegetables

Eindhoven
High-tech industries

'S Hertogenbosch Cathedral

Breda

Tilburg

BAARLE-HERTOG (BELGIUM)

Sugar beet

Vegetables

Chemicals
Antwerp
Diamond cutting

Dockside cranes, Antwerp port

Mussels

Oysters

Wheat

High-tech industries

Brugge

Ostende

Tourism

Damme Canal

Pigs

Sugar beet

Textiles

Ghent

Iron and steel

Vegetables

Dairy cattle

Wheat

Barley

FRANCE

Atomium building

★ **BRUSSELS**

Beer

Chocolate

Vegetables

Sugar beet

Louvain Town Hall

Bicycle racing

Wheat

Dairy cattle

Crystal

Liège

Iron and steel

Red deer

Ardennes

Wild boars

Red squirrel

Beef cattle

Fortress and town of Dinant

BELGIUM

LUXEMBOURG

National Savings Bank

★ **LUXEMBOURG**

Wine

Iron and steel

● Esch-sur-Alzette

SCALE
MILES
0 10 20 30
0 10 20 30 40 50
KILOMETRES

N E S W

◆ PROJECT: *Make a Paper Windmill* ◆

At one time, much of the land in the western part of the Netherlands lay under water. Windmills were used to pump and drain water from land as well as to grind grain. Windmills harness the force of the wind to produce energy. The wind turns the sails of the windmill, which are connected to a pillar. This pillar transmits the energy through a system of gears to a vertical shaft that carries the power to a water pump or mill. You can make a paper windmill and power it by blowing on it.

❶ Cut a 19- x 19-centimetre (7½- x 7½-in) piece of paper. Draw an **X** across the paper. Draw a circle in the centre about 2.5 cm (1 in) across, using a compass.

❷ Cut along the four diagonal lines to the edge of the circle. Without folding the paper, bend every second point in to the centre of the circle.

❸ Stick a drawing pin through the centre of the circle and through all the bent-in points. Now stick the drawing pin into the side of a rubber at the end of a pencil. Hold the windmill by the pencil tip and blow on it.

ALKMAAR CHEESE MARKET
Every Friday during summer in the Dutch town of Alkmaar, round balls of cheese are carried to the market on traditional wooden 'sledges'.

Western Central Europe

AFTER WORLD WAR II, GERMANY was divided into two countries: East Germany and West Germany. They were reunited in 1990, and Germany is now home to more than 80 million people, the largest population of any European country except Russia. Many of Germany's cities lie on rivers. The Rhine river connects the country's most important industrial region, the Ruhr Valley, to the ports of the Netherlands and the Swiss city of Basel. On its journey northwards, the Rhine winds past forests of spruce and fir, steep hillsides covered with vineyards, and cliffs crowned by medieval castles. From southern Germany, the spectacular Alps mountain range stretches across the countries of Switzerland and Austria, where it covers about two-thirds of the land. Throughout these mountains, roads and railways wind through narrow river valleys and cross steep passes. In summer, cows graze in the alpine meadows; in winter, skiers hurtle down the slopes. Switzerland is a peaceful country which hasn't been involved in a war since 1814. This has encouraged people from all over the world to deposit money in Swiss banks, and the country is now a leading financial centre. In Austria, many farms and industries lie on the north-eastern lowlands. This area is crossed by the Danube, Europe's second-longest river. The Danube passes through Austria's capital, Vienna – home to one-fifth of Austria's population and one of Europe's grandest cities.

AUSTRIA
POPULATION: 8,140,000 ✴ CAPITAL: VIENNA

GERMANY
POPULATION: 82,088,000 ✴ CAPITAL: BERLIN

LIECHTENSTEIN
POPULATION: 32,100 ✴ CAPITAL: VADUZ

SWITZERLAND
POPULATION: 7,276,000 ✴ CAPITAL: BERN

✦ PROJECT: *Swiss Chocolate Fondue* ✦

The Swiss eat a dish called fondue, which is often made from cheese. They dip pieces of bread in a mixture of hot melted cheese and white wine. Try making this chocolate fondue.

❶ Place 250 g (8 oz) plain chocolate pieces in a saucepan with 250 ml (8 oz) whipping cream.

❷ Ask an adult to help you warm the ingredients gently until the chocolate has melted. Beat the mixture until it becomes glossy.

❸ Let the mixture cool a little. Then spear a piece of fruit (strawberries or grapes are good) on a fork, dip it in the fondue and eat it straight away.

✦ AMAZING FACT ✦

The country of Liechtenstein is home to only 30,700 people and is just 6 kilometres (4 mi) wide. That means you could walk across it in less than two hours! The prince of Liechtenstein lives in this castle in the capital, Vaduz.

SCALE

MILES
0   25   50   75

KILOMETRES
0   25   50   75   100   125

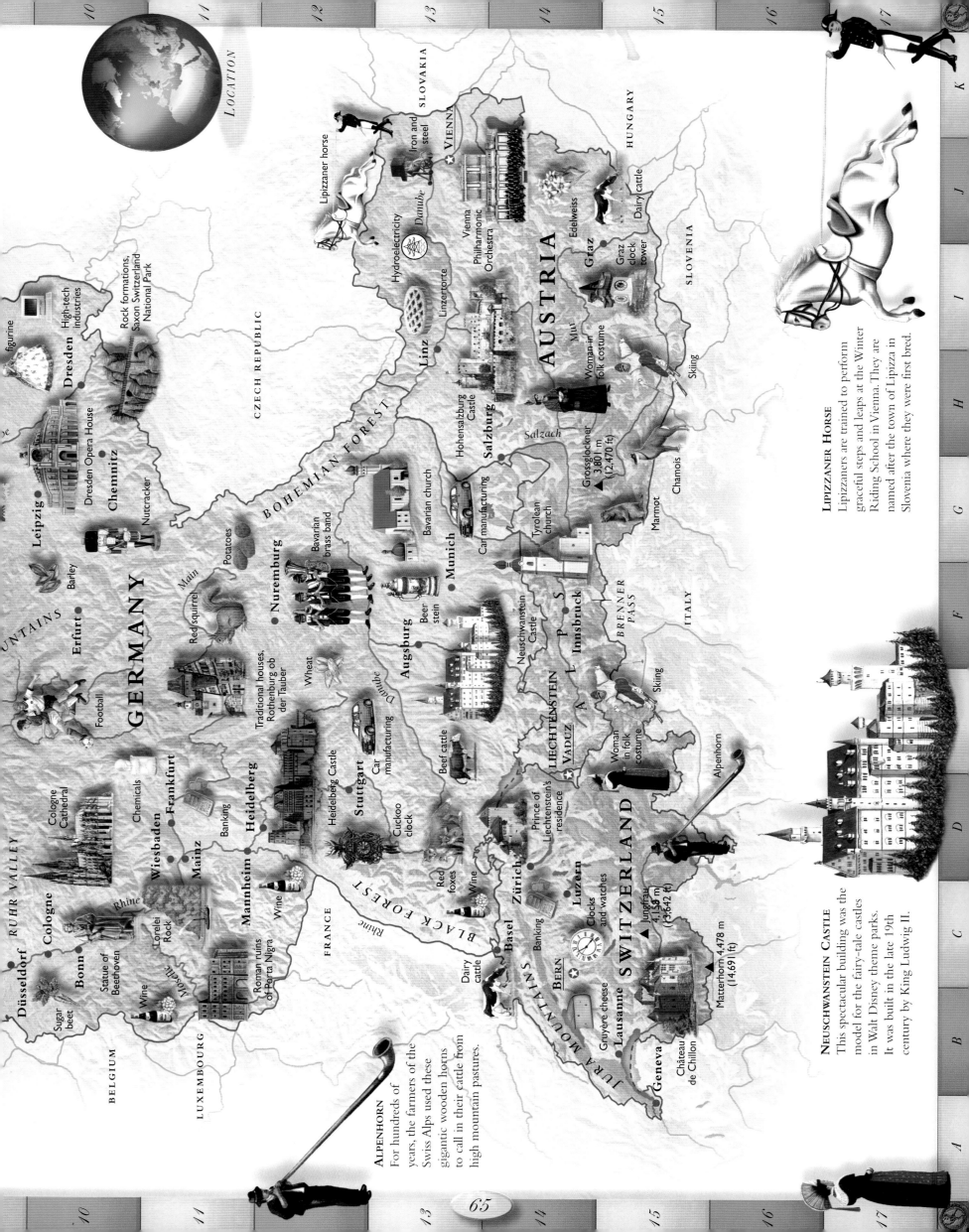

GERMANY

Düsseldorf
Sugar beet
Cologne
Bonn
Cologne Cathedral
Statue of Beethoven
Wine
Moselle
Lorelei Rock
Rhine
Roman ruins of Porta Nigra
Wine
Mainz
Wiesbaden
Frankfurt
Mannheim
Heidelberg
Banking
Chemicals
Wine
Heidelberg Castle
Stuttgart
Car manufacturing
Cuckoo clock
Red foxes
BLACK FOREST
Traditional houses, Rothenburg ob der Tauber
Wheat
Danube
Augsburg
Beer stein
Munich
Beef cattle
Bavarian brass band
Bavarian church
Nuremburg
Potatoes
Red squirrel
Main
Barley
Erfurt
Football
Leipzig
Nutcracker
Chemnitz
Dresden
Dresden Opera House
High-tech industries
Rock formations, Saxon Switzerland National Park
figurine

UNTAINS
RUHR VALLEY
BELGIUM
LUXEMBOURG
FRANCE

BOHEMIAN FOREST
CZECH REPUBLIC
SLOVAKIA

AUSTRIA

VIENNA
Iron and steel
Lipizzaner horse
Danube
Hydroelectricity
Vienna Philharmonic Orchestra
Linz
Linzertorte
Hohensalzburg Castle
Salzburg
Salzach
Car manufacturing
Grossglockner ▲ 3,801 m (12,470 ft)
Chamois
Marmot
Graz
Graz clock tower
Mut
Woman in folk costume
Edelweiss
Dairy cattle
Skiing
HUNGARY
SLOVENIA

SWITZERLAND

Dairy cattle
Basel
Zürich
Banking
Luzern
Bern
Clocks and watches
Jungfrau ▲ 4,158 m (13,642 ft)
Matterhorn 4,478 m (14,691 ft) ▲
Lausanne
Geneva
Château de Chillon
Gruyère cheese
JURA MOUNTAINS
A L P S

LIECHTENSTEIN
VADUZ
Prince of Liechtenstein's residence
Woman in folk costume
Neuschwanstein Castle
Innsbruck
Tyrolean church
BRENNER PASS
Skiing
Alpenhorn
ITALY

LIPIZZANER HORSE
Lipizzaners are trained to perform graceful steps and leaps at the Winter Riding School in Vienna. They are named after the town of Lipizza in Slovenia where they were first bred.

ALPENHORN
For hundreds of years, the farmers of the Swiss Alps used these gigantic wooden horns to call in their cattle from high mountain pastures.

NEUSCHWANSTEIN CASTLE
This spectacular building was the model for the fairy-tale castles in Walt Disney theme parks. It was built in the late 19th century by King Ludwig II.

THE READER'S DIGEST CHILDREN'S ATLAS OF THE WORLD

Italy

ITALY CONSISTS OF A LONG, boot-shaped peninsula, the large islands of Sicily and Sardinia, and about 70 smaller islands. Within Italy lie two other countries: San Marino in the east, and the Vatican City (the world's smallest country) in the city of Rome. The Vatican City is the home of the Pope, the head of the Roman Catholic Church. Most of mainland Italy is mountainous. The Alps form a great arc around the northern border, and the Apennines stretch almost the entire length of the peninsula. Between these two mountain ranges lies the Northern Plain, a flat, fertile region drained by the Po River. This plain has Italy's richest farmland and is home to the country's most important industries, including the car factories of Turin, and Milan's fashion and design houses.

Each year, more than 50 million tourists travel to Italy to visit its ancient ruins and historic cities, and the birthplace of opera, and to enjoy the sunny weather. The country's mild climate allows farmers to grow large quantities of wheat, citrus fruit, olives and grapes – Italy is the world's leading producer of olive oil and wine. Parts of Italy are regularly rocked by earthquakes, and there are active volcanoes. On the island of Sicily, Mount Etna has erupted at least 260 times since the first recorded eruption in 70 BC. About 95 kilometres (60 mi) south of Sicily lie the islands of Malta. Malta has been ruled by the Romans, Arabs, Turks, French and British. It is now an independent republic.

COLOSSEUM

This Roman stadium was built in the first century AD and used for events such as gladiator contests. It was even flooded for mock sea battles.

ITALY
POPULATION: 56,736,000 • CAPITAL: ROME

MALTA
POPULATION: 381,700 • CAPITAL: VALLETTA

SAN MARINO
POPULATION: 25,100 • CAPITAL: SAN MARINO

VATICAN CITY
POPULATION: 830 • CAPITAL: VATICAN CITY

◆ AMAZING FACT ◆

The Leaning Tower of Pisa was constructed as a bell tower between AD 1173 and 1370. Unfortunately, it was built on unstable ground, and it began to sink and tilt to one side after completion of the first three storeys. Although the tower leans about 4.5 metres (15 ft) out of line, it has recently been stabilized so that it will not fall over.

MOUNT VESUVIUS AND POMPEII

In AD 79, Mount Vesuvius erupted, burying the town of Pompeii under stone and ash. The ruins were not uncovered until the 18th century.

66

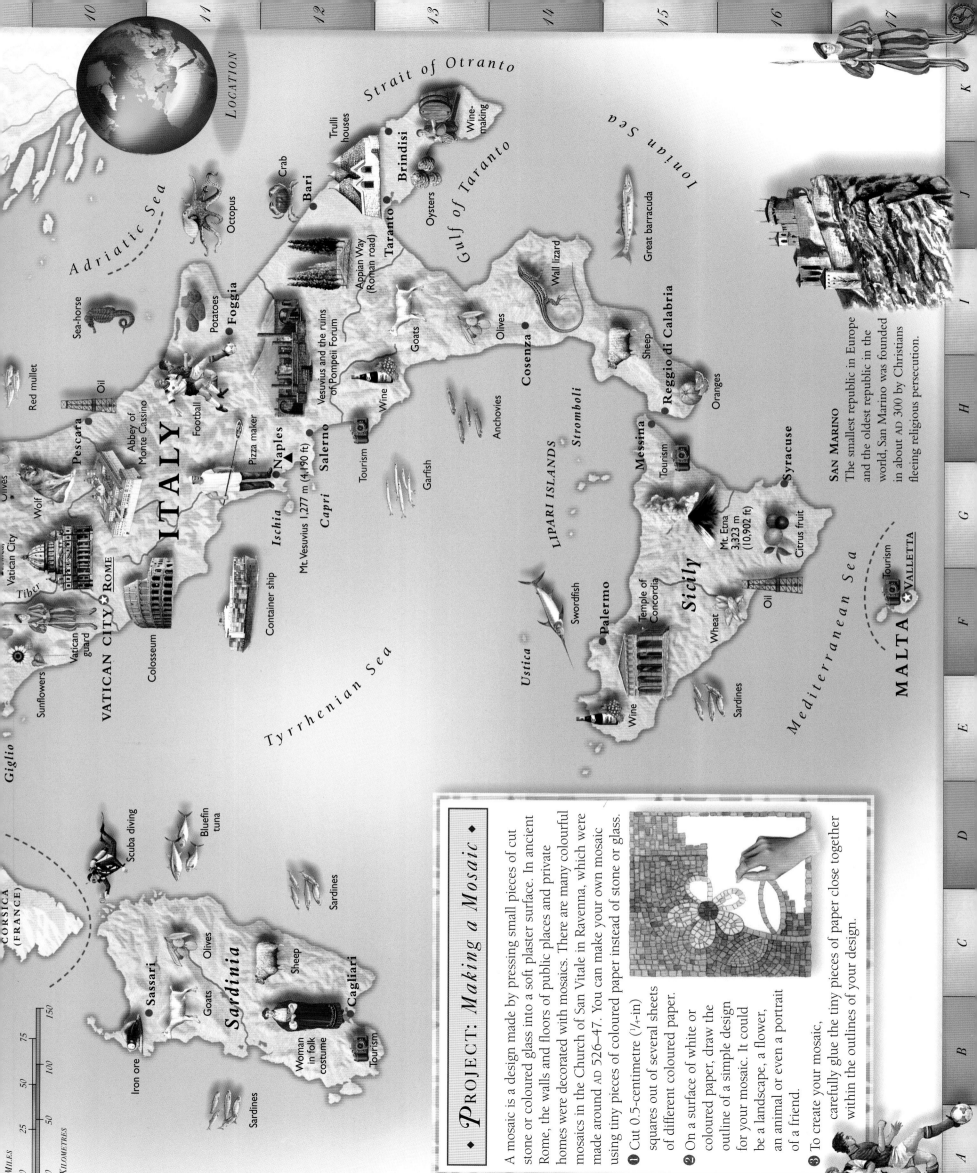

LOCATION

Strait of Otranto

Adriatic Sea

Ionian Sea

Gulf of Taranto

Tyrrhenian Sea

Mediterranean Sea

ITALY

Sicily

Sardinia

LIPARI ISLANDS

Trulli houses

Wine-making

Brindisi

Crab

Bari

Octopus

Oysters

Taranto

Appian Way (Roman road)

Sea-horse

Potatoes

Foggia

Wall lizard

Great barracuda

Red mullet

Oil

Goats

Olives

Cosenza

Sheep

Reggio di Calabria

Pescara

Abbey of Monte Cassino

Football

Pizza maker

Vesuvius and the ruins of Pompeii Forum

Wine

Anchovies

Oranges

Olives

Wolf

Naples

Salerno

Garfish

Stromboli

Messina

Tourism

Syracuse

Vatican City

Capri

Ischia

Mt. Vesuvius 1,277 m (4,190 ft)

Tourism

Citrus fruit

SAN MARINO

The smallest republic in Europe and the oldest republic in the world, San Marino was founded in about AD 300 by Christians fleeing religious persecution.

Tiber

VATICAN CITY

ROME

Container ship

Swordfish

Mt. Etna 3,323 m (10,902 ft)

Palermo

Temple of Concordia

Wheat

Oil

Vatican guard

Colosseum

Ustica

Wine

Sardines

Tourism

MALTA

VALLETTA

Sunflowers

Mediterranean Sea

Giglio

Olives

CORSICA (FRANCE)

Scuba diving

Bluefin tuna

Sardines

Iron ore

Goats

Olives

Sheep

Sassari

Sardinia

Cagliari

Woman in folk costume

Tourism

Sardines

MILES
0   25   50   75   150

KILOMETRES
0   50   100

◆ PROJECT: *Making a Mosaic* ◆

A mosaic is a design made by pressing small pieces of cut stone or coloured glass into a soft plaster surface. In ancient Rome, the walls and floors of public places and private homes were decorated with mosaics. There are many colourful mosaics in the Church of San Vitale in Ravenna, which were made around AD 526–47. You can make your own mosaic using tiny pieces of coloured paper instead of stone or glass.

① Cut 0.5-centimetre (¼-in) squares out of several sheets of different coloured paper.

② On a surface of white or coloured paper, draw the outline of a simple design for your mosaic. It could be a landscape, a flower, an animal or even a portrait of a friend.

③ To create your mosaic, carefully glue the tiny pieces of paper close together within the outlines of your design.

THE READER'S DIGEST CHILDREN'S ATLAS OF THE WORLD

South-eastern Europe

THIS REGION IS OFTEN REFERRED TO as the Balkans. It lies at the edge of Europe, close to Asia, and is home to many peoples from both continents. Throughout history, disputes between countries and ethnic groups have occurred regularly. In 1991, the republics of Slovenia, Croatia, Bosnia and Herzegovina, and Macedonia declared their independence from Yugoslavia. This led to a war that destroyed cities, farms and industries, and left thousands of people homeless. Most of south-eastern Europe is rugged and mountainous. Along the coast of Croatia, rocky slopes rise steeply from the water. Inland, forests and farms surround the peaks that spread eastwards through Yugoslavia and into Romania and Bulgaria. In Bulgaria's Balkan

Mountains, an area known as the Valley of the Roses produces more than two-thirds of the world's rose oil, an essential ingredient in most perfumes. South-eastern Europe's best farmland lies along the Danube River, which connects many of the region's towns to the ports of the Black Sea. In Greece, overgrazing by sheep and goats has stripped some of the land of trees and shrubs, but the warm climate allows farmers to grow olives, grapes, citrus fruit and wheat. Greece's sunny weather and scenic attractions bring tourists from all over the world. In Athens, home to one-third of Greece's population, rush-hour traffic roars past 2,000-year-old temples. On the Greek islands, clusters of white buildings cling to cliffs, and fishing boats drift across clear, turquoise bays.

ALBANIA
POPULATION: 3,365,000 * CAPITAL: TIRANË

BOSNIA AND HERZEGOVINA
POPULATION: 3,483,000 * CAPITAL: SARAJEVO

BULGARIA
POPULATION: 8,195,000 * CAPITAL: SOFIA

CROATIA
POPULATION: 4,677,000 * CAPITAL: ZAGREB

GREECE
POPULATION: 10,708,000 * CAPITAL: ATHENS

MACEDONIA
POPULATION: 2,023,000 * CAPITAL: SKOPJE

ROMANIA
POPULATION: 22,335,000 * CAPITAL: BUCHAREST

SLOVENIA
POPULATION: 1,971,000 * CAPITAL: LJUBLJANA

YUGOSLAVIA
POPULATION: 11,207,000 * CAPITAL: BELGRADE

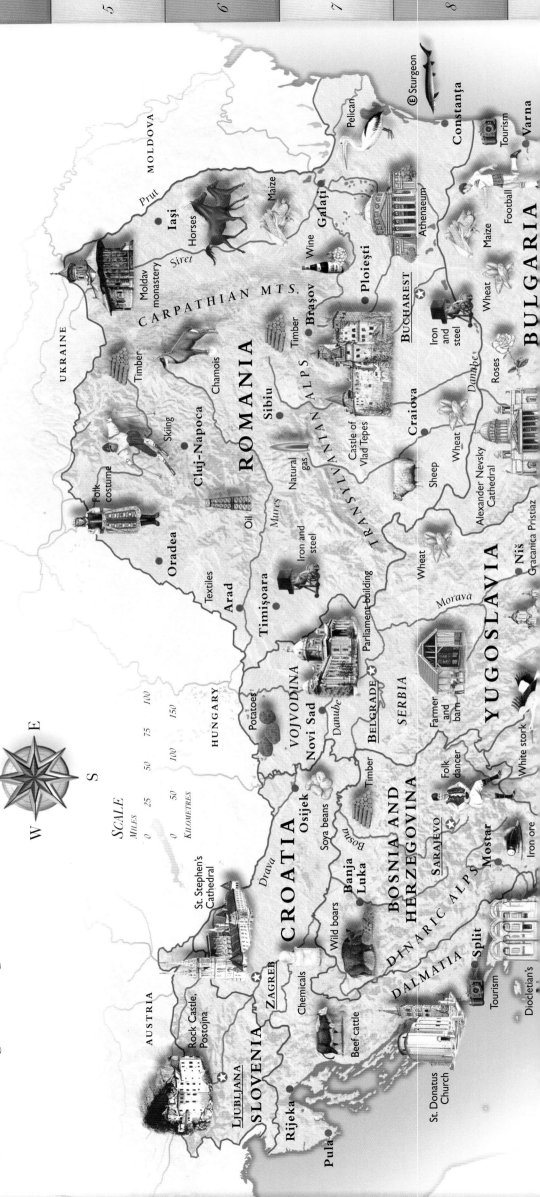

SCALE

MILES
0   25   50   75   100

KILOMETRES
0   50   100   150

N / S / E / W

MOLDOVA

UKRAINE

Prut

Iaşi

Horses

Siret

Maize

Moldav monastery

CARPATHIAN MTS.

Timber

Chamois

Wine

Galaţi

Braşov

Ploieşti

BUCHAREST

Athenaeum

Constanţa

Tourism

Pelican

Sturgeon

Varna

BULGARIA

Wheat

Maize

Football

Iron and steel

Roses

Danube

Alexander Nevsky Cathedral

Gracanica Pristiaz

ROMANIA

Sibiu

Skiing

Folk costume

Cluj-Napoca

Natural gas

Castle of Vlad Tepes

Craiova

Sheep

Wheat

Oradea

Oil

Mureş

TRANSYLVANIAN ALPS

Textiles

Arad

Timişoara

Iron and steel

Wheat

Morava

Niš

YUGOSLAVIA

HUNGARY

Potatoes

VOJVODINA

Novi Sad

Danube

BELGRADE

Parliament building

SERBIA

Farmer and barn

White stork

AUSTRIA

Rock Castle, Postojna

Beef cattle

LJUBLJANA

SLOVENIA

Rijeka

Pula

ZAGREB

Chemicals

St. Stephen's Cathedral

CROATIA

Osijek

Soya beans

Wild boars

Drava

Banja Luka

Bosna

BOSNIA AND HERZEGOVINA

SARAJEVO

Folk dancer

Timber

Mostar

Iron ore

DINARIC ALPS

DALMATIA

Split

Tourism

Diocletian's

St. Donatus Church

Black Sea

LOCATION

Adriatic Sea

ITALY

TURKEY

TURKEY

Shipka Memorial Church

Food processing

Tobacco

Wheat

Plovdiv

Mt. Musala
2,925 m
(9,596 ft) ▲

RHODOPE MTS.

Skiing

Struma

Copper

Shkodër

Black kite

Durrës

ALBANIA

TIRANÉ ★

Vlorë

Inspecting carpets

Tourism

Corfu

Levkás

Olives

IONIAN ISLANDS

Cephalonia

Zákinthos

KOSOVO

★ **SKOPJE**

MACEDONIA

Vardar

Iron and steel

Maze

Eastern Orthodox Church

Bitola

Korçë

Cotton

Goats

Monastery, Meteora

Bouzouki

Wine

Alexandroúpolis

Thásos

Samothráke

Lemnos

Greek Orthodox monk

Thessaloniki

Sardines

Mt. Olympus
2,917 m
(9,570 ft) ▲

Volos

GREECE

Ruins of Delphi

Parthenon

PELOPONNESE

Patras

Ruins of Olympia

King Agamemnon's gold death mask

Aegean Sea

Olives

Sailing

Lesbos

Chios

Mackerel

Skyros

NORTHERN SPORADES

Euboea

Khalkís

Lignite

ATHENS ☆

Piraeus

Evzones guards

Tripolis

Kithira

TURKEY

Sámos

DODECANESE

Rhodes

Andros

Tinos

Mykonos

Naxos

Páros

CYCLADES

Tourism

Thíra

Traditional church

Kárpathos

Bull's head sculpture, Knossos

Iráklion

Canea

Wine

Crete

Sea of Crete

Cruise ship

Windmill

Mediterranean Sea

Ionian Sea

BLACK KITE
These birds of prey are found throughout south-eastern Europe. At night, they roost in trees in huge flocks of as many as 100 birds.

CASTLE OF VLAD TEPES
Vlad Tepes, a 15th-century Romanian prince known as Vlad the Impaler, is said to have inspired the legend of Dracula the vampire.

EVZONES GUARDS
Wearing their traditional skirts and tasselled hats and shoes, the evzones stand guard outside the parliament in Athens.

◆ PROJECT: *Make a Cave* ◆

The Postojna Caves in Slovenia are famous for their stalactites and stalagmites. These formations took thousands of years to develop, but you can make your own cave with stalactites and stalagmites in just a few days.

❶ Draw a cave scene on the inside bottom of a shoe box. Line the outside and inside walls of the box with aluminium foil. Turn the box on its side so that the scene becomes the cave's back wall. Ask an adult to help you punch two holes close together at each end of the top of the box. Place a glass beside each end of the box.

❷ Thread two lengths of string in through holes at one end and out through holes at the other end. Make sure the strings reach the bottom of each glass and hang down a little inside the cave.

❸ Fill the glasses with hot water and stir in washing soda (sodium carbonate) until no more will dissolve, then wash your hands well. Put the ends of the strings in the glasses. Over the next few days, as the water soaks into the strings and then starts to evaporate, small salt formations will appear where the strings sag. At the same time, small mounds of salt will form where the water drips on the cave floor. Gradually, these formations will grow into stalactites and stalagmites.

Eastern Europe

IN RECENT YEARS, MANY POLITICAL CHANGES have occurred within this vast region. During 1990 and 1991, the republics of Latvia, Estonia, Lithuania, Belarus, Moldova and the Ukraine, all formerly part of the Soviet Union, became independent countries. In 1993, Czechoslovakia divided into two countries, the Czech Republic and Slovakia. Mountains line the borders of the Czech Republic and cover most of Slovakia, but elsewhere eastern Europe is generally flat. Wide grasslands cover central Hungary and most of the Ukraine. In Poland, rivers that rise in the southern mountains meander northwards across a wide plain of rich farmland toward coastal swamps and sand dunes. The Baltic States of Lithuania, Latvia and Estonia are covered with meadows, marshes and more than 9,000 lakes. Around the Baltic Sea, winters can be bitterly cold, and ice-breaker ships often have to clear a path between the region's ports. About two-thirds of eastern Europe's people live in cities, and many work in heavy industries such as mining, steel-making and shipbuilding. These industries have created serious pollution problems. Acid rain has destroyed forests in Poland and the Czech Republic, and people are no longer allowed to swim in some polluted lakes in Hungary. In the Ukraine and Belarus, large areas of land can no longer be farmed because they were contaminated by radioactivity after an accident at the Chernobyl nuclear power plant near Kiev in 1986. Despite this, the Ukraine remains one of the largest producers of wheat in the world.

BELARUS
POPULATION: 10,402,000 ∗ CAPITAL: MINSK

CZECH REPUBLIC
POPULATION: 10,281,000 ∗ CAPITAL: PRAGUE

ESTONIA
POPULATION: 1,409,000 ∗ CAPITAL: TALLINN

HUNGARY
POPULATION: 10,187,000 ∗ CAPITAL: BUDAPEST

LATVIA
POPULATION: 2,354,000 ∗ CAPITAL: RIGA

LITHUANIA
POPULATION: 3,585,000 ∗ CAPITAL: VILNIUS

MOLDOVA
POPULATION: 4,461,000 ∗ CAPITAL: CHIŞINĂU

POLAND
POPULATION: 38,609,000 ∗ CAPITAL: WARSAW

SLOVAKIA
POPULATION: 5,397,000 ∗ CAPITAL: BRATISLAVA

UKRAINE
POPULATION: 49,812,000 ∗ CAPITAL: KIEV

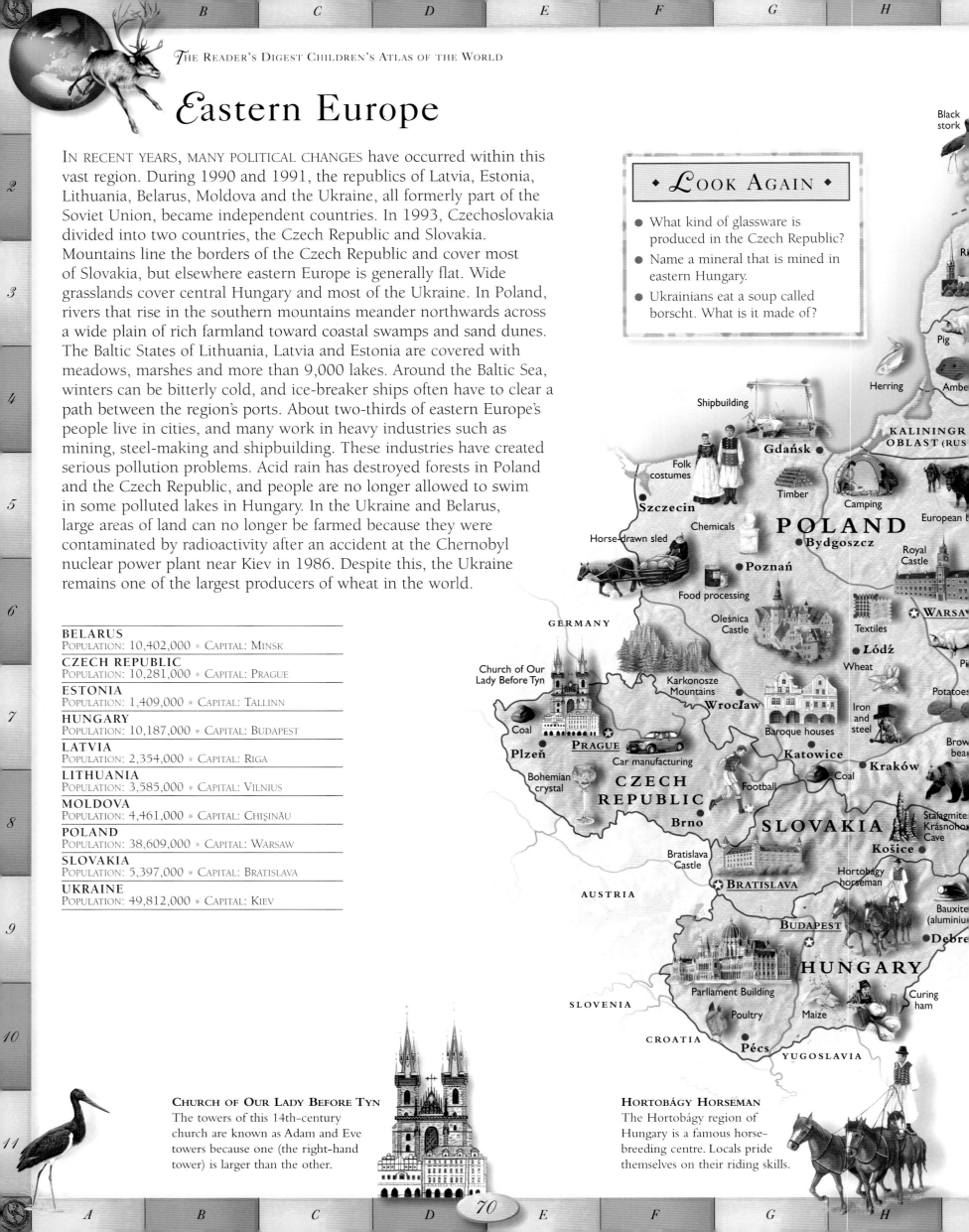

· LOOK AGAIN ·

- What kind of glassware is produced in the Czech Republic?
- Name a mineral that is mined in eastern Hungary.
- Ukrainians eat a soup called borscht. What is it made of?

Black stork

Shipbuilding

Folk costumes

Gdańsk

Herring

Amber

KALININGR OBLAST (RUS

Szczecin

Chemicals

Horse-drawn sled

Timber

Camping

European

POLAND

Bydgoszcz

Royal Castle

Food processing

Poznań

Oleśnica Castle

Textiles

WARSAW

GERMANY

Łódź

Wheat

Church of Our Lady Before Tyn

Karkonosze Mountains

Potatoes

Coal

Wrocław

Iron and steel

Brow bea

Plzeň

Baroque houses

PRAGUE

Car manufacturing

Katowice

Kraków

Bohemian crystal

CZECH REPUBLIC

Football

Coal

Brno

SLOVAKIA

Stalagmite Krásnoho Cave

Košice

Bratislava Castle

Hortobágy horseman

AUSTRIA

BRATISLAVA

Bauxite (aluminiu

BUDAPEST

Debre

HUNGARY

SLOVENIA

Parliament Building

Poultry

Maize

Curing ham

CROATIA

Pécs

YUGOSLAVIA

CHURCH OF OUR LADY BEFORE TYN
The towers of this 14th-century church are known as Adam and Eve towers because one (the right-hand tower) is larger than the other.

HORTOBÁGY HORSEMAN
The Hortobágy region of Hungary is a famous horse-breeding centre. Locals pride themselves on their riding skills.

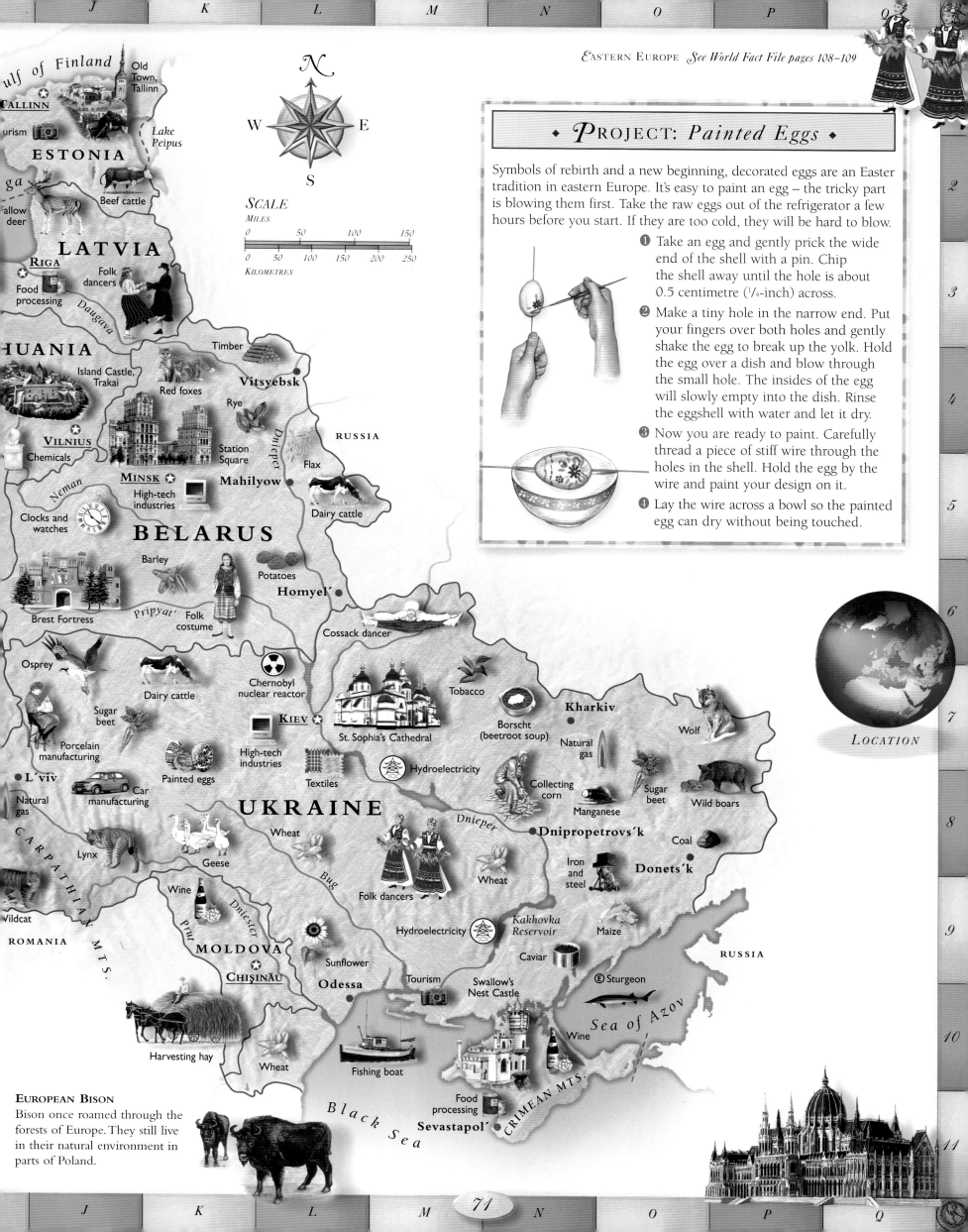

Gulf of Finland

Old Town, Tallinn

TALLINN

urism

ESTONIA

Lake Peipus

Fallow deer

Beef cattle

LATVIA

RIGA

Food processing

Folk dancers

Daugava

LITHUANIA

Island Castle, Trakai

Red foxes

Timber

Vitsyebsk

Rye

RUSSIA

VILNIUS

Chemicals

Station Square

Dnieper

Flax

MINSK

High-tech industries

Mahilyow

Clocks and watches

Neman

Dairy cattle

BELARUS

Barley

Potatoes

Homyel'

Brest Fortress

Pripyat'

Folk costume

Cossack dancer

Osprey

Dairy cattle

Chernobyl nuclear reactor

Tobacco

Kharkiv

Sugar beet

Porcelain manufacturing

KIEV

St. Sophia's Cathedral

Borscht (beetroot soup)

Natural gas

Wolf

L'viv

High-tech industries

Hydroelectricity

Collecting corn

Sugar beet

Wild boars

Natural gas

Painted eggs

Car manufacturing

Textiles

UKRAINE

Wheat

Dnieper

Manganese

Dnipropetrovs'k

Coal

Lynx

Geese

Bug

Wheat

Iron and steel

Donets'k

Wine

Dniester

Folk dancers

ROMANIA

Prut

MOLDOVA

Hydroelectricity

Kakhovka Reservoir

Maize

RUSSIA

Wildcat

CHIŞINĂU

Sunflower

Odessa

Tourism

Caviar

Sturgeon

CARPATHIAN MTS.

Harvesting hay

Wheat

Fishing boat

Swallow's Nest Castle

Wine

Sea of Azov

Food processing

Sevastopol'

CRIMEAN MTS.

Black Sea

EUROPEAN BISON

Bison once roamed through the forests of Europe. They still live in their natural environment in parts of Poland.

N W E S

SCALE

MILES

0   50   100   150

0   50 100 150 200 250

KILOMETRES

• PROJECT: *Painted Eggs* •

Symbols of rebirth and a new beginning, decorated eggs are an Easter tradition in eastern Europe. It's easy to paint an egg – the tricky part is blowing them first. Take the raw eggs out of the refrigerator a few hours before you start. If they are too cold, they will be hard to blow.

❶ Take an egg and gently prick the wide end of the shell with a pin. Chip the shell away until the hole is about 0.5 centimetre (¼-inch) across.

❷ Make a tiny hole in the narrow end. Put your fingers over both holes and gently shake the egg to break up the yolk. Hold the egg over a dish and blow through the small hole. The insides of the egg will slowly empty into the dish. Rinse the eggshell with water and let it dry.

❸ Now you are ready to paint. Carefully thread a piece of stiff wire through the holes in the shell. Hold the egg by the wire and paint your design on it.

❹ Lay the wire across a bowl so the painted egg can dry without being touched.

LOCATION

Northern Europe

THE COUNTRIES OF NORTHERN EUROPE are often referred to as Scandinavia, although strictly speaking Scandinavia is only the wide peninsula occupied by Norway and Sweden. Another name for them is the Nordic countries. On the western side of this peninsula, fjords – spectacular, steep-sided bays formed by glaciers – and more than 150,000 islands create a maze of waterways. Inland, mountain peaks and high plateaux cover most of Norway. To the east, the marshy plains of Sweden and Finland are studded with thousands of lakes and cloaked in coniferous forests that are home to elk, brown bears and wolves. The northern half of this region has a cold climate, with long, dark, snowy winters. In the far south, the climate is more temperate and the land more fertile.

Only one-twentieth of Norway can be farmed, but more than three-quarters of Denmark is used for agriculture. The volcanic island of Iceland, which lies 1,000 kilometres (600 mi) west of Norway, has very little farmland. The island's barren interior consists mainly of volcanoes, hot springs and lava fields. Parts of Iceland are so like the surface of the moon that astronauts trained there for moon landings. Some upland areas are covered by huge sheets of ice. Vatnajökull, an ice sheet in the south-east, is larger than all the glaciers in Europe combined.

DENMARK
POPULATION: 5,357,000 * CAPITAL: COPENHAGEN
FINLAND
POPULATION: 5,159,000 * CAPITAL: HELSINKI
ICELAND
POPULATION: 272,600 * CAPITAL: REYKJAVIK
NORWAY
POPULATION: 4,439,000 * CAPITAL: OSLO
SWEDEN
POPULATION: 8,912,000 * CAPITAL: STOCKHOLM

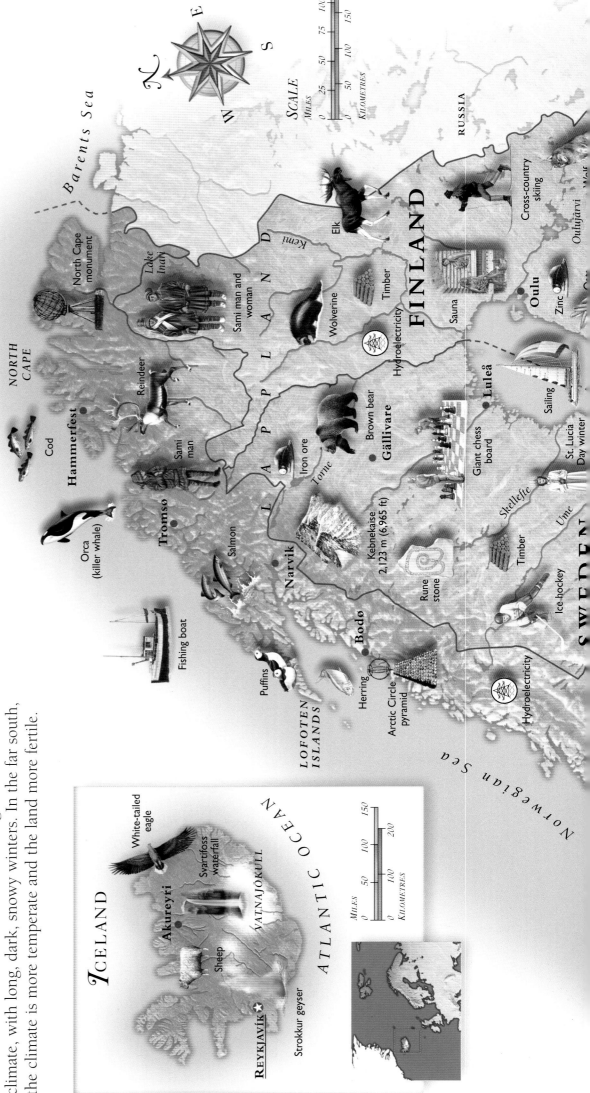

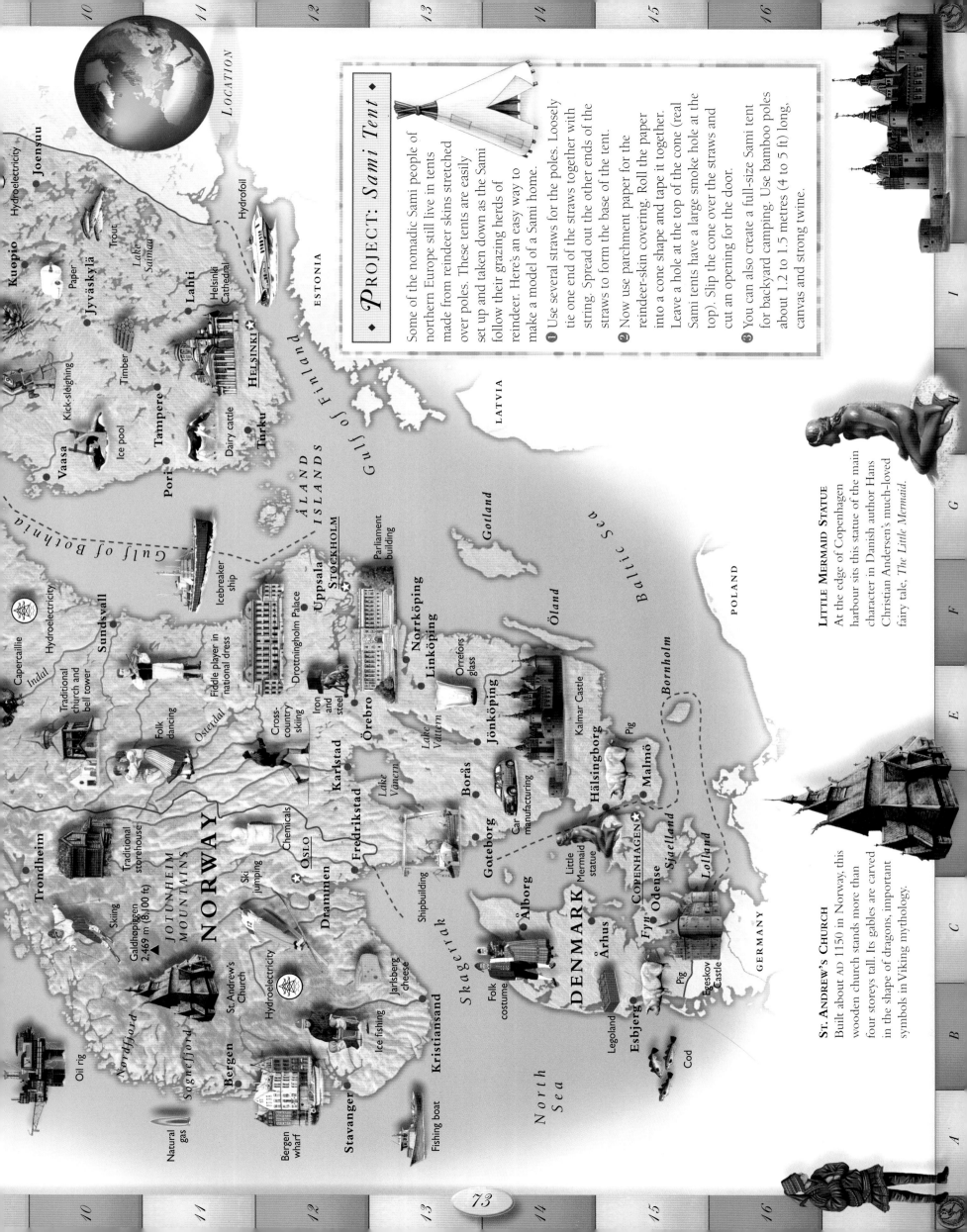

LOCATION

◆ PROJECT: *Sami Tent* ◆

Some of the nomadic Sami people of northern Europe still live in tents made from reindeer skins stretched over poles. These tents are easily set up and taken down as the Sami follow their grazing herds of reindeer. Here's an easy way to make a model of a Sami home.

1. Use several straws for the poles. Loosely tie one end of the straws together with string. Spread out the other ends of the straws to form the base of the tent.

2. Now use parchment paper for the reindeer-skin covering. Roll the paper into a cone shape and tape it together. Leave a hole at the top of the cone (real Sami tents have a large smoke hole at the top). Slip the cone over the straws and cut an opening for the door.

3. You can also create a full-size Sami tent for backyard camping. Use bamboo poles about 1.2 to 1.5 metres (4 to 5 ft) long, canvas and strong twine.

LITTLE MERMAID STATUE
At the edge of Copenhagen harbour sits this statue of the main character in Danish author Hans Christian Andersen's much-loved fairy tale, *The Little Mermaid*.

ST. ANDREW'S CHURCH
Built about AD 1150 in Norway, this wooden church stands more than four storeys tall. Its gables are carved in the shape of dragons, important symbols in Viking mythology.

Map labels:

Hydroelectricity — Joensuu — Kuopio — Paper — Trout — Lake Saimaa — Jyväskylä — Hydrofoil — Lahti — Timber — Helsinki Cathedral — HELSINKI — ESTONIA — Kick-sleighing — Ice pool — Tampere — Dairy cattle — Turku — Vaasa — Pori — ÅLAND ISLANDS — Gulf of Finland — LATVIA

Gulf of Bothnia — Icebreaker ship — Hydroelectricity — Indal — Sundsvall — Capercaillie — Traditional church and bell tower — Fiddle player in national dress — Drottningholm Palace — UPPSALA — STOCKHOLM — Parliament building — Gotland — POLAND — Baltic Sea

Folk dancing — Osterdal — Cross-country skiing — Iron and steel — Örebro — Norrköping — Linköping — Orrefors glass — Öland — Bornholm

Trondheim — Skiing — Traditional storehouse — JOTUNHEIM MOUNTAINS — Galdhøpiggen 2,469 m (8,100 ft) — NORWAY — Ski jumping — Chemicals — OSLO — Drammen — Fredrikstad — Karlstad — Lake Vänern — Lake Vättern — Borås — Jönköping — Kalmar Castle — Hälsingborg — Pig — Malmö

Natural gas — Oil rig — Nordfjord — Sognefjord — Bergen — Bergen wharf — Jarlsberg cheese — St. Andrew's Church — Hydroelectricity — Kristiansand — Ice fishing — Shipbuilding — Skagerrak — Goteborg — Car manufacturing — COPENHAGEN — Sjælland — Lolland

Fishing boat — North Sea — DENMARK — Ålborg — Århus — Little Mermaid statue — Odense — Fyn — Esbjerg — Legoland — Pig — Egeskov Castle — Cod — GERMANY — Folk costume

Asia

THE WORLD'S BIGGEST CONTINENT, Asia stretches almost half-way around the globe and covers one-third of the Earth's land mass. It has the world's tallest mountains, the world's largest lake and the world's lowest point on land. It was the birthplace of many great religions and important civilizations, and is now home to 60 per cent of the people on Earth. Most Asians live in the east and south, where the climate is warm and wet and there are large areas of forest, fertile plains and hundreds of tropical islands. Deserts and barren mountain ranges dominate the south-west and centre of the continent. To the north, the grasslands, or steppes, of central Asia give way to the immense coniferous forests of Russia. A belt of freezing tundra extends along the continent's north coast. Russia is the world's largest country by area, but China has the world's largest population.

Continent Facts

Regional land area: 44,391,162 sq. km (17,139,445 sq. mi), excluding European Russia
Regional population: 3,660,642,000, excluding European Russia
Independent countries: Afghanistan, Armenia, Azerbaijan, Bahrain, Bangladesh, Bhutan, Brunei, Cambodia, China, Cyprus, East Timor, Georgia, India, Indonesia, Iran, Iraq, Israel, Japan, Jordan, Kazakstan, Kuwait, Kyrgyzstan, Laos, Lebanon, Malaysia, Maldives, Mongolia, Myanmar (Burma), Nepal, North Korea, Oman, Pakistan, Philippines, Qatar, Russia, Saudi Arabia, Singapore, South Korea, Sri Lanka, Syria, Taiwan, Tajikistan, Thailand, Turkey, Turkmenistan, United Arab Emirates, Uzbekistan, Vietnam, Yemen

Major Mountains and Rivers

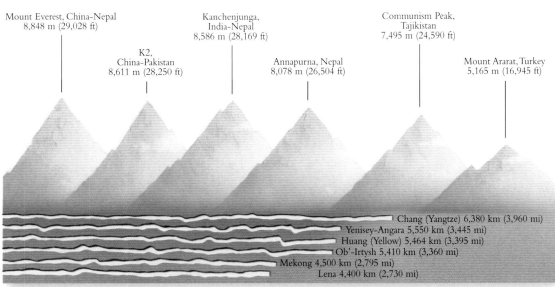

Mount Everest, China-Nepal 8,848 m (29,028 ft)
K2, China-Pakistan 8,611 m (28,250 ft)
Kanchenjunga, India-Nepal 8,586 m (28,169 ft)
Annapurna, Nepal 8,078 m (26,504 ft)
Communism Peak, Tajikistan 7,495 m (24,590 ft)
Mount Ararat, Turkey 5,165 m (16,945 ft)

Chang (Yangtze) 6,380 km (3,960 mi)
Yenisey-Angara 5,550 km (3,445 mi)
Huang (Yellow) 5,464 km (3,395 mi)
Ob'-Irtysh 5,410 km (3,360 mi)
Mekong 4,500 km (2,795 mi)
Lena 4,400 km (2,730 mi)

World Records

WORLD'S HIGHEST MOUNTAIN
MOUNT EVEREST, CHINA-NEPAL, 8,848 M (29,028 FT)

WORLD'S LOWEST POINT ON LAND
DEAD SEA, ISRAEL-JORDAN, 400 M (1,300 FT) BELOW SEA LEVEL

WORLD'S LARGEST LAKE BY AREA
CASPIAN SEA, CENTRAL EURASIA, 371,800 SQ. KM (143,550 SQ. MI)

WORLD'S OLDEST, DEEPEST AND LARGEST (BY VOLUME) LAKE
LAKE BAIKAL, RUSSIA, 25 MILLION YEARS OLD; 1,637 M (5,371 FT) DEEP; 23,000 CUBIC KM (5,500 CUBIC MI) OF WATER

WORLD'S LARGEST COUNTRY BY AREA
RUSSIA, 17,075,383 SQ. KM (6,592,812 SQ. MI)

WORLD'S LARGEST COUNTRY BY POPULATION
CHINA, POPULATION 1,246,872,000

WORLD'S LARGEST CITY BY POPULATION
TOKYO, JAPAN, POPULATION 27,200,000

WORLD'S LONGEST WALL
GREAT WALL OF CHINA, 3,460 KM (2,150 MI)

WORLD'S LONGEST RAILWAY LINE
TRANS-SIBERIAN, RUSSIA, 9,297 KM (5,777 MI)

Continent Records

LONGEST RIVER
CHANG (YANGTZE), 6,380 KM (3,960 MI)

Political Map

RUSSIA
KAZAKSTAN
MONGOLIA
GEORGIA
TURKEY
UZBEKISTAN KYRGYZSTAN
TURKMENISTAN
CYPRUS
SYRIA
TAJIKISTAN
CHINA
NORTH KOREA
SOUTH KOREA
JAPAN
IRAQ
JORDAN
AFGHANISTAN
IRAN
PAKISTAN
NEPAL
SAUDI ARABIA
OMAN
INDIA
MYANMAR (BURMA)
LAOS
TAIWAN
YEMEN
THAILAND
PHILIPPINES
CAMBODIA
VIETNAM
SRI LANKA
MALDIVES
MALAYSIA
INDONESIA
EAST TIMOR

Key to Numbered Countries

1 ARMENIA	7 QATAR
2 AZERBAIJAN	8 UNITED ARAB EMIRATES
3 LEBANON	9 BHUTAN
4 ISRAEL	10 BANGLADESH
5 KUWAIT	■ 11 SINGAPORE
■ 6 BAHRAIN	12 BRUNEI

*P*HYSICAL MAP

ARCTIC OCEAN
× NORTH POLE

Barents Sea

Kara Sea

Laptev Sea

East Siberian Sea

Bering Sea

EUROPE

Arctic Circle

VERKHOYANSKI MTS.

KAMCHATKA PENINSULA

CENTRAL SIBERIAN PLATEAU

Lena

Sea of Okhotsk

Sakhalin

URAL MOUNTAINS

Ob

WEST SIBERIAN PLAIN

Yenisey

Angara

SIBERIA

Lake Baikal

Amur

KURIL ISLANDS

Hokkaidō

Mt. Elbrus ▲

Black Sea

CAUCASUS MTS.

Caspian Sea

Irtysh

Lake Balkhash

ALTAY MTS.

MANCHURIAN PLAIN

Sea of Japan

Honshū

Mt. Ararat ▲

Aral Sea

TIEN MTS.

GOBI DESERT

SYRIAN DESERT

ZAGROS MTS.

TAKLIMAKAN DESERT

Yellow Sea

Shikoku

Kyūshū

Persian Gulf

PLATEAU OF IRAN

Communism Peak ▲

HINDU KUSH

▲ K2

KUNLUN MTS.

Huang (Yellow)

East China Sea

Red Sea

Indus

HIMALAYAS

PLATEAU OF TIBET

PACIFIC OCEAN

ARABIAN PENINSULA

GREAT INDIAN DESERT

INDO-GANGETIC PLAIN

▲ Annapurna
▲ Mt. Everest
▲ Kanchenjunga

Chang (Yangtze)

RYUKYU ISLANDS

Tropic of Cancer

Gulf of Oman

Ganges

NAN MTS.

Gulf of Aden

Taiwan

Arabian Sea

DECCAN

Bay of Bengal

Irrawaddy

Hainan

Luzon

South China Sea

PHILIPPINE ISLANDS

ANDAMAN ISLANDS

Andaman Sea

Mekong

Mindanao

MALDIVES

Sri Lanka

NICOBAR ISLANDS

Gulf of Thailand

MALAY PENINSULA

New Guinea

Sumatra

Borneo

MOLUCCAS

Equator

Sulawesi

INDIAN OCEAN

GREATER SUNDA ISLANDS

Java Sea

Java

LESSER SUNDA ISLANDS

AUSTRALIA AND OCEANIA

Tropic of Capricorn

Russia

RUSSIA IS THE LARGEST country in the world. It covers two-thirds of Asia and one-third of Europe, and is so wide that it has eleven time zones. When the citizens of St. Petersburg are getting ready for bed, the miners and reindeer herders who live in the remote far east are already starting their next day's work. Most of Russia has a cold climate, with mild to cool summers and cold to freezing winters. In the far north, where most of the land is tundra, winter temperatures can drop to –70°C (–94°F). South of the tundra, a wide band of coniferous woodland stretches almost all the way across the country. The Ural Mountains divide Russia into two regions. West of the Urals is European Russia, which has only one-quarter of the land, but four-fifths of the population, the largest industries and the most fertile farmland. East of the Urals, in Asia, is Siberia, a vast wilderness region that is bigger than the U.S.A. and western Europe combined.

In the southern part of this region near Mongolia lies Lake Baikal, the world's deepest lake, which holds one-fifth of the world's fresh water. Siberia is also rich in minerals, such as coal and oil. The Chukchi Peninsula in eastern Siberia is the most easterly point in Asia. It lies only 82 kilometres (50 mi) from North America. Before 1991, Russia was part of an even larger country – the Soviet Union – which also included 14 present-day countries in eastern Europe and central Eurasia.

RUSSIA
POPULATION: 146,394,000 ◦ CAPITAL: MOSCOW

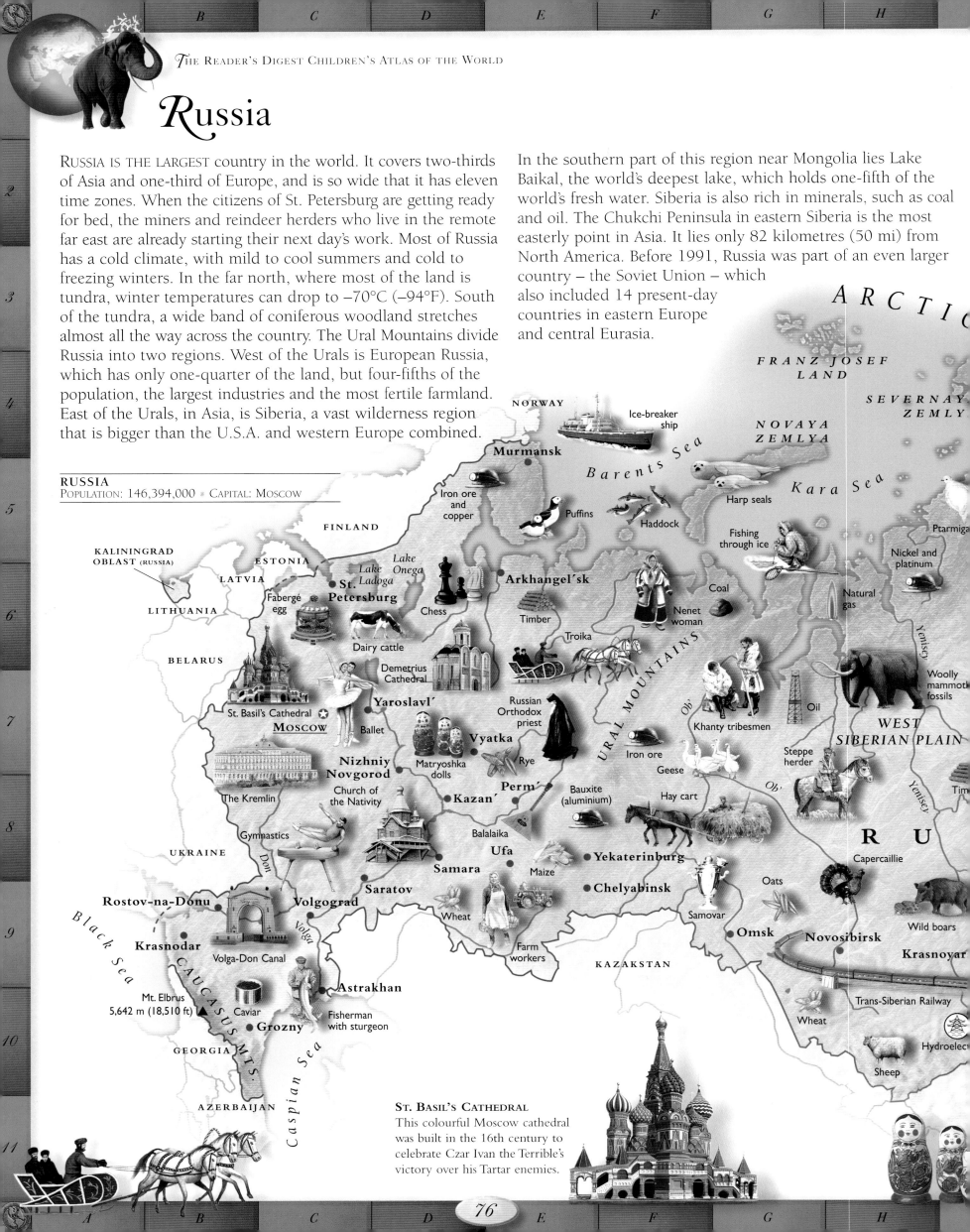

ARCTIC

FRANZ JOSEF LAND

SEVERNAYA ZEMLYA

NOVAYA ZEMLYA

Barents Sea

Kara Sea

NORWAY

Ice-breaker ship

Murmansk

Iron ore and copper

Puffins

Haddock

Harp seals

Fishing through ice

Ptarmigan

Nickel and platinum

Natural gas

FINLAND

KALININGRAD OBLAST (RUSSIA)

ESTONIA

LATVIA

LITHUANIA

Lake Ladoga

Lake Onega

St. Petersburg

Fabergé egg

Arkhangel'sk

Coal

Nenet woman

Timber

Troika

Oil

Woolly mammoth fossils

WEST SIBERIAN PLAIN

BELARUS

Dairy cattle

Chess

Demetrius Cathedral

Russian Orthodox priest

URAL MOUNTAINS

Khanty tribesmen

Steppe herder

St. Basil's Cathedral

MOSCOW

Ballet

Yaroslavl'

Vyatka

Ob'

Iron ore

Geese

Ob'

Yenisey

Nizhniy Novgorod

Church of the Nativity

Matryoshka dolls

Rye

Perm'

Bauxite (aluminium)

Hay cart

The Kremlin

Kazan'

Balalaika

Ufa

Gymnastics

Maize

Yekaterinburg

Capercaillie

Timber

R U

UKRAINE

Don

Samara

Saratov

Chelyabinsk

Oats

Wild boars

Rostov-na-Donu

Volgograd

Wheat

Samovar

Omsk

Novosibirsk

Krasnoyar

Black Sea

CAUCASUS MTS.

Krasnodar

Volga-Don Canal

Volga

Farm workers

KAZAKSTAN

Trans-Siberian Railway

Mt. Elbrus 5,642 m (18,510 ft) ▲

Caviar

Astrakhan

Fisherman with sturgeon

Wheat

Hydroelec

Grozny

GEORGIA

Caspian Sea

Sheep

AZERBAIJAN

ST. BASIL'S CATHEDRAL
This colourful Moscow cathedral was built in the 16th century to celebrate Czar Ivan the Terrible's victory over his Tartar enemies.

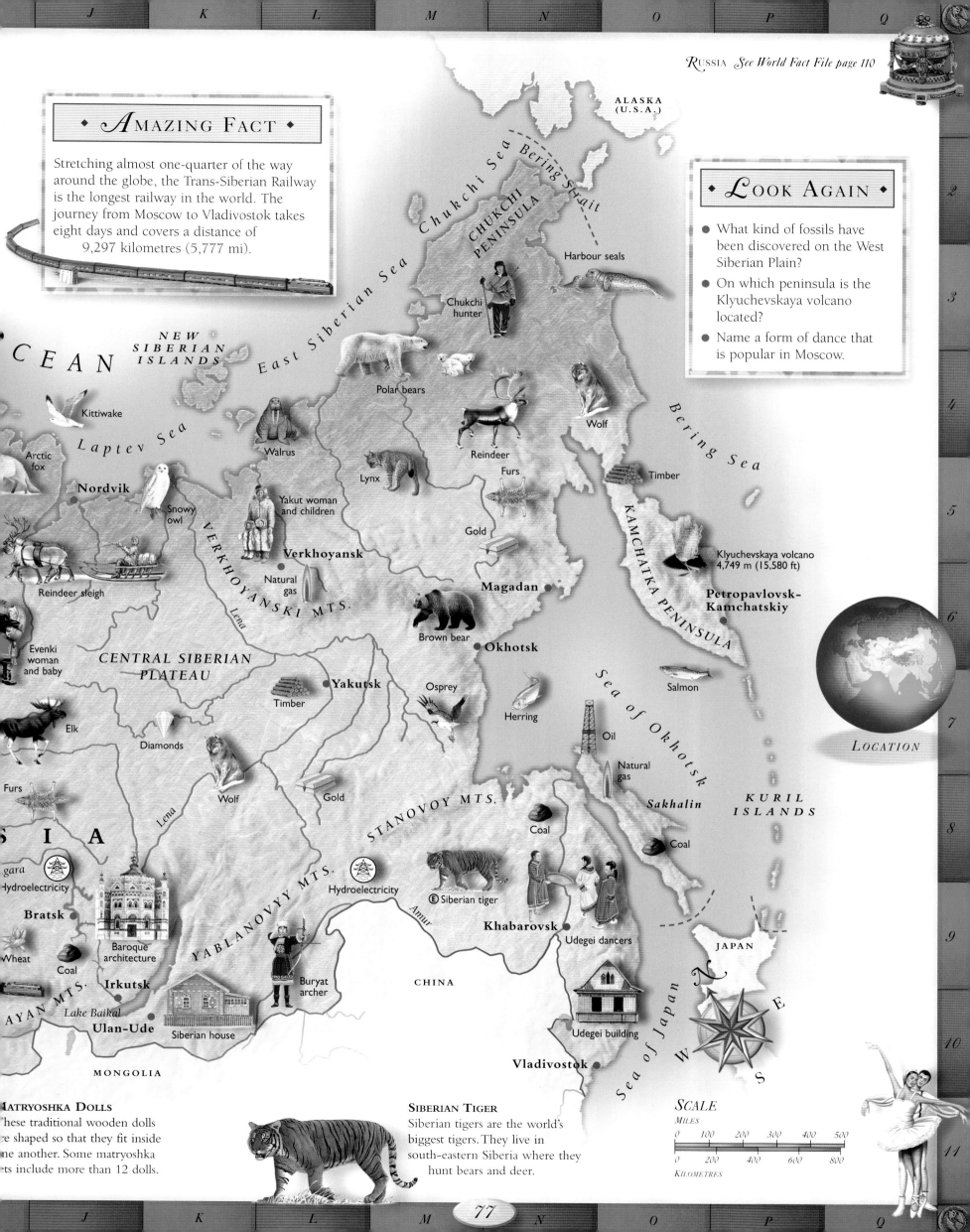

◆ AMAZING FACT ◆

Stretching almost one-quarter of the way around the globe, the Trans-Siberian Railway is the longest railway in the world. The journey from Moscow to Vladivostok takes eight days and covers a distance of 9,297 kilometres (5,777 mi).

◆ LOOK AGAIN ◆

- What kind of fossils have been discovered on the West Siberian Plain?
- On which peninsula is the Klyuchevskaya volcano located?
- Name a form of dance that is popular in Moscow.

ALASKA (U.S.A.)

Chukchi Sea

Bering Strait

CHUKCHI PENINSULA

Harbour seals

Chukchi hunter

NEW SIBERIAN ISLANDS

East Siberian Sea

OCEAN

Polar bears

Wolf

Bering Sea

Laptev Sea

Kittiwake

Walrus

Reindeer

Furs

Timber

Arctic fox

Lynx

Gold

KAMCHATKA PENINSULA

Nordvik

Snowy owl

Yakut woman and children

Klyuchevskaya volcano 4,749 m (15,580 ft)

VERKHOYANSKI MTS.

Verkhoyansk

Natural gas

Magadan

Petropavlovsk-Kamchatskiy

Reindeer sleigh

Lena

Brown bear

Okhotsk

Salmon

Evenki woman and baby

CENTRAL SIBERIAN PLATEAU

Timber

Yakutsk

Osprey

Herring

Sea of Okhotsk

Elk

Diamonds

Wolf

Gold

Oil

Natural gas

Sakhalin

KURIL ISLANDS

Furs

Lena

STANOVOY MTS.

Coal

Coal

SIA

gara Hydroelectricity

Hydroelectricity

Siberian tiger

Khabarovsk

Udegei dancers

JAPAN

Bratsk

Baroque architecture

YABLANOVYY MTS.

Amur

CHINA

Wheat

Coal

Irkutsk

Buryat archer

Udegei building

Sea of Japan

AYAN MTS.

Lake Baikal

Ulan-Ude

Siberian house

Vladivostok

MONGOLIA

MATRYOSHKA DOLLS

These traditional wooden dolls re shaped so that they fit inside ne another. Some matryoshka ts include more than 12 dolls.

SIBERIAN TIGER

Siberian tigers are the world's biggest tigers. They live in south-eastern Siberia where they hunt bears and deer.

SCALE

MILES

0   100   200   300   400   500

0   200   400   600   800

KILOMETRES

LOCATION

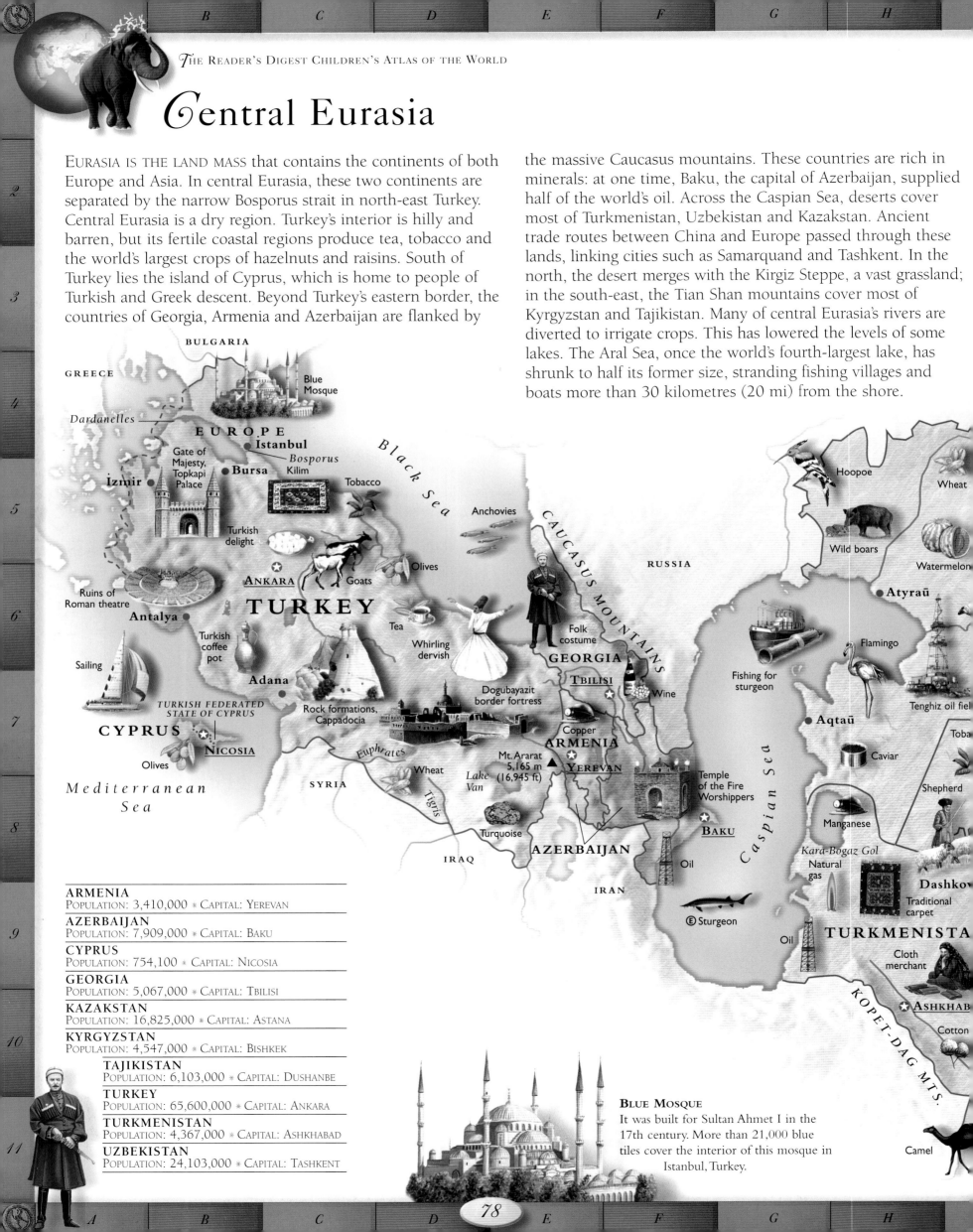

Central Eurasia

EURASIA IS THE LAND MASS that contains the continents of both Europe and Asia. In central Eurasia, these two continents are separated by the narrow Bosporus strait in north-east Turkey. Central Eurasia is a dry region. Turkey's interior is hilly and barren, but its fertile coastal regions produce tea, tobacco and the world's largest crops of hazelnuts and raisins. South of Turkey lies the island of Cyprus, which is home to people of Turkish and Greek descent. Beyond Turkey's eastern border, the countries of Georgia, Armenia and Azerbaijan are flanked by the massive Caucasus mountains. These countries are rich in minerals: at one time, Baku, the capital of Azerbaijan, supplied half of the world's oil. Across the Caspian Sea, deserts cover most of Turkmenistan, Uzbekistan and Kazakstan. Ancient trade routes between China and Europe passed through these lands, linking cities such as Samarquand and Tashkent. In the north, the desert merges with the Kirgiz Steppe, a vast grassland; in the south-east, the Tian Shan mountains cover most of Kyrgyzstan and Tajikistan. Many of central Eurasia's rivers are diverted to irrigate crops. This has lowered the levels of some lakes. The Aral Sea, once the world's fourth-largest lake, has shrunk to half its former size, stranding fishing villages and boats more than 30 kilometres (20 mi) from the shore.

ARMENIA
POPULATION: 3,410,000 * CAPITAL: YEREVAN

AZERBAIJAN
POPULATION: 7,909,000 * CAPITAL: BAKU

CYPRUS
POPULATION: 754,100 * CAPITAL: NICOSIA

GEORGIA
POPULATION: 5,067,000 * CAPITAL: TBILISI

KAZAKSTAN
POPULATION: 16,825,000 * CAPITAL: ASTANA

KYRGYZSTAN
POPULATION: 4,547,000 * CAPITAL: BISHKEK

TAJIKISTAN
POPULATION: 6,103,000 * CAPITAL: DUSHANBE

TURKEY
POPULATION: 65,600,000 * CAPITAL: ANKARA

TURKMENISTAN
POPULATION: 4,367,000 * CAPITAL: ASHKHABAD

UZBEKISTAN
POPULATION: 24,103,000 * CAPITAL: TASHKENT

BLUE MOSQUE
It was built for Sultan Ahmet I in the 17th century. More than 21,000 blue tiles cover the interior of this mosque in Istanbul, Turkey.

◆ PROJECT: *Kilim Weaving* ◆

A kilim is a flat, woven rug traditionally made in Turkey. To make a simple kilim, you will first need to make a loom.

❶ Cut notches into the corners of a rectangular piece of cardboard. Tie a length of string to the left-hand notch and then wrap it around the cardboard, moving from left to right and leaving about one centimetre (½ in) between strings. Tie the string off on the right-hand notch.

❷ Thread wool on a darning needle and weave it under and then over the strings. If you begin the first row weaving under, begin the second

row weaving over, and so on. When you add a new piece of wool, tie it to the old piece. As you weave, push the rows tightly together.

❸ When the loom is full, turn it over so that it is face down and cut the two middle strings. Tie them together at the top and bottom edges of the weaving. Repeat with the rest of the strings.

❹ When all the strings have been cut and tied, remove the weaving from the loom. Trim the ends of the tied-off strings to make a fringe for your kilim.

Step 1   Step 2   Step 3

◆ AMAZING FACT ◆

In Cappadocia in central Turkey, an eerie landscape of strange rock formations has been created by wind and water erosion. Early Christians made homes and churches inside caves cut into the rock. Some of these caves are still in use today.

SNOW LEOPARD
Living high in the mountains, the snow leopard needs strong paws for rock climbing and long, thick fur to keep warm.

LOCATION

Qostanay   Petropavl
Iron ore   Marmot
Wheat   Ishim
Sarsembek herder
ASTANA
Yurts (nomad tents)
Pavlodar
Barley
Irtysh
RUSSIA
Gold
Textiles
KIRGIZ STEPPE
Aktyubinsk
Bearded vulture
Stranded fishing boats, Aral Sea
Manganese   Copper   Qaraghandy   Semey   Oskemen
KAZAKSTAN   Coal   Baking bread in traditional oven   Hydroelectricity   Lake Zaysan
Aral Sea
Baykonur Cosmodrome
Cotton
Syr Dar'ya
Saiga antelope   Lake Balkhash   White-throated kingfisher
Nukus   Folk costume   Cotton   Spoonbill
UZBEKISTAN
Kirgiz farmer   Street vendor selling apples
Registan Square   Chemicals   CHINA
Shymkent   Almaty
Snow leopard
Bukhara   Samarkand   TASHKENT   BISHKEK   TIAN SHAN
Chardzhou   Namangan   KYRGYZSTAN
Cotton   Rice   Sheep
Amu Dar'ya   Osh   Yak
Karakumskiy Canal   Sheep   Cotton   Musician playing longhorn
DUSHANBE   Communism Peak 7,495 m (24,590 ft)
TAJIKISTAN   Hissar fortress
AFGHANISTAN

N
W   E
S

SCALE
MILES
0   100   200   300
0   100   200   300   400   500
KILOMETRES

BAYKONUR COSMODROME
Formerly a Soviet Union space centre, Baykonur is now leased from Kazakstan by Russia for use as its main space shuttle and rocket launching site.

The Middle East

THE MIDDLE EAST IS A LAND of ancient cities and vast deserts. It is home to some of the world's oldest civilizations and was the birthplace of three of the most widespread religions – Islam, Christianity and Judaism. Though there are narrow strips of fertile land on the densely populated Mediterranean coast, along the Tigris and Euphrates rivers in Iraq, and in the highlands of northern Iran and Yemen, most of this region is hot, dry and barren. Deserts extend southwards from Syria, Jordan and Israel, covering most of the Arabian Peninsula. Parts of this peninsula receive no rain for up to 10 years! Deserts also cover two-thirds of Iran. The enormous Dasht-e Kavīr salt desert in eastern Iran has almost no vegetation. Among its few inhabitants are gazelles that survive on tiny amounts of salty water. Over the centuries, the people of the Middle East have made skilful use of their limited water supplies. For thousands of years, the Tigris and Euphrates rivers have been used to water crops. Today, desalination plants on the shores of the Persian Gulf turn sea water into fresh water. The Gulf region holds half the world's reserves of oil and gas, and this has made some countries very wealthy. On average, people in the United Arab Emirates earn twice as much as people in the U.S.A. In contrast, Yemen, which has little oil, is one of the poorest countries in the world.

BAHRAIN
POPULATION: 629,100 ∗ CAPITAL: MANAMA

IRAN
POPULATION: 65,180,000 ∗ CAPITAL: TEHRAN

IRAQ
POPULATION: 22,428,000 ∗ CAPITAL: BAGHDAD

ISRAEL
POPULATION: 5,750,000 ∗ CAPITAL: JERUSALEM

JORDAN
POPULATION: 4,562,000 ∗ CAPITAL: AMMAN

KUWAIT
POPULATION: 1,992,000 ∗ CAPITAL: KUWAIT

LEBANON
POPULATION: 3,563,000 ∗ CAPITAL: BEIRUT

OMAN
POPULATION: 2,447,000 ∗ CAPITAL: MUSCAT

QATAR
POPULATION: 723,600 ∗ CAPITAL: DOHA

SAUDI ARABIA
POPULATION: 21,505,000 ∗ CAPITAL: RIYADH

SYRIA
POPULATION: 17,214,000 ∗ CAPITAL: DAMASCUS

UNITED ARAB EMIRATES
POPULATION: 2,345,000 ∗ CAPITAL: ABU DHABI

YEMEN
POPULATION: 16,943,000 ∗ CAPITAL: SANAA

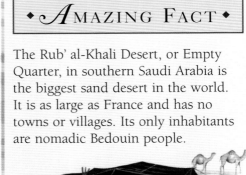

∗ AMAZING FACT ∗

The Rub' al-Khali Desert, or Empty Quarter, in southern Saudi Arabia is the biggest sand desert in the world. It is as large as France and has no towns or villages. Its only inhabitants are nomadic Bedouin people.

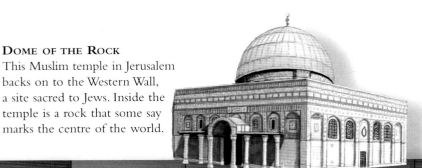

DOME OF THE ROCK
This Muslim temple in Jerusalem backs on to the Western Wall, a site sacred to Jews. Inside the temple is a rock that some say marks the centre of the world.

VEILED WOMAN
Traditionally, Muslim women must keep their face and hair hidden from strangers. Many wear a long black cloak and a veil or eye-mask.

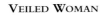

THE MIDDLE EAST *See World Fact File pages 110-111*

ARMENIA AZERBAIJAN

Tobacco
Araks
Tabrīz
Oil
Barley
Rasht
Caspian Sea
TURKMENISTAN
Mosul
Cotton
Caviar
(E) Sturgeon
Mashhad
Turquoise
Friday Mosque, Samarra
TEHRAN
Musician
Winnowing grain
DASHT-E KAVĪR (GREAT SALT DESERT)
BAGHDAD
ZAGROS MOUNTAINS
Kurdish woman
Royal Mosque
PLATEAU OF IRAN
(E) Leopard
Tigris
Q
Eṣfahān
Making rugs
IRAN
DASHT-E LŪT
AFGHANISTAN
Bedouin shepherd
Oil
Ābādān
Kermān
Ziggurat (temple), Ur
Al Basrah
Stone carvings, Persepolis
PAKISTAN
Wine
Shīrāz
Walled city of Bam
Shepherd in traditional felt coat
KUWAIT
Oil
KUWAIT
Oil
Caracal
Camel race
Oil
Persian Gulf
Eurasian griffon
Goats
Strait of Hormuz
BAHRAIN
Ad Dammām
AL MANAMA
QATAR
Oil
Dubai
OMAN
Gulf of Oman
Water tower
AD DAWHAH
Natural gas
ABU DHABI
MUSCAT
Oil tanker
RIYADH
Zubara fort
UNITED ARAB EMIRATES
Al Khuwair Mosque
Date palm
LOCATION
Bedouin with falcon
Arabian horse
(UNDEFINED BORDER)
Şūr
SAUDI ARABIA
Solar-powered telephone
Coconuts
Sardines
Arabian Sea
Great Mosque
Bedouin tent
Collecting frankincense
N
Baboon
RUB' AL-KHALI DESERT (EMPTY QUARTER)
OMAN
W E
Sand cat
(UNDEFINED BORDER)
(E) Arabian oryx
S
Woman at well
Tiger shark
SCALE
MILES
0 50 100 150 200 250
Wheat
Apricots
Salālah
0 100 200 300 400
KILOMETRES
SANAA
YEMEN
Al Hajrah
Men with narghile
Ta'izz
Coffee
Socotra (Yemen)
ARABIAN ORYX
This antelope may have been the origin of the myth of the unicorn. Viewed from the side, the oryx looks as though it has only one horn.
Aden
DJIBOUTI
Gulf of Aden

Southern Asia

SOUTHERN ASIA, OR THE Indian Subcontinent as it is also known, is separated from the rest of Asia by a series of massive mountain ranges. In the north-east, the mighty Himalayas, the highest mountains on Earth, tower over northern India and the two small kingdoms of Nepal and Bhutan. In the north-west, the dry, rugged Hindu Kush – the world's second-highest mountain range – spreads across central Afghanistan. South of these mountains, the land drops steeply to a wide, fertile plain that stretches from Pakistan to Bangladesh and covers most of northern India. Southern India consists of a large triangular plateau, the Deccan, fringed by narrow coastal plains. Just off the south-east coast lies the island of Sri Lanka.

Southern Asia has large areas of fertile land, valuable mineral reserves and expanding industries, but these resources barely support the region's huge population, and many people are very poor. One-fifth of the world's people live in southern Asia, and the population is growing rapidly. In India alone, almost 20 million babies are born each year. Four-fifths of southern Asians live in small villages, and most grow their own food. In India, Sri Lanka and Bangladesh, farmers rely on summer rains to water their crops. These rains are brought by winds known as monsoons. If too little rain falls, the crops fail. If too much rain falls, the crops, as well as buildings and people, can be washed away by devastating floods.

AFGHANISTAN
POPULATION: 25,825,000 * CAPITAL: KABUL

BANGLADESH
POPULATION: 127,118,000 * CAPITAL: DHAKA

BHUTAN
POPULATION: 1,952,000 * CAPITAL: THIMPHU

INDIA
POPULATION: 1,000,849,000 * CAPITAL: NEW DELHI

MALDIVES
POPULATION: 300,300 * CAPITAL: MALE

NEPAL
POPULATION: 24,303,000 * CAPITAL: KATHMANDU

PAKISTAN
POPULATION: 138,124,000 * CAPITAL: ISLAMABAD

SRI LANKA
POPULATION: 19,145,000 * CAPITAL: COLOMBO

◆ PROJECT: *Taj Mahal Tile* ◆

The Taj Mahal in India was built by Emperor Shah Jahan in memory of his beloved wife Mumtaz. Construction began in 1631, and it took 20,000 workers about 20 years to complete the building. It is covered in tiles of dazzling white marble. Each tile is carved with floral designs and inlaid with semi-precious stones. You can make your own paper Taj Mahal tile.

❶ Draw floral patterns on a square of white paper.

❷ Colour the patterns and then use glitter, sequins, buttons or coloured foil to fashion the jewels in the Taj Mahal's intricate designs.

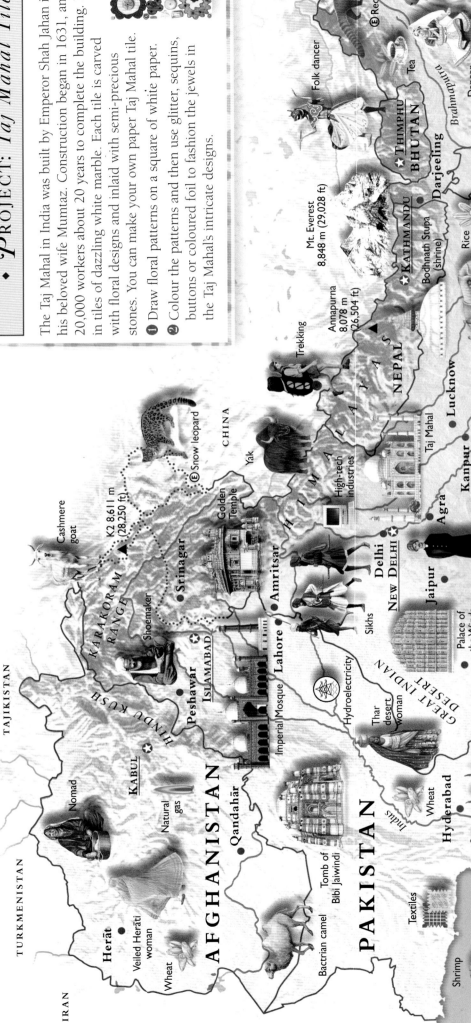

Arabian Sea

Bay of Bengal

INDIAN OCEAN

LOCATION

INDIA

DĚCCAN

SRI LANKA

ANDAMAN ISLANDS

NICOBAR ISLANDS

DHAKA
Ⓔ Ganges dolphin
Chittagong
Transporting jute
Washing in the Ganges
Calcutta
Iron and steel
Ⓔ Garial
Bhubaneswar
Cray fisherman
Mackerel
Weasel shark

Snake charmer
Great Stupa (shrine)
Langur monkeys
Nagpur
Brahman
Ⓔ Tiger
Spice seller
Bharatanyam temple dancer
High-tech industries
Chennai (Madras)
Meenakshi Temple
Fishermen on stilts
Jaffna
Tea
Sloth bear
Cinnamon
COLOMBO

Coal
Bhopal
Cobra and mongoose
Sitar
Hyderabad
Gol Gumbaz Mosque
Cotton
Bangalore
Tea
Blue peacock

Painted elephant
Pangolin
Ahmadabad
Ploughing with cattle
Sardines
Gateway to India
Mumbai (Bombay)
Zebu cow
Millet
Cotton
Panaji (Goa)
Planting rice
Cricket
Fishing boat
Ernakulam (Cochin)
Thiruvananthapuram (Trivandrum)
Fishing boat

W N E S

SCALE
MILES
0 100 200 300
0 100 200 300 400 500
KILOMETRES

BODHNATH STUPA
Begun in the fifth century, this huge shrine in Nepal is decorated with the all-seeing eyes of Buddha, the founder of Buddhism.

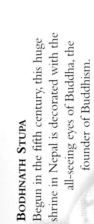

FOLK DANCER
In Bhutan, dancers taking part in religious festivals wear ornate silk costumes and masks to represent gods and spirits.

PAINTED ELEPHANT
During religious processions in India, elephants are painted and then draped in colourful silks and sparkling jewels.

◆ **AMAZING FACT** ◆

The Himalayas were once under the sea! About 40 million years ago the Indian land mass collided with Eurasia, pushing rocks up from the sea floor to form this vast mountain range. Fossilized seashells have been found on many Himalayan peaks.

MALDIVES
Coconut palm
MALE
Tourism
Magnificent frigate bird
MILES
0 100 200 300
0 200 400
KILOMETRES

South-east Asia

SOUTH-EAST ASIA IS MADE UP OF a mainland peninsula and more than 20,000 islands. Throughout this hot, humid region, rugged mountains rise steeply from wide river basins and coastal plains once covered in dense rainforests. Most people live in the river valleys or near the coast, where they fish and grow food. Rice is the most important crop. On the plains, it is planted in wide, flooded fields called rice paddies. On hills and mountains, rice is grown on terraces – narrow strips of land that cover the slopes like giant staircases. In recent years, many South-east Asians have moved from the countryside to cities in search of work. Bangkok, Ho Chi Minh City, Manila and Jakarta are now among the most crowded and fastest-growing cities in the world. South-east Asia has many natural resources. Malaysia is the world's leading exporter of tin, Myanmar supplies most of the world's rubies, and oil has made Brunei one of the world's richest countries. Timber is the most widespread resource, and the region's rainforests supply more than three-quarters of the world's tropical hardwoods. But so many trees are being chopped down that several countries could soon run out of forest, and many animal and plant species are now endangered. Some countries restrict logging activities and have turned large areas of forest into magnificent national parks.

BRUNEI
POPULATION: 323,000 * CAPITAL: BANDAR SERI BEGAWAN

CAMBODIA
POPULATION: 11,627,000 * CAPITAL: PHNOM PENH

EAST TIMOR
POPULATION: 650,000 * CAPITAL: DILI

INDONESIA
POPULATION: 216,109,000 * CAPITAL: JAKARTA

LAOS
POPULATION: 5,408,000 * CAPITAL: VIENTIANE

MALAYSIA
POPULATION: 21,376,000 * CAPITAL: KUALA LUMPUR

MYANMAR (BURMA)
POPULATION: 48,082,000 * CAPITAL: YANGON (RANGOON)

PHILIPPINES
POPULATION: 79,346,000 * CAPITAL: MANILA

SINGAPORE
POPULATION: 3,532,000 * CAPITAL: SINGAPORE

THAILAND
POPULATION: 60,609,000 * CAPITAL: BANGKOK

VIETNAM
POPULATION: 77,312,000 * CAPITAL: HANOI

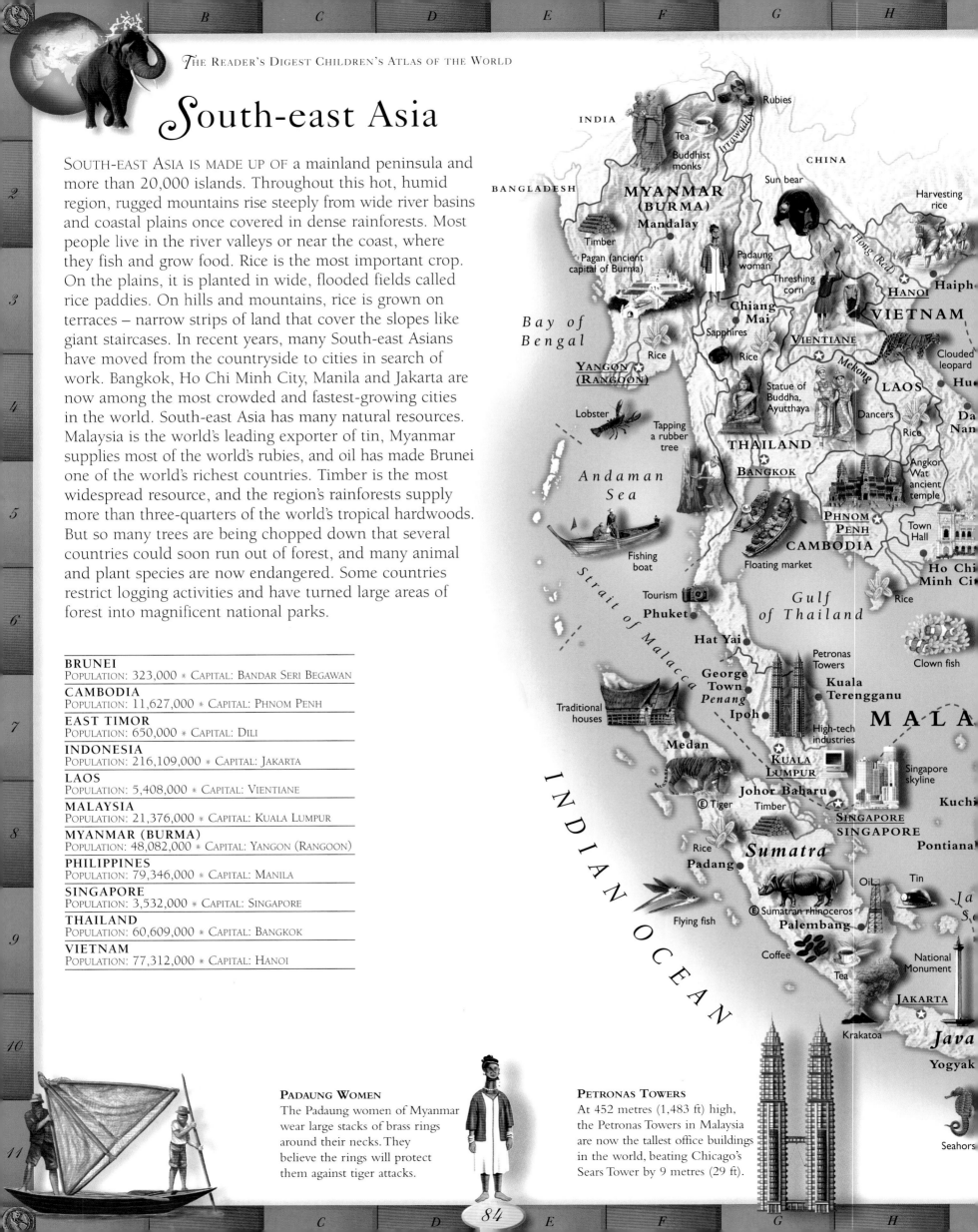

PADAUNG WOMEN
The Padaung women of Myanmar wear large stacks of brass rings around their necks. They believe the rings will protect them against tiger attacks.

PETRONAS TOWERS
At 452 metres (1,483 ft) high, the Petronas Towers in Malaysia are now the tallest office buildings in the world, beating Chicago's Sears Tower by 9 metres (29 ft).

◆ LOOK AGAIN ◆

- In which country could you shop at a floating market?
- Name a weapon used by hunters in Malaysia.
- What kind of dragon lives on an island in Indonesia?

SCALE

MILES

0	100	200	300	400

0	150	300	450	600

KILOMETRES

◆ PROJECT: *Erupting Volcano* ◆

South-east Asia has more active volcanoes than any other part of the world. The island of Java alone has 50 volcanoes that could erupt at any time. Here's a volcano that will erupt whenever you want it to.

❶ Use moist soil to model a mountain on a tray.

❷ Scoop out a hole from the top of the mountain and put in a container, such as the lid from a spray can.

❸ Pour about ¼ cup warm water into the container. Now stir in 1 tablespoon baking powder, a few drops of red food colouring and a few drops of washing-up liquid. Pour in ¼ cup vinegar and watch your volcano erupt.

Adding vinegar to the baking powder produces carbon dioxide gas. This causes pressure to build up until the volcano erupts, forcing lava suds out the top. This is similar to the pressure inside Earth's crust that causes a real volcano to erupt.

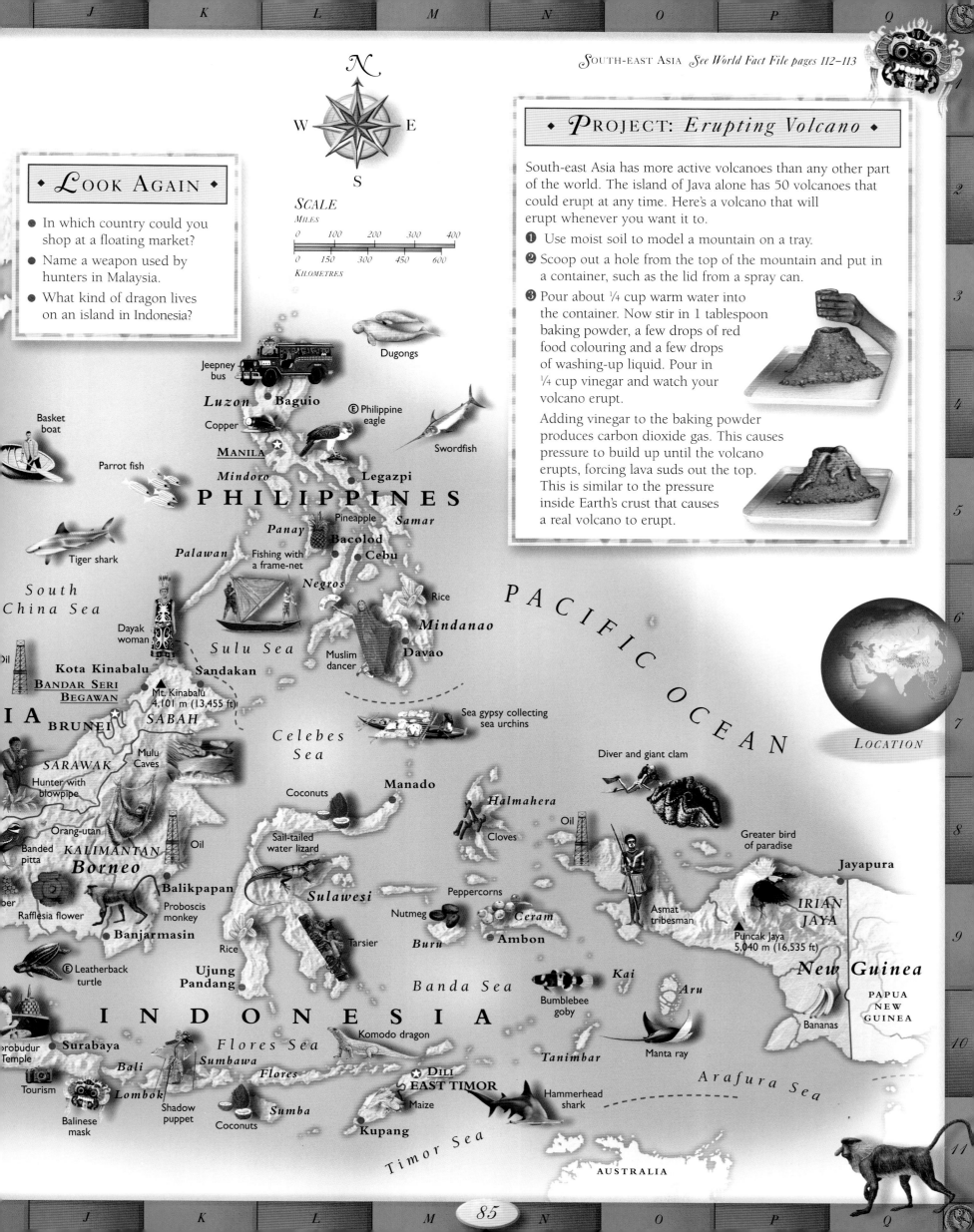

Dugongs

Jeepney bus

Luzon Baguio

Basket boat

Copper Ⓔ Philippine eagle

Swordfish

MANILA

Parrot fish

Mindoro Legazpi

PHILIPPINES

Tiger shark

Panay Pineapple

Samar

Bacolod

Palawan Fishing with a frame-net Cebu

South China Sea *Negros* Rice

Dayak woman

Sulu Sea *Mindanao*

Kota Kinabalu Sandakan Muslim dancer Davao

Oil BANDAR SERI BEGAWAN

Mt. Kinabalu 4,101 m (13,455 ft)

ASIA BRUNEI *SABAH*

Celebes Sea

Sea gypsy collecting sea urchins

SARAWAK Mulu Caves

Hunter with blowpipe

Diver and giant clam

PACIFIC OCEAN

LOCATION

Coconuts *Manado*

Halmahera

Orang-utan

Banded pitta *KALIMANTAN* Oil

Sail-tailed water lizard Cloves Oil

Borneo

Greater bird of paradise

Balikpapan Jayapura

Rafflesia flower Proboscis monkey *Sulawesi* Peppercorns

Nutmeg *Ceram*

IRIAN JAYA

Banjarmasin Tarsier *Buru* Ambon

Rice Asmat tribesman Puncak Jaya 5,040 m (16,535 ft)

Ⓔ Leatherback turtle Ujung Pandang *New Guinea*

Kai

Banda Sea *Aru*

PAPUA NEW GUINEA

INDONESIA

Bumblebee goby

Bananas

Surabaya *Flores Sea* Komodo dragon

robudur Temple *Bali* *Sumbawa* *Tanimbar* Manta ray

Tourism *Flores* DILI EAST TIMOR *Arafura Sea*

Lombok *Sumba* Maize Hammerhead shark

Balinese mask Shadow puppet Coconuts Kupang

Timor Sea

AUSTRALIA

Eastern Asia

EASTERN ASIA INCLUDES PART of the Asian mainland as well as several small islands. It is dominated by China, the third-largest (and most populous) country in the world. China is only slightly larger than the U.S.A., but it has more than four times as many people. Eighty per cent live in the eastern third of the country, where the climate is mild and wet, and most of the land is fertile. There are many large cities in eastern China, but most people live in villages where they raise pigs and chickens, and grow rice, wheat and vegetables. Western China is dry, rugged and sparsely populated. The south-western region – Tibet – is sometimes called the 'roof of the world' because it lies on the highest plateau on Earth and contains part of the tallest mountain range, the Himalayas. In the north, the barren Gobi Desert stretches into Mongolia, where many people are nomadic herders. On and around China's coast lie a number of rapidly developing countries and territories. South Korea and Taiwan have many thriving industries, including textile, car and electrical goods manufacturers. Macao, a tiny Portuguese colony on the south coast of China, is the world's most crowded place, with 22,150 people for every square kilometre (57,100 per sq. mi). Macao will revert to Chinese rule in 1999. Neighbouring Hong Kong, a former British colony which was given back to China in 1997, is the world's third-largest financial centre. Its modern, high-rise office buildings tower over one of Asia's busiest harbours.

CHINA
POPULATION: 1,246,872,000 ∗ CAPITAL: BEIJING
MONGOLIA
POPULATION: 2,618,000 ∗ CAPITAL: ULAANBAATAR
NORTH KOREA
POPULATION: 21,386,000 ∗ CAPITAL: P'YŎNGYANG
SOUTH KOREA
POPULATION: 46,885,000 ∗ CAPITAL: SEOUL
TAIWAN
POPULATION: 22,113,000 ∗ CAPITAL: TAIPEI

∗ AMAZING FACT ∗

The Great Wall of China stretches for 3,460 kilometres (2,150 mi) across northern China and is so large that astronauts can see it from space. It was built in the third century BC to keep out invaders from the north, then rebuilt and expanded in the 14th century AD.

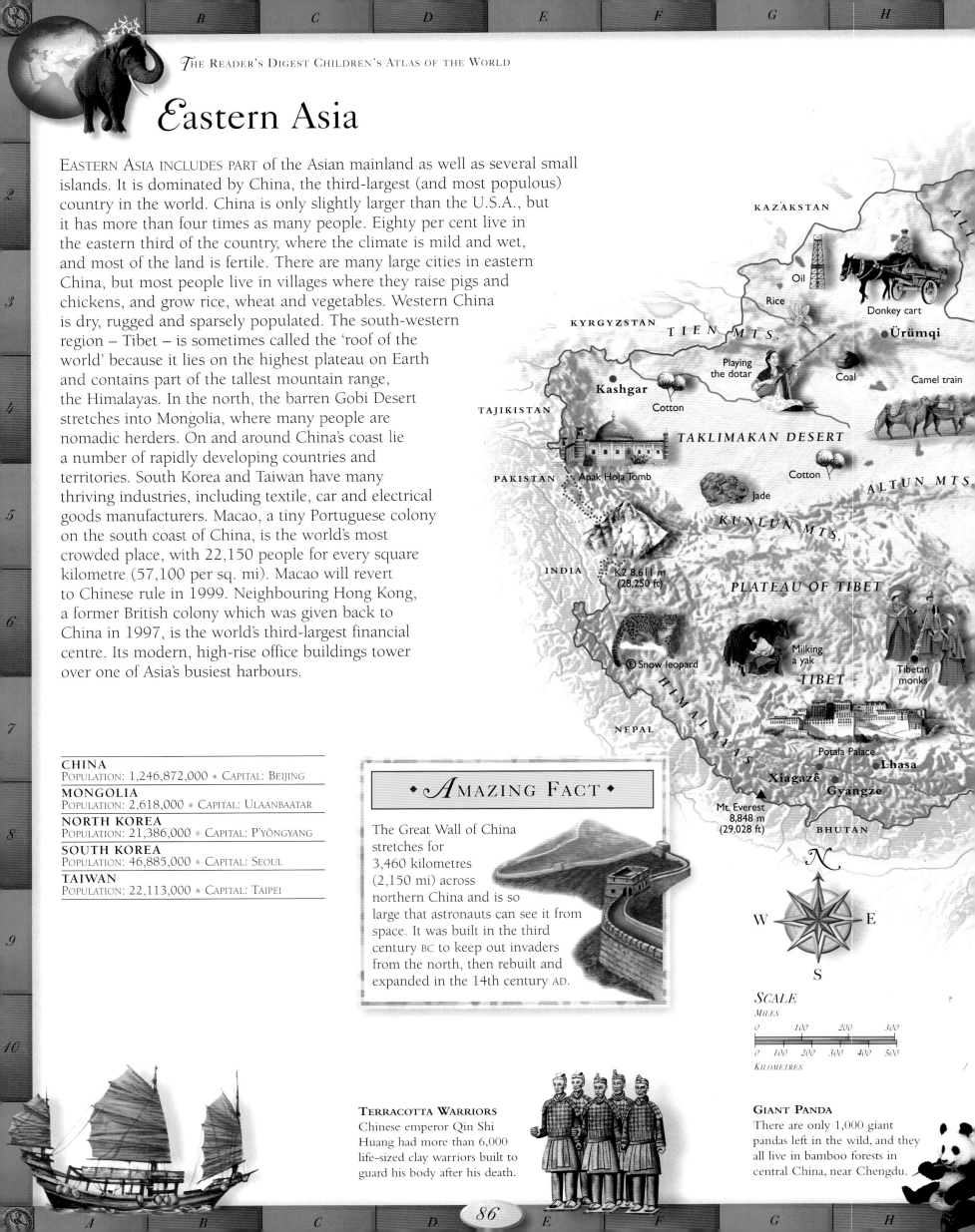

KAZ'AKSTAN

Oil
Rice
Donkey cart
KYRGYZSTAN
TIEN MTS.
Ürümqi
Playing the dotar
Coal
Camel train
Kashgar
Cotton
TAJIKISTAN
TAKLIMAKAN DESERT
ALTUN MTS.
Cotton
PAKISTAN
Apak Hoja Tomb
Jade
KUNLUN MTS.
INDIA
K2 8,611 m (28,250 ft)
PLATEAU OF TIBET
Snow leopard
Milking a yak
Tibetan monks
TIBET
HIMALAYAS
NEPAL
Potala Palace
Lhasa
Xiagazê
Gyangze
Mt. Everest 8,848 m (29,028 ft)
BHUTAN

N
W   E
S

SCALE
MILES
0   100   200   300
0   100   200   300   400   500
KILOMETRES

TERRACOTTA WARRIORS
Chinese emperor Qin Shi Huang had more than 6,000 life-sized clay warriors built to guard his body after his death.

GIANT PANDA
There are only 1,000 giant pandas left in the wild, and they all live in bamboo forests in central China, near Chengdu.

J K L M N O P Q

Lake Uvs

Lake Hövsgöl

Elk

RUSSIA

Amur

Ⓔ Tiger

Coal mining

Qiqihar

Ice sledging

Timber

Darhan

Traditional costume

Choybalsan

Harbin

Car manufacturing

Ⓔ ULAANBAATAR

Soya beans

Wheat

Changchun

Ⓔ Mongolian family and ger (tent)

Wild boar

Coal

Farmer carrying grain

Ch'ŏngjin

MONGOLIA

GREAT KHINGAN MTS.

Corn

Iron and steel

NORTH KOREA

Ⓔ Bactrian camel

Great Wall of China

Shenyang

Fushun

Iron and steel

GOBI DESERT

Oil

Yumen

Goats

Baotou

Iron and steel

Temple of Heaven

BEIJING

P'YŎNGYANG

Sea of Japan

Pallas's cat

Cycling

Forbidden City

Tangshan

Tianjin

Dalian

SEOUL

SOUTH KOREA

Textiles

Pusan

JAPAN

CHINA

Lake Qinghai

Chemicals

Taiyuan

Cotton

Zibo

Jinan

Fortune cookies

Wheat

Traditional costume

Cheju

Korea Strait

Lanzhou

Reeves's pheasant

Terracotta warriors

Xi'an

Chemicals

Huang (Yellow)

Zhengzhou

Taking cabbages to market

Silk worm and cocoon

Grand Canal

Yellow Sea

Ⓔ Giant panda

Golden snub-nosed monkey

Rice

Ping-pong

Tai chi

Nanjing

Nanjing Pagoda

Shanghai

Container ship

LOCATION

Chengdu

Ⓔ Red panda

Iron and steel

Chongqing

Chang (Yangtze)

Lake Dongting

Wuhan

Lychees

Lake Poyang

Nanchang

Ming vase

Hangzhou

Textiles

East China Sea

Grand Buddha

Farmhouse

Changsha

Tea

Sweet potatoes

Fuzhou

Shrimp

Asiatic golden cat

Guiyang

Fishing with cormorants

Limestone hills of Guilin

Rice

Pigs

TAIPEI

Taiwan Strait

Kunming

Herding ducks

Bank of China

High-tech industries

TAIWAN

Stone forest (rock formations)

Guangzhou

Paper

Chiang Kai Shek monument

INDIA

Mekong

Nanning

Hydroelectricity

Hong Kong

Macao

MYANMAR (BURMA)

VIETNAM

LAOS

Coffee

Haikou

South China Sea

Junk

PACIFIC OCEAN

Hainan

Mandarin fish

TRADITIONAL COSTUME
Most Korean men used to wear a
white jacket and baggy trousers,
and a black horsehair hat. Now they
wear these only on special occasions.

2 3 4 5 6 7 8 9 10 11

J K L M N O

THE READER'S DIGEST CHILDREN'S ATLAS OF THE WORLD

Japan

JAPAN CONSISTS OF a long chain of 4 main islands and more than 4,000 smaller islands that lies off the east coast of the Asian mainland. The northern half of Japan has a cold temperate climate with snowy winters and mild summers. In the south the weather is more tropical, with mild winters and a summer wet season. Most of the land is mountainous, and almost two-thirds is covered in forests. Earthquakes are common, and there are many active volcanoes. Three-quarters of the population live in cities, the largest of which are located on the large island of Honshū. Japan's capital, Tokyo, sprawls across more than 80 neighbouring towns, forming the biggest urban area in the world, and is home to almost 27 million people. So many workers commute to the city centre each day that railway stations employ guards known as 'pushers' to cram passengers into trains. Despite having little farmland, Japan manages to produce most of its food, including large quantities of rice. Fish is the country's most important resource, and the Japanese fishing fleet is the largest in the world. Although it has few other natural resources, Japan has become a major industrial power by importing raw materials and manufacturing high-quality goods. It is the world's top car manufacturer, has the world's foremost shipbuilding industry, and is a leading exporter of electronic goods.

JAPAN
POPULATION: 126,182,000 • CAPITAL: TOKYO

◆ LOOK AGAIN ◆

- What kind of festival takes place in Sapporo?
- Name two kinds of shark found off the west coast of Honshū.
- Which famous mountain lies south-west of Japan's capital?

RUSSIA

Sea of Okhotsk

Hokkaidō

RUSSIA

Salmon

Dairy cattle

Kushiro

Great white shark

Coal

Pollock

Ainu man

Brown bear

Timber

Sapporo snow festival

Sapporo

Asahikawa

Rice

Skiing

Wakkanai

Rebun

Rishiri

Halibut

Otaru

Serows

Hakodate

Japanese crane

Mako shark

Tsugaru Strait

Macaques

Aomori

Apples

Japanese spider crab

Akita

Morioka

Sushi

Mackerel

Making chopsticks

Rice

Kokechi doll

Carp streamers

Sendai

Shiogama festival

Dancer in traditional costume

Sardines

Fukushima

Niigata

JAPAN

Shinano

Sado

Ninja

Sea of Japan

RYUKYU ISLANDS

East China Sea

Rice

Long-tailed carpet shark

AMAMI ISLANDS

Karate

OKINAWA ISLANDS

Tourism

Pineapple

Naha

MILES
0   25   50   75

0   50   100   150
KILOMETRES

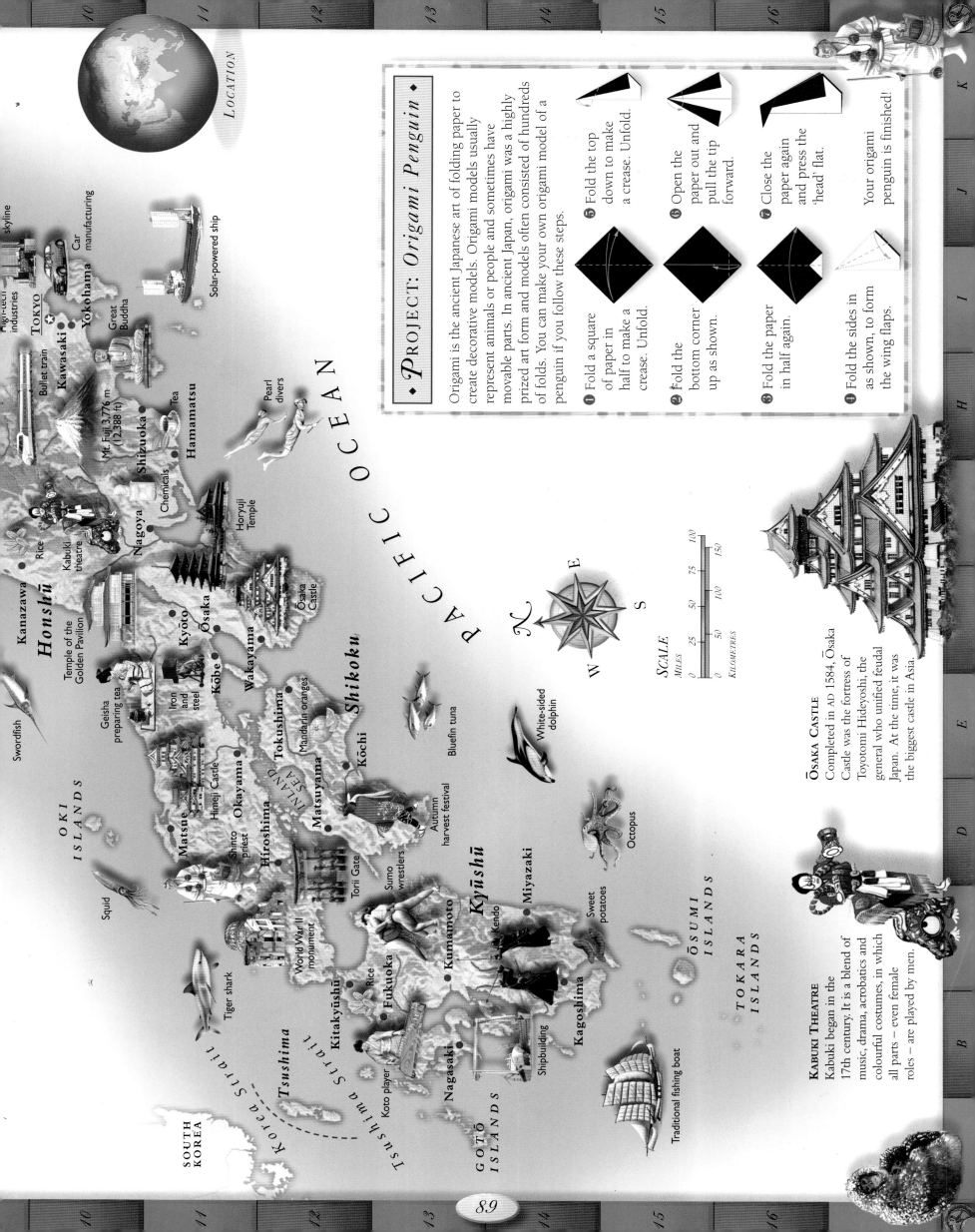

LOCATION

◆ PROJECT: *Origami Penguin* ◆

Origami is the ancient Japanese art of folding paper to create decorative models. Origami models usually represent animals or people and sometimes have movable parts. In ancient Japan, origami was a highly prized art form and models often consisted of hundreds of folds. You can make your own origami model of a penguin if you follow these steps.

❶ Fold a square of paper in half to make a crease. Unfold.

❷ Fold the bottom corner up as shown.

❸ Fold the paper in half again.

❹ Fold the sides in as shown, to form the wing flaps.

❺ Fold the top down to make a crease. Unfold.

❻ Open the paper out and pull the tip forward.

❼ Close the paper again and press the 'head' flat.

Your origami penguin is finished!

SOUTH KOREA

Korea Strait

OKI ISLANDS

Tsushima

Tsushima Strait

GOTŌ ISLANDS

Honshū

Kanazawa

Tokyo

Yokohama

High-tech industries

skyline

Car manufacturing

Solar-powered ship

Kawasaki

Great Buddha

Bullet train

Mt. Fuji 3,776 m (12,388 ft)

Shizuoka

Tea

Hamamatsu

Pearl divers

Nagoya

Chemicals

Rice

Kabuki theatre

Temple of the Golden Pavilion

Horyuji Temple

Kyōto

Ōsaka

Ōsaka Castle

Kōbe

Wakayama

Geisha preparing tea

Iron and steel

Mandarin oranges

Shikoku

Tokushima

Matsuyama

Kōchi

INLAND SEA

Swordfish

Squid

Tiger shark

Matsue

Shinto priest

Hineji Castle

Okayama

Hiroshima

Torii Gate

Sumo wrestlers

Autumn harvest festival

Bluefin tuna

White-sided dolphin

Octopus

Kyūshū

Koto player

Nagasaki

Kitakyūshū

Fukuoka

Rice

Kumamoto

Kendo

Miyazaki

Sweet potatoes

Kagoshima

Shipbuilding

World War II monument

Traditional fishing boat

ŌSUMI ISLANDS

TOKARA ISLANDS

P A C I F I C   O C E A N

N E S W

SCALE

MILES   0   25   50   75   100

KILOMETRES   0   50   100   150

ŌSAKA CASTLE
Completed in AD 1584, Ōsaka Castle was the fortress of Toyotomi Hideyoshi, the general who unified feudal Japan. At the time, it was the biggest castle in Asia.

KABUKI THEATRE
Kabuki began in the 17th century. It is a blend of music, drama, acrobatics and colourful costumes, in which all parts – even female roles – are played by men.

Africa

THE WORLD'S SECOND-LARGEST CONTINENT, Africa is an enormous plateau surrounded by narrow coastal plains. A thick band of tropical rainforest covers much of the centre of the continent. To the north and south of this forest lie grasslands, known as savannahs, and deserts. The Sahara Desert, the biggest desert in the world, spans the entire width of northern Africa, from the Atlantic Ocean to the Red Sea, and covers an area almost as large as the U.S.A. The Kalahari and Namib deserts extend across much of the south-west. In the east, the Great Rift Valley, a series of valleys formed by cracks in Earth's crust, stretches from Syria, in Asia, to Mozambique. Africa includes 53 countries ranging from vast, mainly arid Sudan to the tiny tropical islands of the Seychelles. Arab peoples form the majority of the population in the north. The south's mainly black population is made up of hundreds of native tribes.

Major Mountains and Rivers

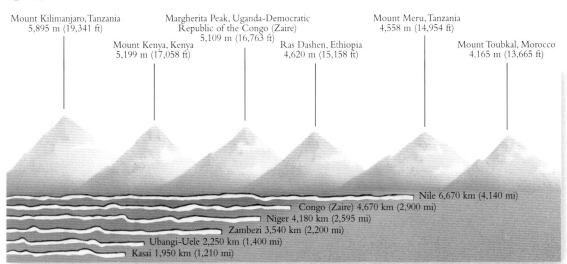

Mount Kilimanjaro, Tanzania
5,895 m (19,341 ft)

Mount Kenya, Kenya
5,199 m (17,058 ft)

Margherita Peak, Uganda-Democratic
Republic of the Congo (Zaire)
5,109 m (16,763 ft)

Ras Dashen, Ethiopia
4,620 m (15,158 ft)

Mount Meru, Tanzania
4,558 m (14,954 ft)

Mount Toubkal, Morocco
4,165 m (13,665 ft)

Nile 6,670 km (4,140 mi)
Congo (Zaire) 4,670 km (2,900 mi)
Niger 4,180 km (2,595 mi)
Zambezi 3,540 km (2,200 mi)
Ubangi-Uele 2,250 km (1,400 mi)
Kasai 1,950 km (1,210 mi)

Political Map

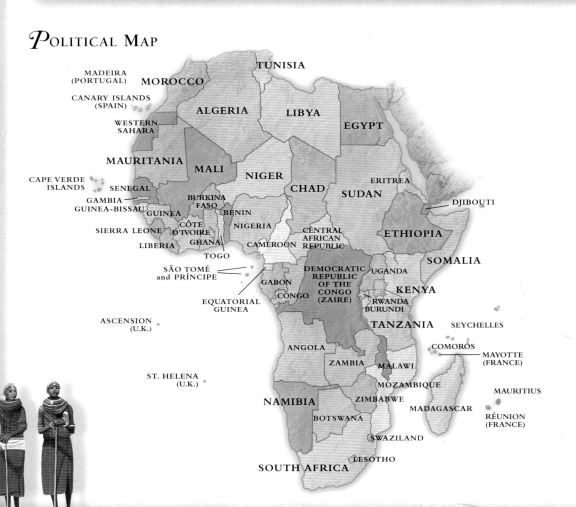

MADEIRA (PORTUGAL)
MOROCCO
CANARY ISLANDS (SPAIN)
WESTERN SAHARA
TUNISIA
ALGERIA
LIBYA
EGYPT
MAURITANIA
MALI
NIGER
CHAD
SUDAN
ERITREA
CAPE VERDE ISLANDS
SENEGAL
GAMBIA
GUINEA-BISSAU
GUINEA
BURKINA FASO
BENIN
NIGERIA
DJIBOUTI
SIERRA LEONE
CÔTE D'IVOIRE
GHANA
TOGO
CAMEROON
CENTRAL AFRICAN REPUBLIC
ETHIOPIA
LIBERIA
SÃO TOMÉ and PRÍNCIPE
EQUATORIAL GUINEA
GABON
CONGO
DEMOCRATIC REPUBLIC OF THE CONGO (ZAIRE)
UGANDA
SOMALIA
RWANDA
BURUNDI
KENYA
ASCENSION (U.K.)
TANZANIA
SEYCHELLES
ANGOLA
ZAMBIA
MALAWI
COMOROS
MAYOTTE (FRANCE)
ST. HELENA (U.K.)
MOZAMBIQUE
ZIMBABWE
MAURITIUS
NAMIBIA
BOTSWANA
MADAGASCAR
RÉUNION (FRANCE)
SWAZILAND
LESOTHO
SOUTH AFRICA

Continent Facts

Regional land area: 30,354,852 sq. km (11,716,972 sq. mi)
Regional population: 777,338,000
Independent countries: Algeria, Angola, Benin, Botswana, Burkina Faso, Burundi, Cameroon, Cape Verde Islands, Central African Republic, Chad, Comoros, Congo, Côte d'Ivoire (Ivory Coast), Democratic Republic of the Congo (Zaire), Djibouti, Egypt, Equatorial Guinea, Eritrea, Ethiopia, Gabon, Gambia, Ghana, Guinea, Guinea-Bissau, Kenya, Lesotho, Liberia, Libya, Madagascar, Malawi, Mali, Mauritania, Mauritius, Morocco, Mozambique, Namibia, Niger, Nigeria, Rwanda, São Tomé and Príncipe, Senegal, Seychelles, Sierra Leone, Somalia, South Africa, Sudan, Swaziland, Tanzania, Togo, Tunisia, Uganda, Zambia, Zimbabwe

World Records

WORLD'S LARGEST DESERT
SAHARA DESERT, NORTHERN AFRICA, 9,269,000 SQ. KM (3,579,000 SQ. MI)

WORLD'S LONGEST RIVER
NILE RIVER, NORTHERN AFRICA, 6,670 KM (4,140 MI)

WORLD'S LARGEST ARTIFICIAL LAKE
LAKE VOLTA, GHANA, 8,482 SQ. KM (3,275 SQ. MI)

WORLD'S HIGHEST TEMPERATURE
AL-'AZĪZĪYA, LIBYA, SHADE TEMPERATURE OF 58°C (136°F) RECORDED ON SEPTEMBER 13, 1922

Continent Records

HIGHEST MOUNTAIN
KILIMANJARO, TANZANIA, 5,895 M (19,341 FT)

LOWEST POINT
LAKE ASSAL, DJIBOUTI, 152 M (500 FT) BELOW SEA LEVEL

LARGEST LAKE
LAKE VICTORIA, EAST AFRICA, 69,485 SQ. KM (26,828 SQ. MI)

LARGEST COUNTRY BY AREA
SUDAN, 2,505,825 SQ. KM (967,500 SQ. MI)

LARGEST COUNTRY BY POPULATION
NIGERIA, POPULATION 113,829,000

LARGEST CITY BY POPULATION
CAIRO, EGYPT, POPULATION 9,700,000

◆ Amazing Fact ◆

The huge volume of water that pours over Victoria Falls, on the border between Zambia and Zimbabwe, creates a deafening roar and a cloud of spray that can be seen from more than 32 kilometres (20 mi) away. Because of this, locals refer to the Falls as 'the smoke that thunders'.

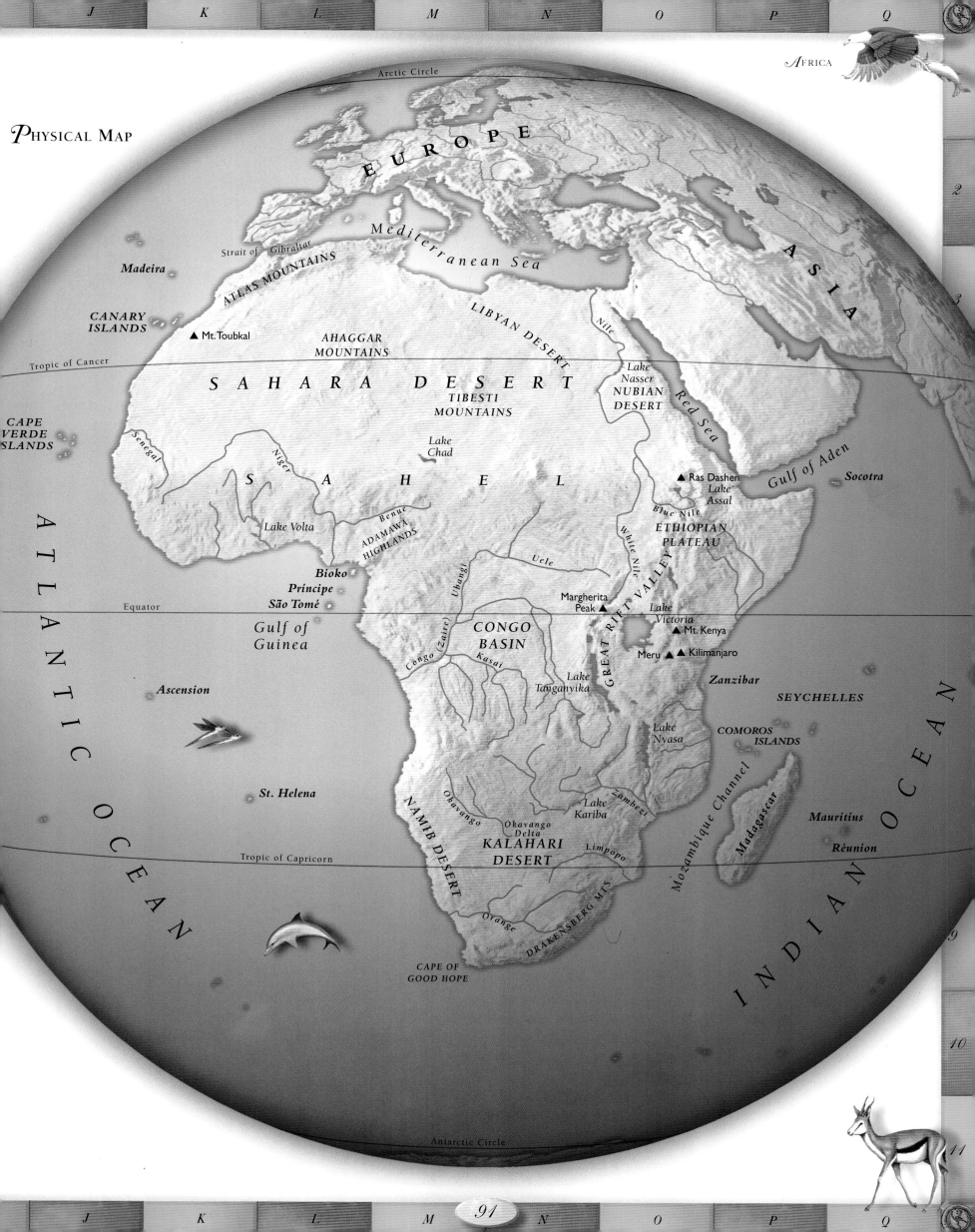

P*HYSICAL* MAP

EUROPE

ASIA

Madeira

Strait of Gibraltar

Mediterranean Sea

ATLAS MOUNTAINS

CANARY
ISLANDS

▲ Mt. Toubkal

AHAGGAR
MOUNTAINS

LIBYAN DESERT

Nile

Tropic of Cancer

SAHARA DESERT

TIBESTI
MOUNTAINS

Lake
Nasser
NUBIAN
DESERT

Red Sea

CAPE
VERDE
SLANDS

Senegal

S   A   H   E   L

Niger

*Lake
Chad*

▲ Ras Dashen
*Lake
Assal*

Gulf of Aden

Socotra

*Lake
Volta*

Benue

ADAMAWA
HIGHLANDS

Uele

Blue Nile

White Nile

ETHIOPIAN
PLATEAU

ATLANTIC

Bioko

Príncipe

São Tomé

Ubangi

Margherita
Peak ▲

GREAT RIFT VALLEY

Equator

Gulf of
Guinea

CONGO
BASIN

Congo (Zaire)

Kasai

*Lake
Victoria*

▲ Mt. Kenya

Meru ▲ ▲ Kilimanjaro

Ascension

*Lake
Tanganyika*

Zanzibar

SEYCHELLES

St. Helena

*Lake
Nyasa*

COMOROS
ISLANDS

OCEAN

NAMIB DESERT

Okavango

Okavango
Delta

*Lake
Kariba*

Zambezi

Mozambique Channel

Madagascar

Mauritius

KALAHARI
DESERT

Limpopo

Réunion

Tropic of Capricorn

Orange

DRAKENSBERG MTS.

INDIAN OCEAN

CAPE OF
GOOD HOPE

Arctic Circle

Antarctic Circle

Northern Africa

The Sahara Desert, the largest desert in the world, covers more than half of northern Africa. On its barren, rocky plains and rolling sand dunes, the heat is fierce, water is scarce and there is little land that can be farmed. Most of the people of the Sahara are nomads who move their camels, sheep and goats around the desert in search of water and pasture. The only usable fertile land north or east of the Sahara lies in the valleys of the Atlas Mountains and along the banks of the River Nile in Egypt. People have farmed the Nile valley for thousands of years, and it is now one of the most densely populated places on Earth. There is little farmland in Algeria and Libya, but both countries possess large oil and gas reserves which have helped them overcome serious poverty. South of the Sahara lies a wide belt of dry grasslands known as the Sahel. These grasslands suffer frequent droughts, and overfarming is turning some areas into desert. Further south, the Sahel gives way to the tropical rainforests of central Africa. Around the Gulf of Guinea, much of the forest has been cleared to make way for farms and large plantations where cocoa beans, coffee and cotton are grown. Oil and other minerals have been discovered in a number of Gulf countries, and this has created some wealth and industries. However, only a minority of the region's huge population benefit and most people are still very poor.

ALGERIA
Population: 31,134,000 * Capital: Algiers

BENIN
Population: 6,306,000 * Capitals: Cotonou, Porto-Novo

BURKINA FASO
Population: 11,576,000 * Capital: Ouagadougou

CAMEROON
Population: 15,456,000 * Capital: Yaoundé

CAPE VERDE ISLANDS
Population: 405,800 * Capital: Praia

CENTRAL AFRICAN REPUBLIC
Population: 3,445,000 * Capital: Bangui

CHAD
Population: 7,558,000 * Capital: N'Djamena

CÔTE D'IVOIRE (IVORY COAST)
Population: 15,818,000 * Capitals: Abidjan, Yamoussoukro

DJIBOUTI
Population: 447,500 * Capital: Djibouti

EGYPT
Population: 67,274,000 * Capital: Cairo

EQUATORIAL GUINEA
Population: 465,800 * Capital: Malabo

ERITREA
Population: 3,985,000 * Capital: Asmara

ETHIOPIA
Population: 59,681,000 * Capital: Addis Ababa

GAMBIA
Population: 1,337,000 * Capital: Banjul

GHANA
Population: 18,888,000 * Capital: Accra

GUINEA
Population: 7,539,000 * Capital: Conakry

GUINEA-BISSAU
Population: 1,235,000 * Capital: Bissau

LIBERIA
Population: 2,924,000 * Capital: Monrovia

LIBYA
Population: 4,993,000 * Capital: Tripoli

MALI
Population: 10,429,000 * Capital: Bamako

MAURITANIA
Population: 2,582,000 * Capital: Nouakchott

MOROCCO
Population: 29,662,000 * Capital: Rabat

NIGER
Population: 9,963,000 * Capital: Niamey

NIGERIA
Population: 113,829,000 * Capital: Abuja

SENEGAL
Population: 10,052,000 * Capital: Dakar

SIERRA LEONE
Population: 5,297,000 * Capital: Freetown

SOMALIA
Population: 7,141,000 * Capital: Mogadishu

SUDAN
Population: 34,476,000 * Capital: Khartoum

TOGO
Population: 5,082,000 * Capital: Lomé

TUNISIA
Population: 9,514,000 * Capital: Tunis

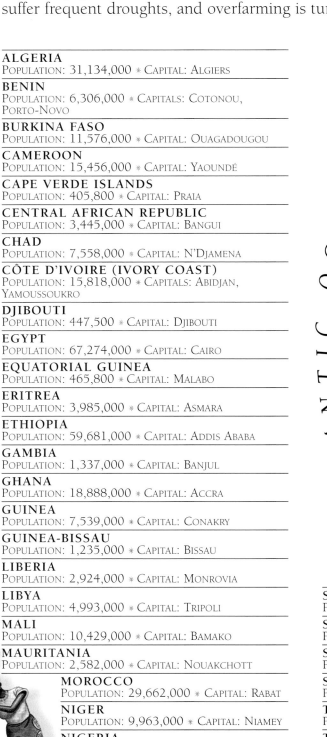

OSTRICH
The largest bird in the world, the ostrich cannot fly, but can run at up to 65 kilometres per hour (40 mph).

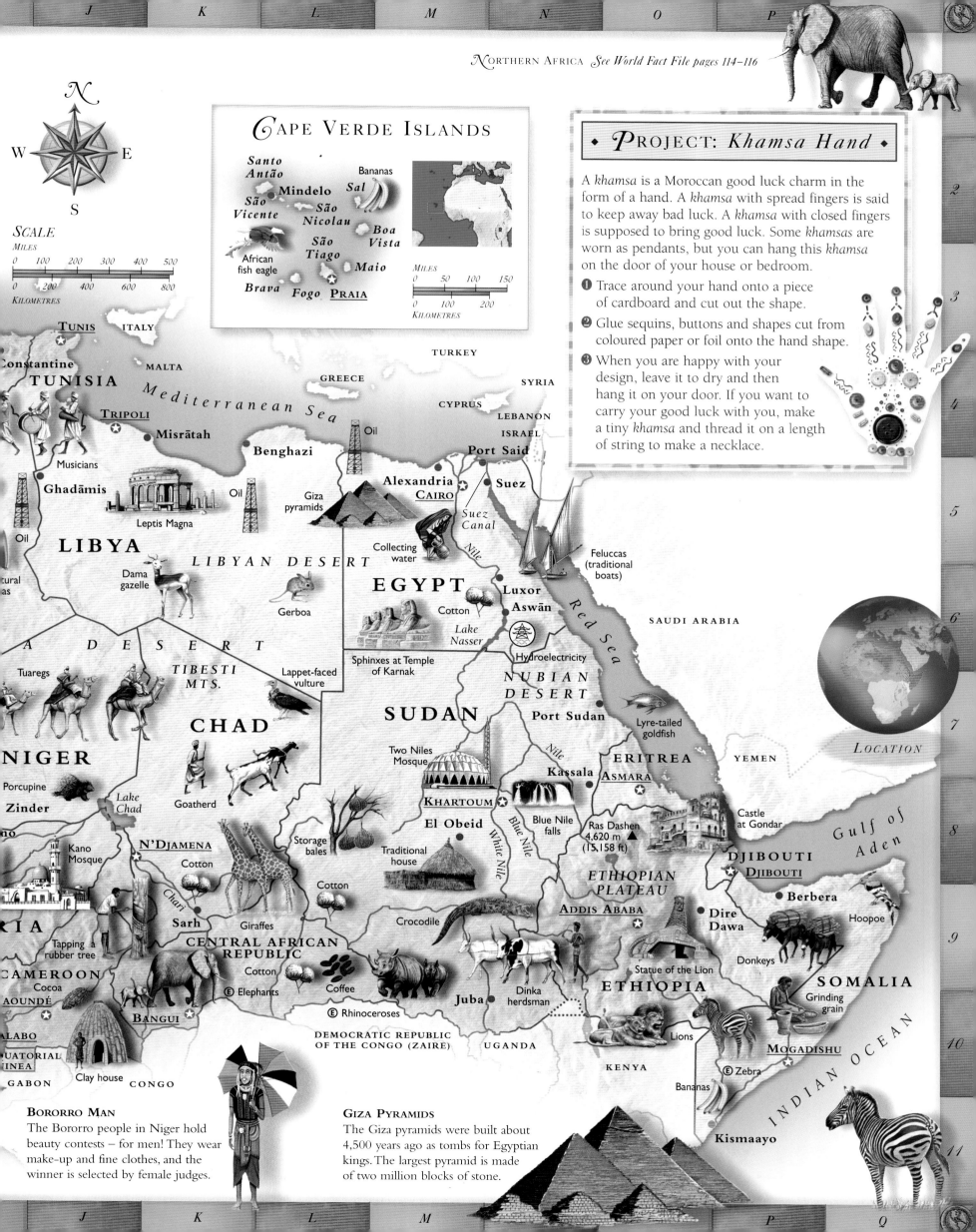

J K L M N O P

CAPE VERDE ISLANDS

Santo Antão
Mindelo
São Vicente
Bananas
Sal
São Nicolau
African fish eagle
Boa Vista
São Tiago
Maio
Brava **Fogo** **PRAIA**

MILES
0   50   100   150
0   100   200
KILOMETRES

◆ PROJECT: *Khamsa Hand* ◆

A *khamsa* is a Moroccan good luck charm in the form of a hand. A *khamsa* with spread fingers is said to keep away bad luck. A *khamsa* with closed fingers is supposed to bring good luck. Some *khamsas* are worn as pendants, but you can hang this *khamsa* on the door of your house or bedroom.

❶ Trace around your hand onto a piece of cardboard and cut out the shape.

❷ Glue sequins, buttons and shapes cut from coloured paper or foil onto the hand shape.

❸ When you are happy with your design, leave it to dry and then hang it on your door. If you want to carry your good luck with you, make a tiny *khamsa* and thread it on a length of string to make a necklace.

N
W ⊕ E
S

SCALE
MILES
0   100   200   300   400   500
0   200   400   600   800
KILOMETRES

TUNIS ITALY
Constantine MALTA
TUNISIA
TRIPOLI **Misrātah** **Benghazi**
Musicians
Oil
Ghadāmis
Oil
Leptis Magna
Oil
LIBYA
LIBYAN DESERT
Dama gazelle
Gerboa
EGYPT
Giza pyramids
Alexandria
CAIRO **Suez**
Port Said
Suez Canal
Collecting water
Nile
Feluccas (traditional boats)
Luxor
Cotton
Aswān
Lake Nasser
Sphinxes at Temple of Karnak
Hydroelectricity
Red Sea
SAUDI ARABIA
TURKEY
GREECE
Mediterranean Sea
CYPRUS
SYRIA
LEBANON
ISRAEL

SAHARA DESERT
TIBESTI MTS.
Tuaregs
Lappet-faced vulture
CHAD
NUBIAN DESERT
SUDAN
Port Sudan
Lyre-tailed goldfish
YEMEN
ERITREA
ASMARA
LOCATION

NIGER
Porcupine
Zinder
Lake Chad
Goatherd
Two Niles Mosque
Kassala
Castle at Gondar
Gulf of Aden

Kano Mosque
N'DJAMENA
Cotton
Storage bales
KHARTOUM
El Obeid
Traditional house
White Nile
Blue Nile
Blue Nile falls
Ras Dashen 4,620 m ▲ (15,158 ft)
ETHIOPIAN PLATEAU
DJIBOUTI
Djibouti
Berbera

RIA
Tapping a rubber tree
Sarh
Giraffes
Cotton
Coffee
Crocodile
ADDIS ABABA
Statue of the Lion
Dire Dawa
Hoopoe
Donkeys

CAMEROON
Cocoa
BANGUI
CENTRAL AFRICAN REPUBLIC
Cotton
Ⓔ Elephants
Cotton
Coffee
Ⓔ Rhinoceroses
Juba
Dinka herdsman
ETHIOPIA
Lions
SOMALIA
Grinding grain

ALABO
QUATORIAL INEA
GABON
Clay house CONGO
DEMOCRATIC REPUBLIC OF THE CONGO (ZAIRE)
UGANDA
KENYA
Bananas
Ⓔ Zebra
MOGADISHU
INDIAN OCEAN
Kismaayo

BORORRO MAN
The Bororro people in Niger hold beauty contests – for men! They wear make-up and fine clothes, and the winner is selected by female judges.

GIZA PYRAMIDS
The Giza pyramids were built about 4,500 years ago as tombs for Egyptian kings. The largest pyramid is made of two million blocks of stone.

Southern Africa

IN THE NORTH-WESTERN PART of this region, the Congo River and its many tributaries flow through immense tropical rainforests. Crocodiles swim the waterways, and the jungles are home to chimpanzees, gorillas and tropical birds. Most of the local people live in villages near the rivers and grow their own food on small plots of cleared land. The rainforests stretch eastwards across the continent toward the Great Rift Valley, a chain of dramatic, steep-sided valleys that runs down the eastern side of Africa. Within these valleys lie many deep lakes as well as a number of volcanoes, including Mount Kilimanjaro, Africa's highest mountain. On the valley floors and across the surrounding grassland plateaus, enormous herds of zebras, wildebeests and antelopes are hunted by lions, cheetahs and other predators. To protect the region's wildlife, many countries have created nature reserves, which attract tourists from all over the world. From the southern end of the Rift Valley, in Mozambique, high grasslands known as the veld spread westwards toward the Kalahari and Namib deserts. In South Africa the veld is an important farming region rich in mineral resources including copper, gold and diamonds. Off the coast of Mozambique lies the large island of Madagascar. Madagascar is famous for its unique wildlife, which includes many species of lemurs, unusual types of monkeys.

ANGOLA
POPULATION: 11,178,000 * CAPITAL: LUANDA

BOTSWANA
POPULATION: 1,465,000 * CAPITAL: GABORONE

BURUNDI
POPULATION: 5,736,000 * CAPITAL: BUJUMBURA

COMOROS
POPULATION: 562,800 * CAPITAL: MORONI

CONGO
POPULATION: 2,717,000 * CAPITAL: BRAZZAVILLE

DEMOCRATIC REPUBLIC OF THE CONGO (ZAIRE)
POPULATION: 50,482,000 * CAPITAL: KINSHASA

GABON
POPULATION: 1,226,000 * CAPITAL: LIBREVILLE

KENYA
POPULATION: 28,809,000 * CAPITAL: NAIROBI

LESOTHO
POPULATION: 2,129,000 * CAPITAL: MASERU

MADAGASCAR
POPULATION: 14,874,000 * CAPITAL: ANTANANARIVO

MALAWI
POPULATION: 10,001,000 * CAPITAL: LILONGWE

MAURITIUS
POPULATION: 1,183,000 * CAPITAL: PORT LOUIS

MOZAMBIQUE
POPULATION: 19,125,000 * CAPITAL: MAPUTO

NAMIBIA
POPULATION: 1,649,000 * CAPITAL: WINDHOEK

RWANDA
POPULATION: 8,155,000 * CAPITAL: KIGALI

SÃO TOMÉ AND PRÍNCIPE
POPULATION: 154,900 * CAPITAL: SÃO TOMÉ

SEYCHELLES
POPULATION: 79,200 * CAPITAL: VICTORIA

SOUTH AFRICA
POPULATION: 43,427,000 * CAPITALS: BLOEMFONTEIN, CAPE TOWN, PRETORIA

SWAZILAND
POPULATION: 986,000 * CAPITAL: MBABANE

TANZANIA
POPULATION: 31,271,000 * CAPITALS: DAR ES SALAAM, DODOMA

UGANDA
POPULATION: 22,805,000 * CAPITAL: KAMPALA

ZAMBIA
POPULATION: 9,664,000 * CAPITAL: LUSAKA

ZIMBABWE
POPULATION: 11,164,000 * CAPITAL: HARARE

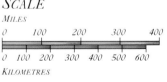

SCALE

MILES

0   100   200   300   400

0 100 200 300 400 500 600

KILOMETRES

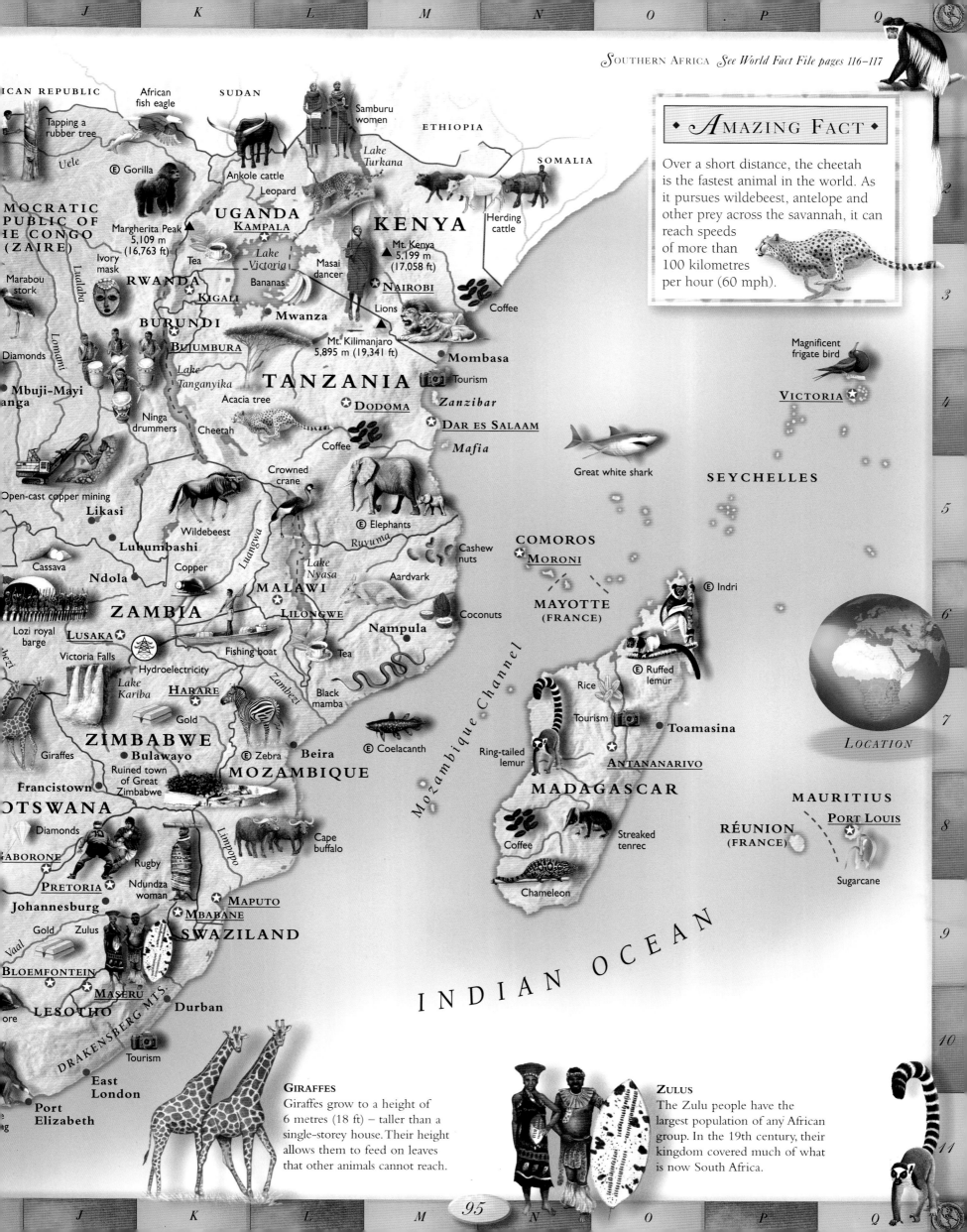

CENTRAL AFRICAN REPUBLIC

Tapping a rubber tree

African fish eagle

Uele

ⓔ Gorilla

SUDAN

Ankole cattle

Leopard

Samburu women

ETHIOPIA

SOMALIA

Herding cattle

DEMOCRATIC REPUBLIC OF THE CONGO (ZAIRE)

Margherita Peak 5,109 m (16,763 ft) ▲

Ivory mask

Marabou stork

Lualaba

Lomami

RWANDA

UGANDA

★ **KAMPALA**

Tea

Lake Victoria

Bananas

Masai dancer

KENYA

Mt. Kenya 5,199 m (17,058 ft) ▲

★ **NAIROBI**

Lions

Coffee

★ **KIGALI**

Mwanza

BURUNDI

★ **BUJUMBURA**

Diamonds

Ninga drummers

Lake Tanganyika

Mt. Kilimanjaro 5,895 m (19,341 ft) ▲

Mbuji-Mayi

Kananga

Acacia tree

TANZANIA

★ **DODOMA**

Zanzibar

☆ **DAR ES SALAAM**

Mafia

Mombasa

Tourism 📷

Open-cast copper mining

Cheetah

Coffee

Crowned crane

ⓔ Elephants

Ruvuma

Cashew nuts

Likasi

Wildebeest

Lubumbashi

Copper

Luangwa

Lake Nyasa

Aardvark

Coconuts

Cassava

Ndola

MALAWI

★ **LILONGWE**

ZAMBIA

Lozi royal barge

★ **LUSAKA**

Victoria Falls

Hydroelectricity

Lake Kariba

Fishing boat

Tea

Nampula

Zambezi

COMOROS

★ **MORONI**

MAYOTTE (FRANCE)

ⓔ Indri

SEYCHELLES

★ **VICTORIA**

Magnificent frigate bird

Great white shark

ZIMBABWE

★ **HARARE**

Gold

Giraffes

Bulawayo

Ruined town of Great Zimbabwe

Francistown

Zambezi

Black mamba

ⓔ Zebra

Beira

ⓔ Coelacanth

MOZAMBIQUE

Mozambique Channel

Ring-tailed lemur

ⓔ Ruffed lemur

Rice

Tourism 📷

Toamasina

★ **ANTANANARIVO**

MADAGASCAR

Coffee

Streaked tenrec

Chameleon

MAURITIUS

★ **PORT LOUIS**

RÉUNION (FRANCE)

Sugarcane

BOTSWANA

Diamonds

★ **GABORONE**

Rugby

★ **PRETORIA**

Ndundza woman

Johannesburg

Gold   Zulus

Vaal

★ **BLOEMFONTEIN**

★ **MASERU**

LESOTHO

DRAKENSBERG MTS.

Tourism 📷

East London

Port Elizabeth

Durban

Cape buffalo

Limpopo

★ **MAPUTO**

☆ **MBABANE**

SWAZILAND

INDIAN OCEAN

🌍 *LOCATION*

GIRAFFES

Giraffes grow to a height of 6 metres (18 ft) – taller than a single-storey house. Their height allows them to feed on leaves that other animals cannot reach.

ZULUS

The Zulu people have the largest population of any African group. In the 19th century, their kingdom covered much of what is now South Africa.

Australia and Oceania

STRETCHING FROM THE INDIAN OCEAN to the centre of the Pacific Ocean, Australia and Oceania cover a vast area of the globe. But because most of this region is ocean, it has a relatively small population. Australia is by far the largest land mass. This island is so big that it is considered a continent. Oceania consists of thousands of much smaller islands that are scattered across the Pacific Ocean to the east of Australia. They are divided into three groups: Micronesia, Melanesia and Polynesia, which includes the large islands of New Zealand. There are two main types of Pacific island: high, rugged islands that are the peaks of undersea volcanoes and submerged mountain ranges; and coral atolls – low, sandy islands formed by coral reefs growing on the tops of undersea mountains. Many of the Pacific islands are so small that they do not appear on regular maps.

CONTINENT FACTS

Regional land area: 8,507,753 sq. km (3,283,993 sq. mi)
Regional population: 29,300,000
Independent countries: Australia, Federated States of Micronesia, Fiji, Kiribati, Marshall Islands, Nauru, New Zealand, Palau, Papua New Guinea, Solomon Islands, Tonga, Tuvalu, Vanuatu, Western Samoa

WORLD RECORDS

WORLD'S LONGEST CORAL REEF
THE GREAT BARRIER REEF, AUSTRALIA, 2,025 KM (1,260 MI)

WORLD'S LARGEST ROCK
ULURU (AYERS ROCK), AUSTRALIA, 348 M (1,143 FT) HIGH; 2.5 KM (1.5 MI) LONG; 1.6 KM (1 MI) WIDE

WORLD'S LARGEST SAND ISLAND
FRASER ISLAND, AUSTRALIA, 120 KM (75 MI) LONG

CONTINENT RECORDS

HIGHEST MOUNTAIN
MOUNT WILHELM, PAPUA NEW GUINEA, 4,500 M (14,762 FT)

LOWEST POINT
LAKE EYRE, AUSTRALIA, 52 FT (16 M) BELOW SEA LEVEL

LARGEST LAKE
LAKE EYRE, AUSTRALIA, 9,324 SQ. KM (3,600 SQ. MI)

LONGEST RIVER
MURRAY-DARLING, AUSTRALIA, 3,750 KM (2,330 MI)

LARGEST COUNTRY BY AREA
AUSTRALIA, 7,686,884 SQ. KM (2,967,909 SQ. MI)

LARGEST COUNTRY BY POPULATION
AUSTRALIA, POPULATION 18,784,000

LARGEST CITY BY POPULATION
SYDNEY, AUSTRALIA, POPULATION 3,934,000

MAJOR MOUNTAINS AND RIVERS

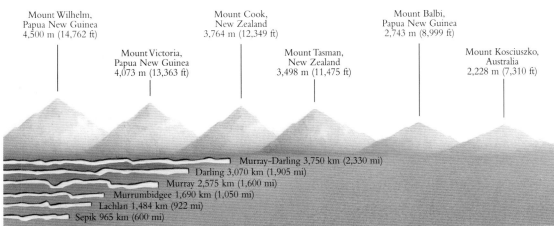

Mount Wilhelm, Papua New Guinea 4,500 m (14,762 ft)
Mount Victoria, Papua New Guinea 4,073 m (13,363 ft)
Mount Cook, New Zealand 3,764 m (12,349 ft)
Mount Tasman, New Zealand 3,498 m (11,475 ft)
Mount Balbi, Papua New Guinea 2,743 m (8,999 ft)
Mount Kosciuszko, Australia 2,228 m (7,310 ft)

Murray-Darling 3,750 km (2,330 mi)
Darling 3,070 km (1,905 mi)
Murray 2,575 km (1,600 mi)
Murrumbidgee 1,690 km (1,050 mi)
Lachlan 1,484 km (922 mi)
Sepik 965 km (600 mi)

POLITICAL MAP

WAKE ISLAND (U.S.A.)
NORTHERN MARIANA ISLANDS (U.S.A)
GUAM (U.S.A.)
MARSHALL ISLANDS
PALAU
FEDERATED STATES of MICRONESIA
PAPUA NEW GUINEA
NAURU
KIRIBATI
SOLOMON ISLANDS
TUVALU
TOKELAU (N.Z.)
WESTERN SAMOA
WALLIS and FUTUNA (FRANCE)
AMERICAN SAMOA (U.S.A.)
VANUATU
TONGA
NIUE (N.Z.)
COOK ISLANDS (N.Z.)
FRENCH POLYNESIA (FRANCE)
FIJI
NEW CALEDONIA (FRANCE)
PITCAIRN ISLANDS (U.K.)
AUSTRALIA
KERMADEC ISLANDS (N.Z.)
NORFOLK ISLAND (AUSTRALIA)
NEW ZEALAND
CHATHAM ISLANDS (N.Z.)

Australia and Papua New Guinea

AUSTRALIA IS MORE THAN 30 times as big as the U.K., but its population is three times smaller. The vast, dry interior, known as the outback, consists mainly of deserts and grasslands. The outback contains mineral reserves and is used for grazing enormous numbers of sheep, but few people live there. Most Australians live in or near cities along the east, south-east and south-west coasts, where the climate is temperate and the land fertile. The far north-east is tropical, with areas of dense rainforest. The south-east is cooler, and mountain snowfalls are common. Most of Australia's native peoples, the Aborigines, live in towns and cities, but some still follow old traditions in the outback. Aborigines originally came to Australia more than 40,000 years ago, having crossed over from the island of New Guinea when it was still attached to Australia. Papua New Guinea, an Australian territory until 1975, is made up of several island chains and half the island of New Guinea. This main island is covered in jungle and surrounded by swampy plains. Most people live in small villages, where they grow food in gardens and raise animals. Many communities have little contact with the outside world and have retained their own traditions and languages. Papua New Guinea has over 700 languages – more than any other country.

AUSTRALIA
POPULATION: 18,784,000 * CAPITAL: CANBERRA
PAPUA NEW GUINEA
POPULATION: 4,705,000 * CAPITAL: PORT MORESBY

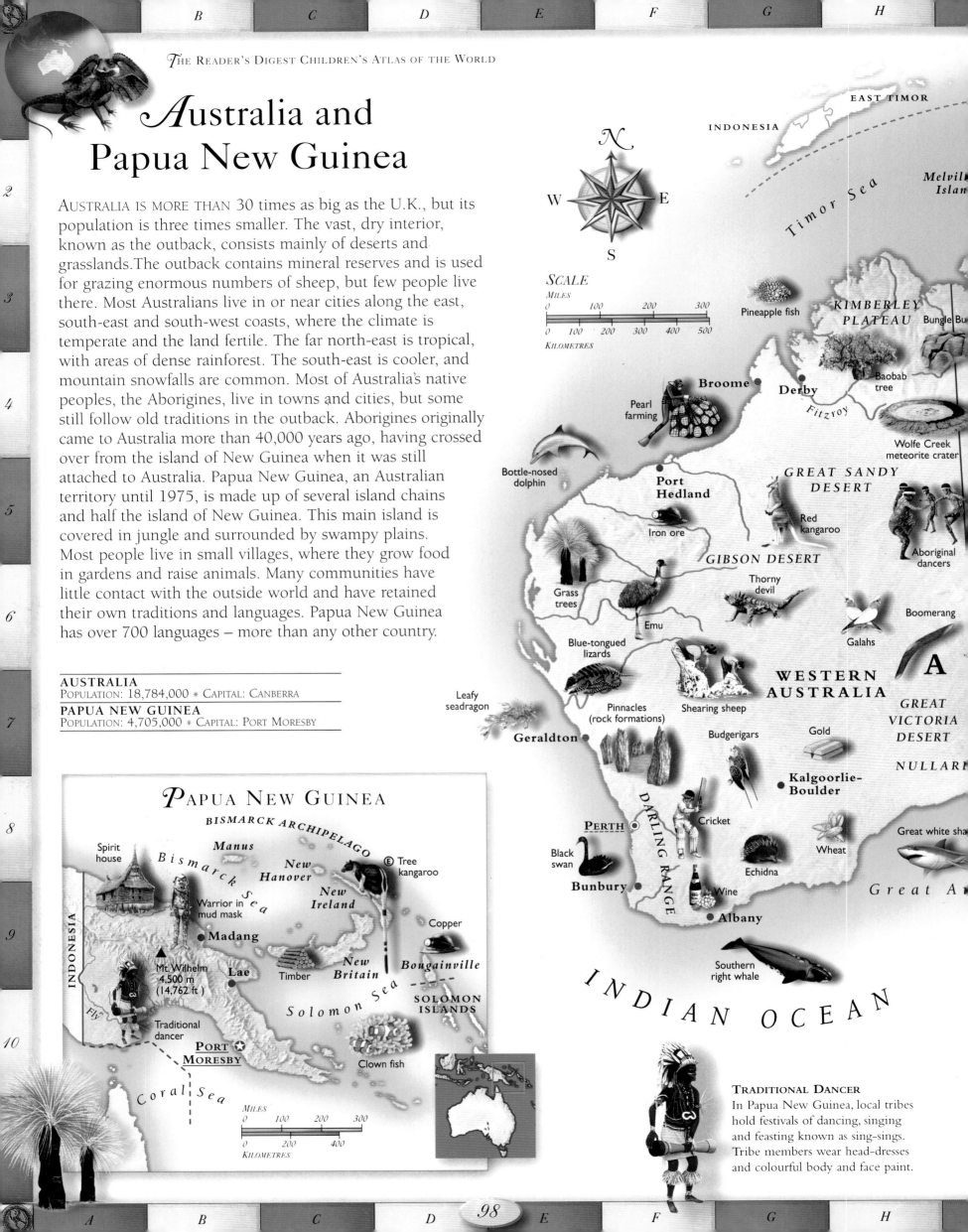

SCALE
MILES
0   100   200   300
0 100 200 300 400 500
KILOMETRES

EAST TIMOR
INDONESIA
Melvill
Islan
Timor Sea
Pineapple fish
KIMBERLEY PLATEAU
Bungle Bu
Baobab tree
Broome
Derby
Fitzroy
Pearl farming
Wolfe Creek meteorite crater
Bottle-nosed dolphin
GREAT SANDY DESERT
Port Hedland
Iron ore
Red kangaroo
Aboriginal dancers
GIBSON DESERT
Thorny devil
Grass trees
Emu
Boomerang
Blue-tongued lizards
Galahs
WESTERN AUSTRALIA
A
Leafy seadragon
Pinnacles (rock formations)
Shearing sheep
GREAT VICTORIA DESERT
Geraldton
Budgerigars
Gold
NULLARB
Kalgoorlie-Boulder
PERTH
Cricket
Black swan
DARLING RANGE
Wheat
Great white sha
Bunbury
Echidna
Wine
Great A
Albany
Southern right whale
INDIAN OCEAN

PAPUA NEW GUINEA

BISMARCK ARCHIPELAGO
Spirit house
Manus
New Hanover
Tree kangaroo
Bismarck Sea
Warrior in mud mask
New Ireland
Madang
Copper
Mt. Wilhelm 4,500 m (14,762 ft)
Lae
New Britain
Bougainville
Timber
Solomon Sea
SOLOMON ISLANDS
INDONESIA
Fly
Traditional dancer
PORT MORESBY
Clown fish
Coral Sea
MILES
0   100   200   300
0   200   400
KILOMETRES

TRADITIONAL DANCER
In Papua New Guinea, local tribes hold festivals of dancing, singing and feasting known as sing-sings. Tribe members wear head-dresses and colourful body and face paint.

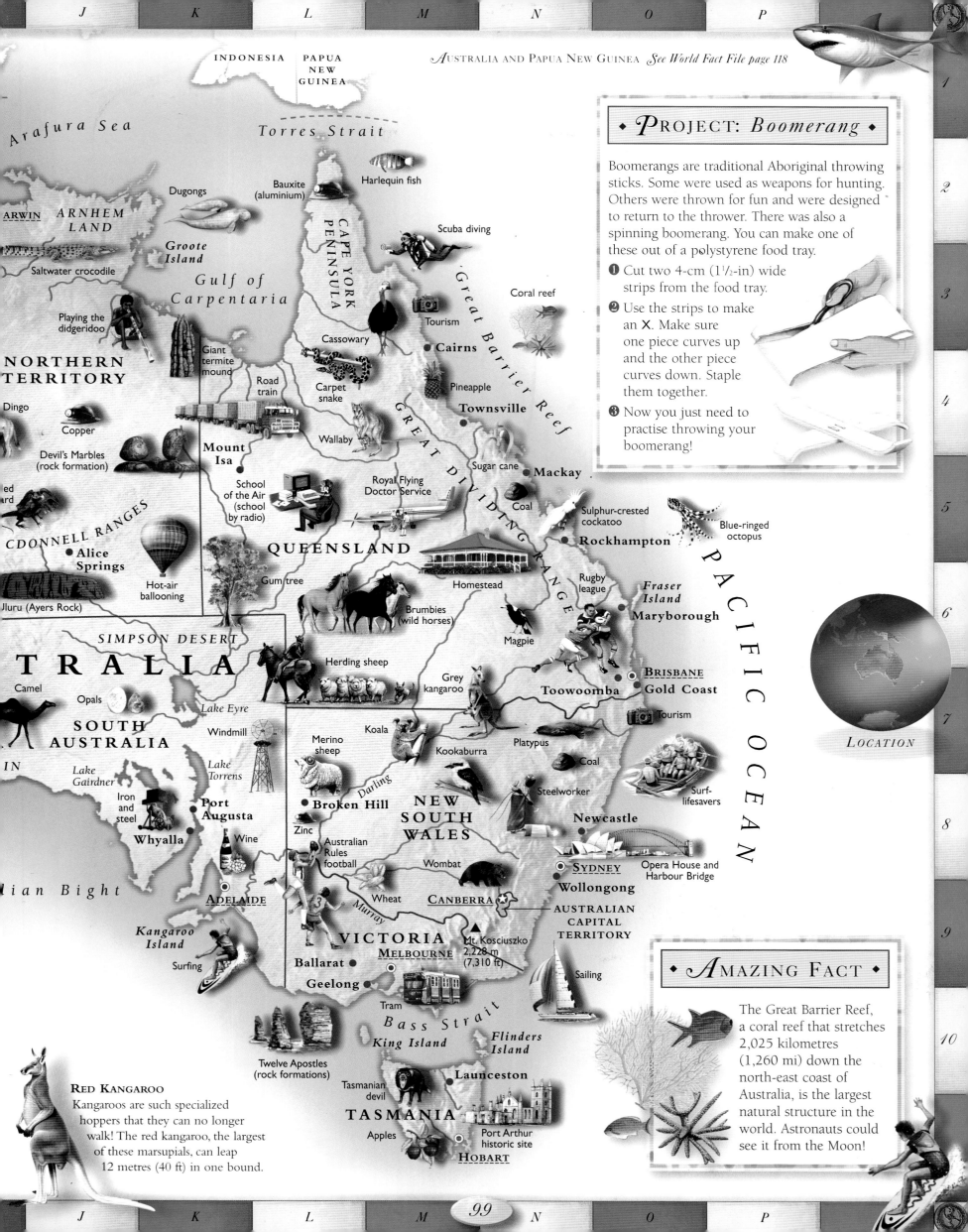

INDONESIA · PAPUA NEW GUINEA

Arafura Sea

Torres Strait

AUSTRALIA AND PAPUA NEW GUINEA *See World Fact File page 118*

Harlequin fish

Bauxite (aluminium)

Dugongs

ARNHEM LAND

Groote Island

Saltwater crocodile

Gulf of Carpentaria

CAPE YORK PENINSULA

Scuba diving

Coral reef

Playing the didgeridoo

NORTHERN TERRITORY

Giant termite mound

Road train

Cassowary

Carpet snake

Tourism

Cairns

GREAT BARRIER REEF

Dingo

Copper

Devil's Marbles (rock formation)

Wallaby

Pineapple

Townsville

Sugar cane

Mackay

Mount Isa

School of the Air (school by radio)

Royal Flying Doctor Service

Coal

GREAT DIVIDING RANGE

Sulphur-crested cockatoo

Rockhampton

Blue-ringed octopus

CDONNELL RANGES

Alice Springs

Hot-air ballooning

Gum tree

QUEENSLAND

Homestead

Rugby league

Fraser Island

Maryborough

PACIFIC OCEAN

Jluru (Ayers Rock)

SIMPSON DESERT

Brumbies (wild horses)

Magpie

TRALIA

Herding sheep

Grey kangaroo

Toowoomba

BRISBANE

Gold Coast

Camel

Opals

Lake Eyre

SOUTH AUSTRALIA

Windmill

Koala

Merino sheep

Kookaburra

Platypus

Coal

Steelworker

Tourism

Surf-lifesavers

Lake Gairdner

Lake Torrens

Darling

Iron and steel

Port Augusta

Broken Hill

NEW SOUTH WALES

Newcastle

Whyalla

Zinc

Wine

Australian Rules football

Wombat

Opera House and Harbour Bridge

lian *Bight*

ADELAIDE

Murray

Wheat

CANBERRA

SYDNEY

Wollongong

AUSTRALIAN CAPITAL TERRITORY

Kangaroo Island

Surfing

VICTORIA

Ballarat

MELBOURNE

▲ Mt. Kosciuszko 2,228 m (7,310 ft)

Sailing

Geelong

Tram

Twelve Apostles (rock formations)

Bass Strait

King Island

Flinders Island

Launceston

Tasmanian devil

TASMANIA

Apples

Port Arthur historic site

HOBART

LOCATION

◆ PROJECT: *Boomerang* ◆

Boomerangs are traditional Aboriginal throwing sticks. Some were used as weapons for hunting. Others were thrown for fun and were designed to return to the thrower. There was also a spinning boomerang. You can make one of these out of a polystyrene food tray.

❶ Cut two 4-cm (1½-in) wide strips from the food tray.

❷ Use the strips to make an X. Make sure one piece curves up and the other piece curves down. Staple them together.

❸ Now you just need to practise throwing your boomerang!

◆ AMAZING FACT ◆

The Great Barrier Reef, a coral reef that stretches 2,025 kilometres (1,260 mi) down the north-east coast of Australia, is the largest natural structure in the world. Astronauts could see it from the Moon!

RED KANGAROO

Kangaroos are such specialized hoppers that they can no longer walk! The red kangaroo, the largest of these marsupials, can leap 12 metres (40 ft) in one bound.

New Zealand and the South-western Pacific

SCATTERED ACROSS A VAST EXPANSE of ocean and separated from each other by great distances, the islands of the south-western Pacific are among the most isolated places on Earth. The largest and most southerly group is New Zealand, consisting of two large islands – the North Island and the South Island – and several smaller islands. New Zealand is a modern, industrialized country. About 70 per cent of the population live on the North Island, which has several active volcanoes. Lake Taupo, New Zealand's largest lake, lies in a crater that formed when a volcano exploded. The nearby volcanoes, Ruapehu and Ngauruhoe, have erupted several times in recent years. The Southern Alps form the 'backbone' of the South Island. On their western side, temperate rainforests have grown up around a line of mighty glaciers that run down to the coast. More than half of New Zealand is used for growing crops and grazing animals – there are 20 sheep for every New Zealander! The country's original inhabitants, the Maori people, make up one-sixth of the population. Most other New Zealanders are descendants of British immigrants. Thousands of tropical islands lie to the north and east of New Zealand. Tourism is a growing industry in countries such as Fiji and Vanuatu. Some islands have developing towns with new businesses, but most islanders live in small villages. They fish for crabs, lobsters, turtles and tuna, and grow sweet potatoes and bananas. One of the most important export products is copra (dried coconut meat), which is used in making soap and candles.

FIJI
POPULATION: 813,000 * CAPITAL: SUVA

NEW ZEALAND
POPULATION: 3,663,000 * CAPITAL: WELLINGTON

SOLOMON ISLANDS
POPULATION: 455,500 * CAPITAL: HONIARA

TONGA
POPULATION: 109,100 * CAPITAL: NUKU'ALOFA

VANUATU
POPULATION: 189,100 * CAPITAL: PORT VILA

WESTERN SAMOA
POPULATION: 230,000 * CAPITAL: APIA

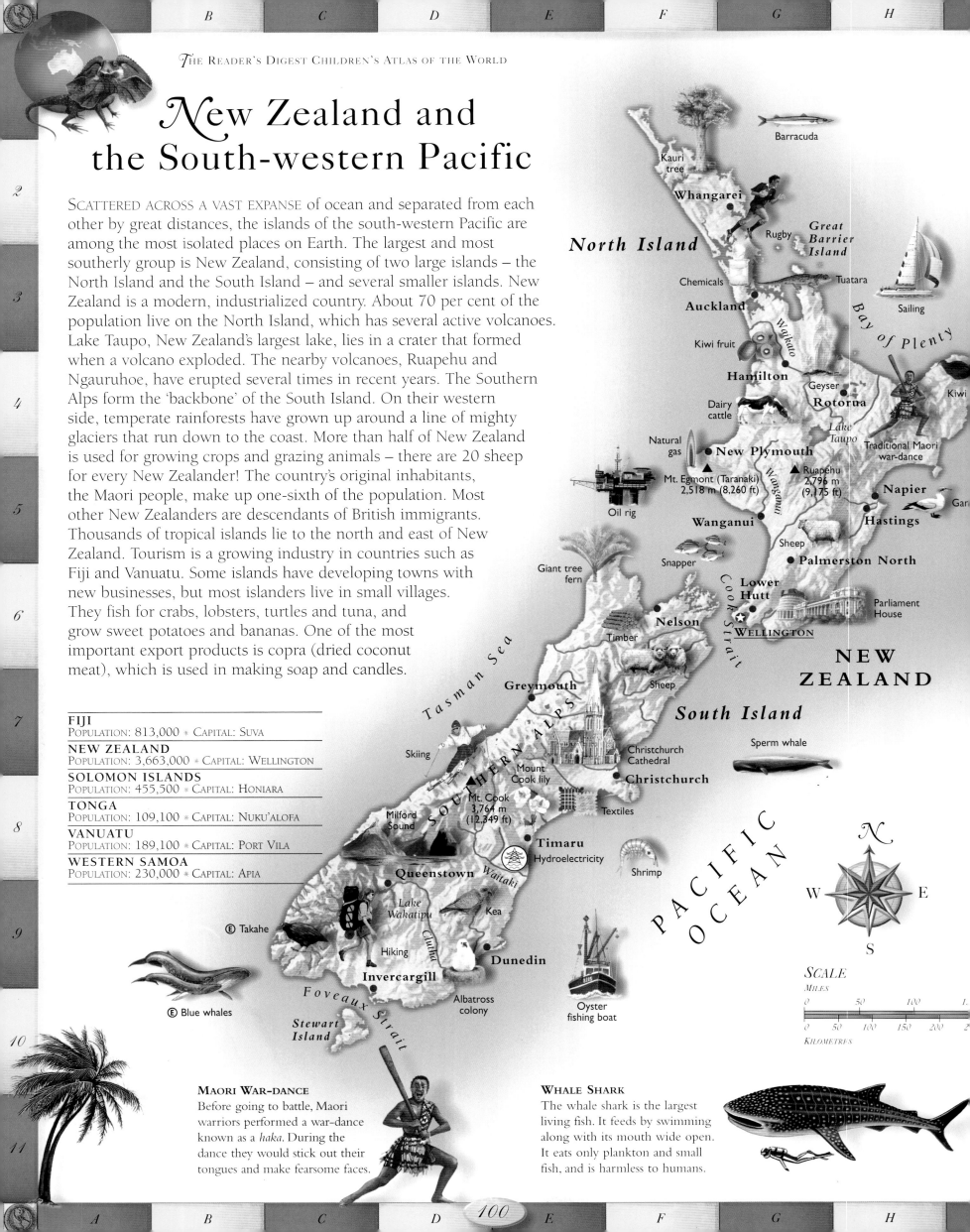

Barracuda

Kauri tree

Whangarei

North Island

Rugby

Great Barrier Island

Chemicals

Tuatara

Sailing

Auckland

Waikato

Bay of Plenty

Kiwi fruit

Hamilton

Geyser

Rotorua

Kiwi

Dairy cattle

Lake Taupo

Traditional Maori war-dance

Natural gas

New Plymouth

Mt. Egmont (Taranaki) 2,518 m (8,260 ft)

▲ Ruapehu 2,796 m (9,175 ft)

Napier

Oil rig

Wanganui

Wanganui

Snapper

Sheep

Hastings

Gan

Palmerston North

Giant tree fern

Lower Hutt

Cook Strait

Parliament House

Timber

Nelson

WELLINGTON

NEW ZEALAND

Tasman Sea

Sheep

South Island

Greymouth

Sperm whale

Christchurch Cathedral

Skiing

Mount Cook lily

Christchurch

SOUTHERN ALPS

Mt. Cook 3,764 m (12,349 ft)

Textiles

Milford Sound

Timaru
Hydroelectricity

Shrimp

PACIFIC OCEAN

Queenstown

Waitaki

Lake Wakatipu

Kea

Ⓔ Takahe

Hiking

Clutha

Dunedin

Invercargill

Foveaux Strait

Albatross colony

Oyster fishing boat

Ⓔ Blue whales

Stewart Island

N
W E
S

SCALE
MILES
0   50   100   1.
0   50   100   150   200   2
KILOMETRES

MAORI WAR-DANCE
Before going to battle, Maori warriors performed a war-dance known as a *haka*. During the dance they would stick out their tongues and make fearsome faces.

WHALE SHARK
The whale shark is the largest living fish. It feeds by swimming along with its mouth wide open. It eats only plankton and small fish, and is harmless to humans.

Solomon Islands

House on stilts
Choiseul
Santa Isabel
Spotted cuscus
MILES
0   100   200
0   100   200   300
KILOMETRES
NEW GEORGIA ISLANDS
Malaita
HONIARA
Guadalcanal
Timber
Bananas
San Cristóbal
Harlequin tuskfish
Rennell
Coral Sea
SANTA CRUZ ISLANDS

Samoa Islands

WESTERN SAMOA
Coconuts
Savai'i
Making tapa cloth
Bottle-nosed dolphin
Sala'ilua
AMERICAN SAMOA (U.S.A.)
APIA
Upolu
Pago-Pago
Preparing copra
Tau
Tutuila
MANUA ISLANDS
MILES
0   25   50
0   25   50   75
KILOMETRES
Manta ray
Bluefin tuna

Vanuatu and New Caledonia

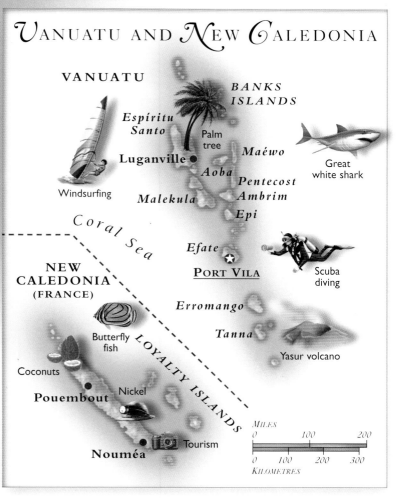

VANUATU
BANKS ISLANDS
Espíritu Santo
Palm tree
Luganville
Maéwo
Great white shark
Aoba
Pentecost
Malekula
Ambrim
Windsurfing
Epi
Coral Sea
Efate
PORT VILA
Scuba diving
NEW CALEDONIA (FRANCE)
Erromango
Tanna
Butterfly fish
Yasur volcano
Coconuts
LOYALTY ISLANDS
Nickel
Pouembout
Tourism
Nouméa
MILES
0   100   200
0   100   200   300
KILOMETRES

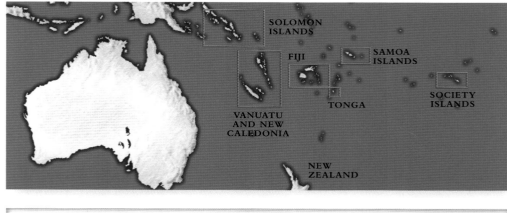

SOLOMON ISLANDS
FIJI
SAMOA ISLANDS
VANUATU AND NEW CALEDONIA
TONGA
SOCIETY ISLANDS
NEW ZEALAND

Fiji

Sugar cane
Vanua Levu
Taveuni
Koro
Cocoa
Tourism
Viti Levu
Koro Sea
LAU GROUP
Walking on hot coals
SUVA
Gau
Lakeba
Moala
Magnificent frigate bird
Coconuts
Kandavu
Angelfish
MILES
0   25   50   75
0   50   100   150
KILOMETRES

LOCATION

Tonga

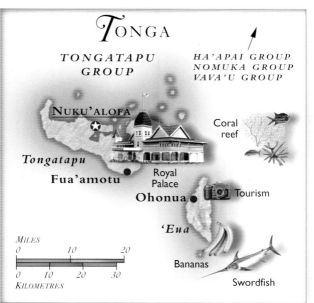

TONGATAPU GROUP
HA'APAI GROUP
NOMUKA GROUP
VAVA'U GROUP
NUKU'ALOFA
Coral reef
Tongatapu
Fua'amotu
Royal Palace
Ohonua
Tourism
'Eua
MILES
0   10   20
0   10   20   30
KILOMETRES
Bananas
Swordfish

Society Islands

Tupai Atoll
Bora-Bora
Lobster
FRENCH POLYNESIA (FRANCE)
Maupiti
Green turtle
Tahaa
HUAHINE ISLANDS
Raiatea
Tourism
Outrigger boat
LEEWARD ISLANDS
Pearls
Tetiaroa Atoll
Surfer in traditional dress
WINDWARD ISLANDS
Paopao
Papeete
Moorea
Whale shark
Palm trees
Maiao
Tahiti
Bananas
Taravao
MILES
0   25   50
0   25   50   75
KILOMETRES

The Polar Regions

THE REGIONS THAT SURROUND the North and South poles are the coldest and windiest parts of our planet. Both are permanently covered in snow and ice, and during winter months there is little or no daylight. Antarctica is a frozen continent surrounded by ocean. The Arctic is an area of frozen ocean surrounded by continents. In winter, the Arctic ice spreads southwards, reaching North America, Europe and Asia. The northern fringes of these continents are home to native peoples who have adapted to Arctic life. They include the Saami (Lapps) of Scandinavia and the Inuit of Canada, Alaska, Greenland and Russia. A Danish territory, Greenland is the world's largest island. Most of it lies under a thick sheet of ice. Antarctica is the only continent with no permanent population. Scientists spend part of the year at research stations, but many leave Antarctica before the cold, dark winter sets in. The continent is covered by a vast ice sheet which is three kilometres (2 mi) thick in some places. Along the coast, the ice sheet forms huge ice shelves over the ocean. Giant blocks of ice break off and float away as icebergs. Some icebergs are as large as small countries and take years to melt. There is little life in the Antarctic interior, but whales, seals and fish swim just offshore, and during the summer enormous colonies of seabirds nest along the coast and on nearby islands.

Antarctica

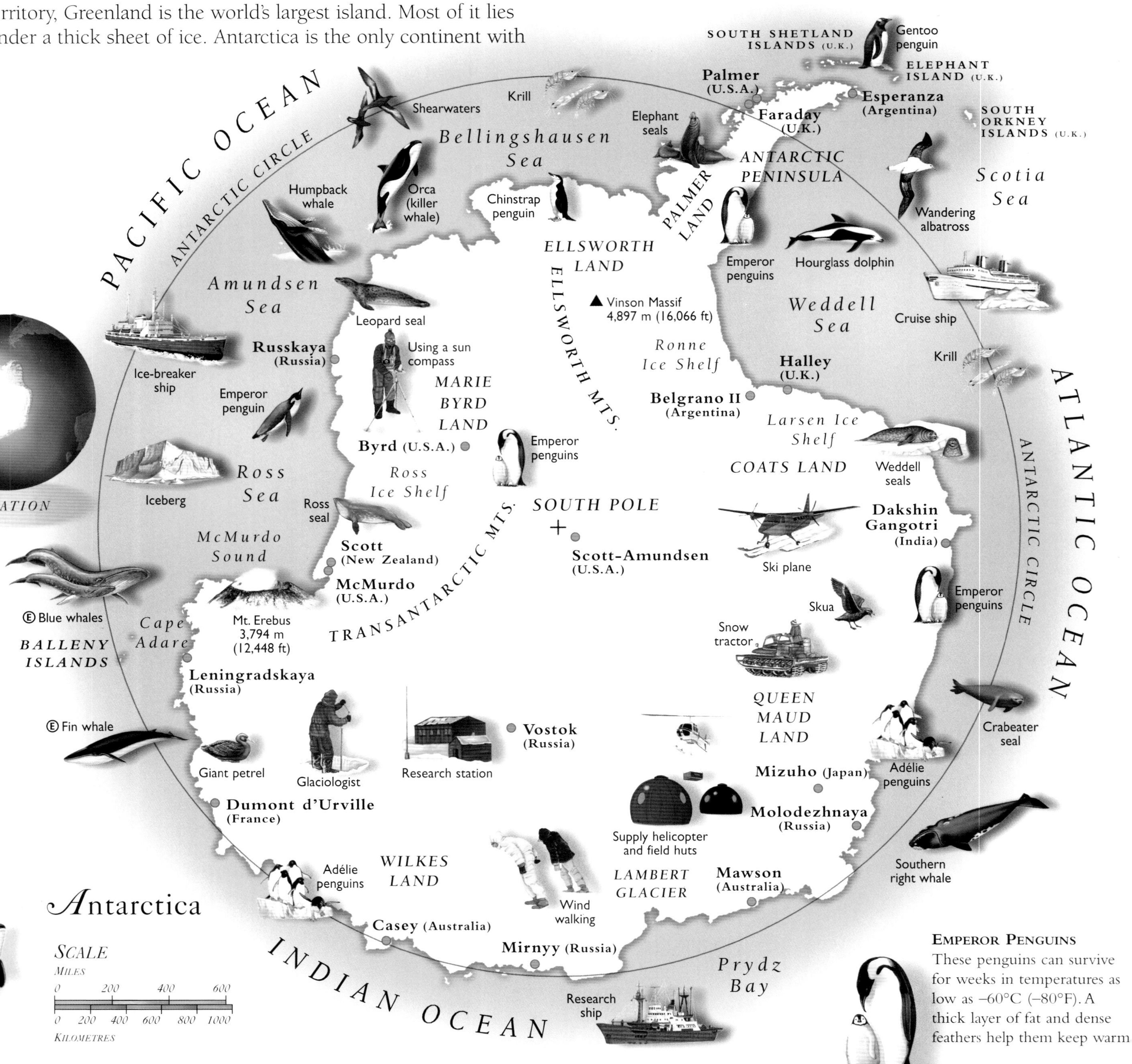

EMPEROR PENGUINS
These penguins can survive for weeks in temperatures as low as −60°C (−80°F). A thick layer of fat and dense feathers help them keep warm.

SCALE
MILES
0 200 400 600
0 200 400 600 800 1000
KILOMETRES

LOCATION

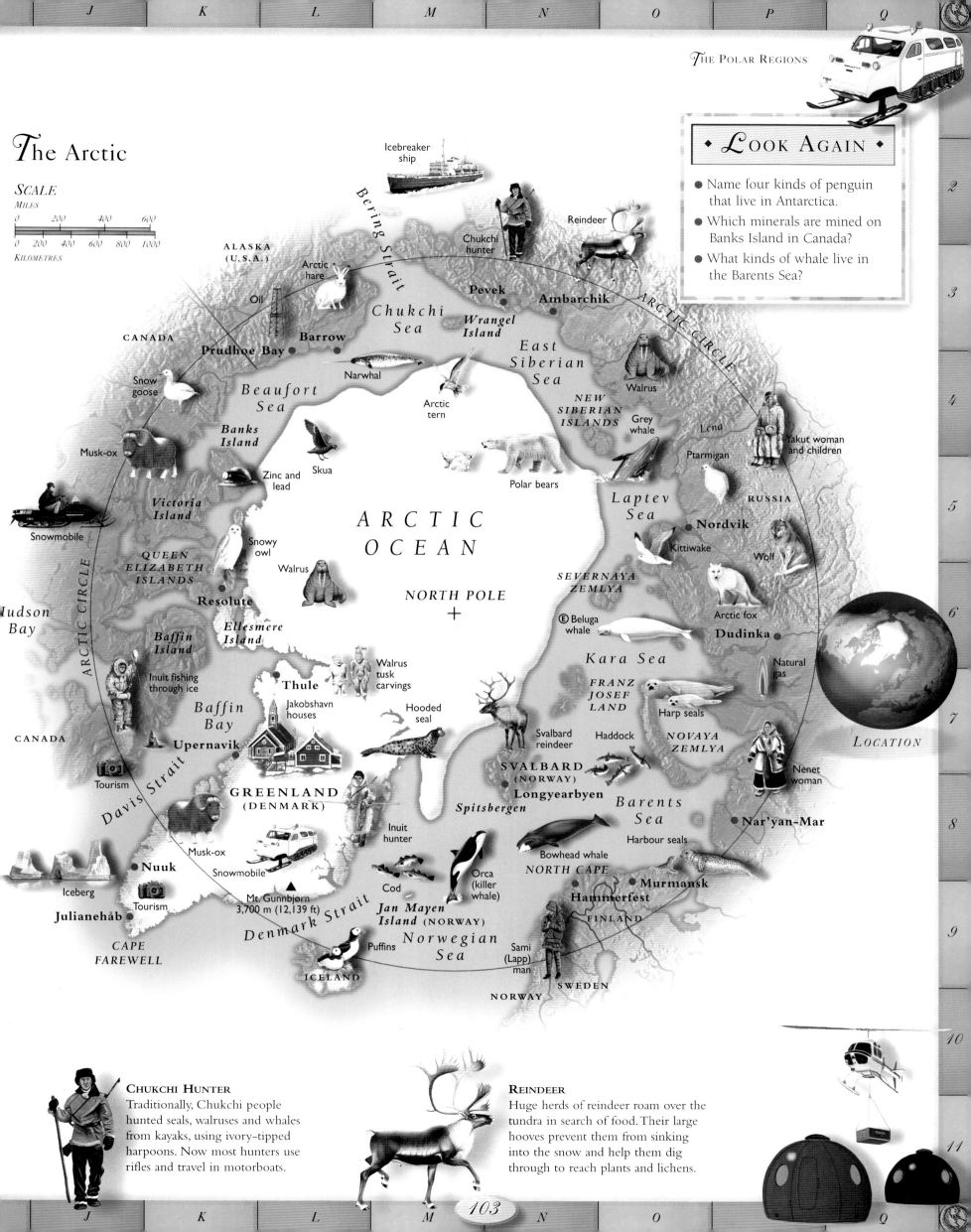

The Arctic

SCALE

MILES

0   200   400   600

0 200 400 600 800 1000

KILOMETRES

◆ LOOK AGAIN ◆

- Name four kinds of penguin that live in Antarctica.
- Which minerals are mined on Banks Island in Canada?
- What kinds of whale live in the Barents Sea?

Icebreaker ship

Reindeer

Chukchi hunter

ALASKA (U.S.A.)

Arctic hare

Oil

Chukchi Sea

Pevek

Ambarchik

ARCTIC CIRCLE

CANADA

Prudhoe Bay

Barrow

Wrangel Island

East Siberian Sea

Narwhal

Snow goose

Beaufort Sea

Arctic tern

NEW SIBERIAN ISLANDS

Walrus

Banks Island

Skua

Grey whale

Musk-ox

Zinc and lead

Polar bears

Lena

Ptarmigan

Yakut woman and children

Victoria Island

Snowmobile

Snowy owl

Walrus

ARCTIC OCEAN

Laptev Sea

Nordvik

Kittiwake

Wolf

RUSSIA

QUEEN ELIZABETH ISLANDS

Resolute

NORTH POLE
+

SEVERNAYA ZEMLYA

Arctic fox

ARCTIC CIRCLE

Hudson Bay

Ellesmere Island

Beluga whale

Dudinka

Baffin Island

Kara Sea

Natural gas

Inuit fishing through ice

Thule

Walrus tusk carvings

FRANZ JOSEF LAND

LOCATION

CANADA

Baffin Bay

Jakobshavn houses

Hooded seal

Harp seals

NOVAYA ZEMLYA

Upernavik

Svalbard reindeer

Haddock

Nenet woman

Tourism

GREENLAND (DENMARK)

SVALBARD (NORWAY)

Nar'yan-Mar

Musk-ox

Inuit hunter

Longyearbyen

Barents Sea

Davis Strait

Snowmobile

Spitsbergen

Harbour seals

Nuuk

Cod

Bowhead whale

NORTH CAPE

Murmansk

Iceberg

Tourism

Mt. Gunnbjørn 3,700 m (12,139 ft)

Orca (killer whale)

Hammerfest

Julianehåb

Jan Mayen Island (NORWAY)

Denmark Strait

Norwegian Sea

FINLAND

CAPE FAREWELL

Puffins

Sami (Lapp) man

SWEDEN

ICELAND

NORWAY

CHUKCHI HUNTER

Traditionally, Chukchi people hunted seals, walruses and whales from kayaks, using ivory-tipped harpoons. Now most hunters use rifles and travel in motorboats.

REINDEER

Huge herds of reindeer roam over the tundra in search of food. Their large hooves prevent them from sinking into the snow and help them dig through to reach plants and lichens.

World Fact File

NORTH AMERICA

CANADA
AREA: 9,976,185 sq. km
(3,851,809 sq. mi)
POPULATION: 31,007,000
CAPITAL: Ottawa
CURRENCY: 100 cents = 1 Canadian dollar (Can$)
OFFICIAL LANGUAGES: English, French
MAIN RELIGION: Christianity 72%
EXPORTS: Newsprint, wood pulp, timber, crude petroleum, machinery, natural gas, aluminium, motor vehicles and parts, telecommunications equipment

UNITED STATES OF AMERICA
AREA: 9,375,720 sq. km
(3,619,969 sq. mi)
POPULATION: 274,088,480
CAPITAL: Washington, D.C.
CURRENCY: 100 cents = 1 United States dollar (US$)
OFFICIAL LANGUAGE: English
OTHER LANGUAGE: Spanish
MAIN RELIGIONS: Christianity 86%, Judaism 2%
EXPORTS: Motor vehicles, raw materials, consumer goods, agricultural products

MEXICO
AREA: 1,972,544 sq. km
(761,600 sq. mi)
POPULATION: 100,295,000
CAPITAL: Mexico City
CURRENCY: 100 centavos = 1 Mexican peso (Mex$)
OFFICIAL LANGUAGE: Spanish
OTHER LANGUAGES: Regional languages
MAIN RELIGION: Christianity 95%
EXPORTS: Crude oil, oil products, coffee, silver, engines, motor vehicles, cotton, electronic goods

GUATEMALA
AREA: 108,889 sq. km (42,042 sq. mi)
POPULATION: 12,336,000
CAPITAL: Guatemala
CURRENCY: 100 centavos = 1 Guatemalan quetzal (Q)
OFFICIAL LANGUAGE: Spanish
OTHER LANGUAGES: Quiche, Cakchiquel, Kekchi and other regional languages
MAIN RELIGIONS: Christianity 99%, traditional Mayan religions
EXPORTS: Coffee, bananas, cotton, sugar, minerals, textiles

BELIZE
AREA: 22,966 sq. km
(8,867 sq. mi)
POPULATION: 235,800
CAPITAL: Belmopan
CURRENCY: 100 cents = 1 Belizian dollar (Bz$)
OFFICIAL LANGUAGE: English
OTHER LANGUAGES: Spanish, Maya, Garifuna
MAIN RELIGION: Christianity 92%
EXPORTS: Sugar, molasses, citrus fruit, bananas, clothing, fish products, timber

HONDURAS
AREA: 112,087 sq. km
(43,277 sq. mi)
POPULATION: 5,998,000
CAPITAL: Tegucigalpa
CURRENCY: 100 centavos = 1 lempira (L)
OFFICIAL LANGUAGE: Spanish
OTHER LANGUAGES: Regional languages
MAIN RELIGION: Christianity 97%
EXPORTS: Bananas, coffee, shrimp, lobsters, minerals, meat, timber

EL SALVADOR
AREA: 21,393 sq. km
(8,260 sq. mi)
POPULATION: 5,840,000
CAPITAL: San Salvador
CURRENCY: 100 centavos = 1 Salvadorean colón (C)
OFFICIAL LANGUAGE: Spanish
OTHER LANGUAGE: Nahuatl
MAIN RELIGION: Christianity 92%
EXPORTS: Coffee, sugar cane, shrimp

NICARAGUA
AREA: 128,410 sq. km
(49,579 sq. mi)
POPULATION: 4,718,000
CAPITAL: Managua
CURRENCY: 100 centavos = 1 gold cordoba (C$)
OFFICIAL LANGUAGE: Spanish
OTHER LANGUAGES: English, Indian
MAIN RELIGION: Christianity 100%
EXPORTS: Meat, coffee, cotton, sugar, bananas, seafood, gold

COSTA RICA
AREA: 50,899 sq. km
(19,652 sq. mi)
POPULATION: 3,675,000
CAPITAL: San José
CURRENCY: 100 centimos = 1 Costa Rican colón (C)
OFFICIAL LANGUAGE: Spanish
OTHER LANGUAGE: English
MAIN RELIGION: Christianity 95%
EXPORTS: Coffee, bananas, sugar, textiles

PANAMA
AREA: 87,177 sq. km
(33,659 sq. mi)
POPULATION: 2,779,000
CAPITAL: Panama City
CURRENCY: 100 centesimos = 1 balboa (B)

*F*LAGS OF THE WORLD

Next to the name of each country in this World Fact File is an illustration of that country's flag. Flags come in many different designs and colours

The First Flags
We will never know who invented flags, but we do know that about 5,000 years ago Egyptian soldiers carried into battle long poles with symbols made of cloth, wood or metal attached to the top. The soldiers hoped that these symbols would bring them good luck. At about the same time, silk banners were made in China. Both of these were early forms of flags.

National Flags
Today's national flags remind us of a country's history, religion and culture. The flags of many Islamic countries, for example, include a crescent and star, while the flags of Christian countries often include a cross. Countries with a shared history often have similar flags. For example, some countries in Central America have blue and white flags, because they were once part of the same country. The flags of several Arab countries are green, white, red and black, as these colours are the symbols of Arab unity. Every country's flag is special to the people of that country.

OFFICIAL LANGUAGE: Spanish
OTHER LANGUAGES: English, regional languages
MAIN RELIGION: Christianity 100%
EXPORTS: Bananas, shrimp, sugar, coffee, clothing

THE BAHAMAS

AREA: 13,950 sq. km
(5,386 sq. mi)
POPULATION: 284,800
CAPITAL: Nassau
CURRENCY: 100 cents = 1 Bahamian dollar (B$)
OFFICIAL LANGUAGE: English
OTHER LANGUAGE: Bahamian creole
MAIN RELIGION: Christianity 95%
EXPORTS: Pharmaceuticals, cement, rum, crayfish, refined petroleum products

CUBA

AREA: 110,862 sq. km
(42,804 sq. mi)
POPULATION: 11,097,000
CAPITAL: Havana
CURRENCY: 100 centavos = 1 Cuban peso (Cu$)
OFFICIAL LANGUAGE: Spanish
MAIN RELIGION: Christianity 85%
EXPORTS: Sugar, shellfish, citrus fruit, coffee, tobacco, nickel, medical products

JAMAICA

PRONUNCIATION: juh-MAY-kuh
AREA: 11,580 sq. km (4,471 sq. mi)
POPULATION: 2,653,000
CAPITAL: Kingston
CURRENCY: 100 cents = 1 Jamaican dollar (J$)
OFFICIAL LANGUAGE: English
OTHER LANGUAGE: Jamaican creole
MAIN RELIGION: Christianity 65%
EXPORTS: Bauxite, sugar, bananas, rum

HAITI

AREA: 27,749 sq. km
(10,714 sq. mi)
POPULATION: 6,885,000
CAPITAL: Port-au-Prince
CURRENCY: 100 centimes = 1 gourde (G)
OFFICIAL LANGUAGE: French
OTHER LANGUAGE: Haitian creole
MAIN RELIGION: Christianity 96%
EXPORTS: Clothing, coffee, sugar

DOMINICAN REPUBLIC

AREA: 48,322 sq. km
(18,657 sq. mi)
POPULATION: 8,130,000
CAPITAL: Santo Domingo
CURRENCY: 100 centavos = 1 Dominican peso (RD$)
OFFICIAL LANGUAGE: Spanish
MAIN RELIGION: Christianity 95%
EXPORTS: Minerals, sugar, coffee, cocoa, gold

ANTIGUA AND BARBUDA

AREA: 443 sq. km
(171 sq. mi)
POPULATION: 64,300
CAPITAL: St. John's
CURRENCY: 100 cents = 1 East Caribbean dollar (EC$)
OFFICIAL LANGUAGE: English
OTHER LANGUAGES: Regional languages
MAIN RELIGIONS: Christianity 97%, indigenous religions 3%
EXPORTS: Petroleum products, manufactured goods, machinery and transport equipment, food and livestock

ST. KITTS–NEVIS

AREA: 269 sq. km
(104 sq. mi)
POPULATION: 42,900
CAPITAL: Basseterre
CURRENCY: 100 cents = 1 East Caribbean dollar (EC$)
OFFICIAL LANGUAGE: English
MAIN RELIGION: Christianity 86%
EXPORTS: Machinery, food, beverages, electronics, tobacco

DOMINICA

AREA: 749 sq. km (289 sq. mi)
POPULATION: 64,900
CAPITAL: Roseau
CURRENCY: 100 cents = 1 East Caribbean dollar (EC$)
OFFICIAL LANGUAGE: English
OTHER LANGUAGE: French patois
MAIN RELIGION: Christianity 92%
EXPORTS: Bananas, grapefruit, oranges, vegetables, soap, bay oil

ST. LUCIA

AREA: 616 sq. km
(238 sq. mi)
POPULATION: 154,100
CAPITAL: Castries
CURRENCY: 100 cents = 1 East Caribbean dollar (EC$)
OFFICIAL LANGUAGE: English
OTHER LANGUAGE: French patois
MAIN RELIGION: Christianity 100%
EXPORTS: Bananas, clothing, cocoa, fruit and vegetables, coconut oil

BARBADOS

AREA: 430 sq. km (166 sq. mi)
POPULATION: 259,200
CAPITAL: Bridgetown
CURRENCY: 100 cents = 1 Barbadian dollar (Bds$)
OFFICIAL LANGUAGE: English
OTHER LANGUAGE: Barbadian creole
MAIN RELIGION: Christianity 71%
EXPORTS: Sugar, molasses, rum, other foods and beverages, chemicals, electrical components, clothing

ST. VINCENT AND THE GRENADINES

AREA: 389 sq. km (150 sq. mi)
POPULATION: 120,600
CAPITAL: Kingstown
CURRENCY: 100 cents = 1 East Caribbean dollar (EC$)
OFFICIAL LANGUAGE: English
OTHER LANGUAGE: French patois
MAIN RELIGION: Christianity 75
EXPORTS: Bananas, taro (food plant), tennis racquets

GRENADA

AREA: 344 sq. km (133 sq. mi)
POPULATION: 97,100
CAPITAL: St. George's
CURRENCY: 100 cents = 1 East Caribbean dollar (EC$)
OFFICIAL LANGUAGE: English
OTHER LANGUAGE: French patois
MAIN RELIGION: Christianity 85%
EXPORTS: Bananas, cocoa, nutmeg, fruit and vegetables, clothing, mace (spice)

TRINIDAD AND TOBAGO

AREA: 5,128 sq. km
(1,980 sq. mi)
POPULATION: 1,103,000
CAPITAL: Port-of-Spain
CURRENCY: 100 cents = 1 Trinidad and Tobago dollar (TT$)
OFFICIAL LANGUAGE: English
OTHER LANGUAGES: Hindi, French, Spanish
MAIN RELIGIONS: Christianity 60%, Hinduism 24%, Islam 6%
EXPORTS: Petroleum and petroleum products, chemicals, steel products, fertilizer, sugar, cocoa, coffee, citrus fruit, flowers

SOUTH AMERICA

COLOMBIA
AREA: 1,138,914 sq. km
(439,735 sq. mi)
POPULATION: 39,310,000
CAPITAL: Bogotá
CURRENCY: 100 centavos = 1 Colombian
peso (Col$)
OFFICIAL LANGUAGE: Spanish
MAIN RELIGION: Christianity 95%
EXPORTS: Petroleum, coffee, coal, bananas, flowers

VENEZUELA
AREA: 912,050 sq. km
(352,143 sq. mi)
POPULATION: 23,204,000
CAPITAL: Caracas
CURRENCY: 100 centimos = 1 bolivar (B)
OFFICIAL LANGUAGE: Spanish
OTHER LANGUAGES: Regional languages
MAIN RELIGION: Christianity 98%
EXPORTS: Petroleum, bauxite and aluminium,
steel, chemicals, agricultural products,
manufactured goods

GUYANA
AREA: 214,970 sq. km
(83,000 sq. mi)
POPULATION: 705,200
CAPITAL: Georgetown
CURRENCY: 100 cents = 1 Guyanese dollar (G$)
OFFICIAL LANGUAGE: English
OTHER LANGUAGES: Regional languages
MAIN RELIGIONS: Christianity 57%,
Hinduism 33%, Islam 9%
EXPORTS: Sugar, molasses, bauxite, rice, shrimp

SURINAME
AREA: 163,820 sq. km
(63,251 sq. mi)
POPULATION: 431,200
CAPITAL: Paramaribo
CURRENCY: 100 cents = 1 Surinamese guilder or
florin (Sf)
OFFICIAL LANGUAGE: Dutch
OTHER LANGUAGES: English, Sranang Tongo,
Hindustani, Javanese
MAIN RELIGIONS: Christianity 48%,
Hinduism 27%, Islam 20%, regional religions 5%
EXPORTS: Aluminium, shrimp, fish, rice, bananas

ECUADOR
AREA: 283,561 sq. km
(109,483 sq. mi)
POPULATION: 12,563,000
CAPITAL: Quito
CURRENCY: 100 centavos = 1 sucre (S/.)
OFFICIAL LANGUAGE: Spanish
OTHER LANGUAGES: Quechua, other regional
languages
MAIN RELIGION: Christianity 95%
EXPORTS: Petroleum, bananas, shrimp,
cocoa, coffee

PERU
AREA: 1,285,215 sq. km
(496,222 sq. mi)
POPULATION: 26,625,000
CAPITAL: Lima
CURRENCY: 100 centimos = 1 nuevo sol (S/.)
OFFICIAL LANGUAGES: Spanish, Quechua
OTHER LANGUAGE: Aymara
MAIN RELIGION: Christianity 90%
EXPORTS: Copper, zinc, petroleum and petroleum
products, lead, refined silver, coffee, cotton

BRAZIL
AREA: 8,506,663 sq. km
(3,284,426 sq. mi)
POPULATION: 171,854,000
CAPITAL: Brasília
CURRENCY: 100 centavos = 1 real (R$)
OFFICIAL LANGUAGE: Portuguese
OTHER LANGUAGES: Spanish, English, French
MAIN RELIGION: Christianity 96%
EXPORTS: Iron ore, soya bean bran, bananas,
orange juice, shoes, coffee, motor vehicle parts

BOLIVIA
AREA: 1,098,579 sq. km
(424,162 sq. mi)
POPULATION: 7,983,000
CAPITALS: La Paz (seat of government),
Sucre (legal and judicial)
CURRENCY: 100 centavos = 1 boliviano ($B)
OFFICIAL LANGUAGES: Spanish, Quechua, Aymara
MAIN RELIGION: Christianity 100%
EXPORTS: Metals, natural gas, soya beans,
jewellery, timber

CHILE
AREA: 756,946 sq. km
(292,257 sq. mi)
POPULATION: 14,974,000
CAPITAL: Santiago
CURRENCY: 100 centavos = 1 Chilean peso (Ch$)
OFFICIAL LANGUAGE: Spanish
OTHER LANGUAGES: Regional languages
MAIN RELIGION: Christianity 99%
EXPORTS: Copper, other metals and minerals,
timber products, fish, fruit

PARAGUAY
AREA: 406,741 sq. km
(157,043 sq. mi)
POPULATION: 5,435,000
CAPITAL: Asunción
CURRENCY: 100 centimos = 1 guarani (G)
OFFICIAL LANGUAGE: Spanish
OTHER LANGUAGE: Guarani
MAIN RELIGION: Christianity 97%
EXPORTS: Cotton, soya beans, timber, vegetable
oils, meat products, coffee

ARGENTINA
AREA: 2,776,884 sq. km
(1,072,156 sq. mi)
POPULATION: 36,738,000
CAPITAL: Buenos Aires
CURRENCY: 100 centavos = 1 peso
OFFICIAL LANGUAGE: Spanish
OTHER LANGUAGES: English, Italian,
German, French
MAIN RELIGIONS: Christianity 94%, Judaism 2%
EXPORTS: Manufactured goods, meat, wheat,
maize, oilseed

URUGUAY
AREA: 176,221 sq. km
(68,039 sq. mi)
POPULATION: 3,309,000
CAPITAL: Montevideo
CURRENCY: 100 centesimos = 1 Uruguayan
peso ($Ur)
OFFICIAL LANGUAGE: Spanish
MAIN RELIGIONS: Christianity 68%, Judaism 2%
EXPORTS: Wool, textiles, beef and other animal
products, leather, rice

EUROPE

UNITED KINGDOM

AREA: 244,110 sq. km
(94,251 sq. mi)
POPULATION: 59,114,000
CAPITAL: London
CURRENCY: 100 pence = 1 British pound (£)
OFFICIAL LANGUAGE: English
OTHER LANGUAGES: Welsh, Scottish Gaelic, Irish Gaelic
MAIN RELIGIONS: Christianity 90%, Islam 3%, Sikh 1%, Hinduism 1%, Judaism 1%
EXPORTS: Manufactured goods, machinery, fuels, chemicals, transport equipment

IRELAND

AREA: 68,894 sq. km
(26,600 sq. mi)
POPULATION: 3,633,000
CAPITAL: Dublin
CURRENCY: 100 pence = 1 Irish pound (£Ir)
OFFICIAL LANGUAGES: English, Irish (Gaelic)
MAIN RELIGION: Christianity 96%
EXPORTS: Chemicals, data processing equipment, industrial machinery, livestock, animal products

PORTUGAL

AREA: 91,642 sq. km
(35,383 sq. mi)
POPULATION: 9,919,000
CAPITAL: Lisbon
CURRENCY: 100 centavos = 1 Portuguese escudo (Esc)
OFFICIAL LANGUAGE: Portuguese
MAIN RELIGION: Christianity 98%
EXPORTS: Clothing, shoes, machinery, cork, paper products, animal skins

SPAIN

AREA: 504,742 sq. km
(194,881 sq. mi)
POPULATION: 39,168,000
CAPITAL: Madrid
CURRENCY: 100 centimos = 1 peseta (pta)
OFFICIAL LANGUAGE: Castilian Spanish
OTHER LANGUAGES: Catalan, Galician, Basque
MAIN RELIGION: Christianity 99%
EXPORTS: Motor vehicles, manufactured goods, food, machinery

ANDORRA

AREA: 482 sq. km (180 sq. mi)
POPULATION: 66,000
CAPITAL: Andorra
CURRENCIES: 100 centimes = 1 French franc (F), 100 centimos = 1 peseta (Pta)
OFFICIAL LANGUAGE: Catalan
OTHER LANGUAGES: French, Spanish
MAIN RELIGION: Christianity 95%
EXPORTS: Electricity, tobacco products, furniture

FRANCE

AREA: 551,458 sq. km
(212,918 sq. mi)
POPULATION: 58,979,000
CAPITAL: Paris
CURRENCY: 100 centimes = 1 French franc (F)
OFFICIAL LANGUAGE: French
OTHER LANGUAGES: Occitan, German, Breton, Catalan, Arabic
MAIN RELIGIONS: Christianity 92%, Judaism 1%, Islam 1%
EXPORTS: Machinery and transport equipment, chemicals, food, agricultural products, iron and steel products, textiles, clothing

MONACO

AREA: 1.5 sq. km (0.58 sq. mi)
POPULATION: 32,200
CAPITAL: Monaco
CURRENCY: 100 centimes = 1 French franc (F)
OFFICIAL LANGUAGE: French
OTHER LANGUAGES: English, Italian, Monégasque
MAIN RELIGION: Christianity 95%
EXPORTS: Pharmaceuticals, perfumes, clothing

THE NETHERLANDS

AREA: 41,525 sq. km
(16,033 sq. mi)
POPULATION: 15,808,000
CAPITALS: Amsterdam; The Hague (judicial)
CURRENCY: 100 cents = 1 Dutch florin (f)
OFFICIAL LANGUAGE: Dutch
MAIN RELIGIONS: Christianity 59%, Islam 3%
EXPORTS: Metal products, chemicals, processed food, tobacco, agricultural products

BELGIUM

AREA: 30,513 sq. km
(11,781 sq. mi)
POPULATION: 10,183,000
CAPITAL: Brussels
CURRENCY: 100 centimes = 1 Belgian franc (BF)
OFFICIAL LANGUAGES: Dutch (Flemish), French
OTHER LANGUAGE: German
MAIN RELIGION: Christianity 100%
EXPORTS: Iron and steel, transport equipment, tractors, diamonds, petroleum products

LUXEMBOURG

AREA: 2,587 sq. km (999 sq. mi)
POPULATION: 429,100
CAPITAL: Luxembourg
CURRENCY: 100 centimes = 1 Luxembourg franc (LuxF)
OFFICIAL LANGUAGES: Letzeburgesh, German, French
OTHER LANGUAGE: English
MAIN RELIGIONS: Christianity 99%, Judaism 1%
EXPORTS: Steel products, chemicals, rubber products, glass, aluminium

GERMANY

AREA: 356,734 sq. km
(137,735 sq. mi)
POPULATION: 82,088,000
CAPITAL: Berlin
CURRENCY: 100 pfennig = 1 Deutschmark (DM)
OFFICIAL LANGUAGE: German
MAIN RELIGIONS: Christianity 72%, Islam 2%
EXPORTS: Machines and machine tools, chemicals, motor vehicles, iron and steel products, agricultural products, raw materials, fuels

SWITZERLAND

AREA: 41,287 sq. km
(15,941 sq. mi)
POPULATION: 7,276,000
CAPITAL: Bern
CURRENCY: 100 centimes = 1 Swiss franc (SFR)
OFFICIAL LANGUAGES: German, French, Italian, Romansch
MAIN RELIGION: Christianity 86%
EXPORTS: Machinery, precision instruments, metal products, food, textiles

LIECHTENSTEIN

AREA: 161 sq. km
(62 sq. mi)
POPULATION: 32,100
CAPITAL: Vaduz
CURRENCY: 100 centimes = 1 Swiss franc (SwF)
OFFICIAL LANGUAGE: German
MAIN RELIGION: Christianity 88%
EXPORTS: Machinery, dental products, stamps, hardware, pottery

AUSTRIA

AREA: 83,851 sq. km
(32,375 sq. mi)
POPULATION: 8,140,000
CAPITAL: Vienna
CURRENCY: 100 groschen = 1 Austrian
schilling (AS)
OFFICIAL LANGUAGE: German
MAIN RELIGION: Christianity 83%
EXPORTS: Machinery, electrical equipment,
iron and steel, timber, textiles, paper
products, chemicals

ITALY

AREA: 301,251 sq. km
(116,313 sq. mi)
POPULATION: 56,736,000
CAPITAL: Rome
CURRENCY: 100 centesimi = Italian lira (Lit)
OFFICIAL LANGUAGE: Italian
OTHER LANGUAGES: German, French, Slovene
MAIN RELIGION: Christianity 98%
EXPORTS: Metals, textiles, clothing, machinery,
motor vehicles, transport equipment,
chemicals

SAN MARINO

AREA: 62 sq. km (24 sq. mi)
POPULATION: 25,100
CAPITAL: San Marino
CURRENCY: 100 centesimi = Italian lira (Lit)
OFFICIAL LANGUAGE: Italian
MAIN RELIGION: Christianity 95%
EXPORTS: Building stone, lime, timber, chestnuts,
wheat, wine, baked goods, animal skins, ceramics

VATICAN CITY

AREA: 0.44 sq. km (0.17 sq. mi)
POPULATION: 850
CAPITAL: Vatican City
CURRENCY: Vatican lira (VLit)
OFFICIAL LANGUAGES: Italian, Latin
MAIN RELIGION: Christianity 100%
EXPORTS: None

MALTA

AREA: 316 sq. km (122 sq. mi)
POPULATION: 381,700
CAPITAL: Valletta
CURRENCY: 100 cents = 1 Maltese lira (LM)
OFFICIAL LANGUAGES: Maltese, English
MAIN RELIGION: Christianity 98%
EXPORTS: Machinery and transport equipment,
clothing, shoes, printed matter

SLOVENIA

AREA: 20,251 sq. km (7,819 sq. mi)
POPULATION: 1,971,000
CAPITAL: Ljubljana
CURRENCY: 100 stotins = 1 tolar (SIT)
OFFICIAL LANGUAGE: Slovenian
OTHER LANGUAGE: Serbo-Croatian
MAIN RELIGIONS: Christianity 96%, Islam 1%
EXPORTS: Motor vehicles, furniture, machinery,
manufactured goods, chemicals, textiles, food,
raw materials

CROATIA

AREA: 56,537 sq. km
(21,829 sq. mi)
POPULATION: 4,677,000
CAPITAL: Zagreb
CURRENCY: 100 lipa = 1 Croatian kuna (HRK)
OFFICIAL LANGUAGE: Serbo-Croatian
MAIN RELIGIONS: Christianity 88%, Islam 1%
EXPORTS: Machinery and transport
equipment, other manufactured goods,
chemicals, food, livestock, raw materials,
fuels and lubricants

BOSNIA AND HERZEGOVINA

AREA: 51,750 sq. km
(19,904 sq. mi)
POPULATION: 3,483,000
CAPITAL: Sarajevo
CURRENCY: 100 pfenniga = 1 marka (KM)
OFFICIAL LANGUAGE: Serbo-Croatian
MAIN RELIGIONS: Christianity 50%, Islam 40%
EXPORTS: Timber, furniture

YUGOSLAVIA

AREA: 102,173 sq. km (39,449 sq. mi)
POPULATION: 11,207,000
CAPITAL: Belgrade
CURRENCY: 100 paras = 1 Yugoslav new dinar (YD)
OFFICIAL LANGUAGE: Serbo-Croatian
OTHER LANGUAGES: Albanian, Hungarian
MAIN RELIGIONS: Christianity 70%, Islam 19%
EXPORTS: Textiles, leather goods, machinery

ROMANIA

AREA: 237,500 sq. km (91,699 sq. mi)
POPULATION: 22,335,000
CAPITAL: Bucharest
CURRENCY: 100 bani = 1 leu (L)
OFFICIAL LANGUAGE: Romanian
OTHER LANGUAGES: Hungarian, German
MAIN RELIGION: Christianity 82%
EXPORTS: Metals and metal products, mineral
products, textiles, electrical equipment,
transport equipment

BULGARIA

AREA: 110,912 sq. km
(42,823 sq. mi)
POPULATION: 8,195,000
CAPITAL: Sofia
CURRENCY: 100 stotinki = 1 Lev (Lv)
OFFICIAL LANGUAGE: Bulgarian
MAIN RELIGIONS: Christianity 85%, Islam 13%,
Judaism 1%
EXPORTS: Machinery, agricultural products,
manufactured goods, fuels, minerals, raw
materials, metals

ALBANIA

AREA: 28,749 sq. km
(11,100 sq. mi)
POPULATION: 3,365,000
CAPITAL: Tiranë
CURRENCY: 100 qintars = 1 lek (L)
OFFICIAL LANGUAGE: Albanian
OTHER LANGUAGE: Greek
MAIN RELIGIONS: Islam 70%, Christianity 30%
EXPORTS: Asphalt, metals and metallic ores,
electricity, crude oil, fruit and vegetables, tobacco

MACEDONIA

AREA: 25,714 sq. km (9,928 sq. mi)
POPULATION: 2,023,000
CAPITAL: Skopje
CURRENCY: 100 deni = 1 Macedonian denar (MKD)
OFFICIAL LANGUAGE: Macedonian
OTHER LANGUAGES: Albanian, Turkish,
Serbo-Croatian
MAIN RELIGIONS: Christianity 67%, Islam 30%
EXPORTS: Manufactured goods, machinery and
transport equipment, raw materials, food,
livestock, beverages, tobacco, chemicals

GREECE

AREA: 131,945 sq. km
(50,944 sq. mi)
POPULATION: 10,708,000
CAPITAL: Athens
CURRENCY: 100 lepta = 1 drachma (Dr)
OFFICIAL LANGUAGE: Greek
OTHER LANGUAGES: English, French
MAIN RELIGIONS: Christianity 98%, Islam 1%
EXPORTS: Manufactured goods, food, fuels

ESTONIA

AREA: 45,100 sq. km
(17,413 sq. mi)
POPULATION: 1,409,000
CAPITAL: Tallinn
CURRENCY: 100 cents = 1 Estonian kroon (EEK)
OFFICIAL LANGUAGE: Estonian
OTHER LANGUAGES: Russian, Ukrainian, English
MAIN RELIGION: Christianity 100%
EXPORTS: Textiles, food, motor vehicles, metals

LATVIA

AREA: 63,701 sq. km
(24,595 sq. mi)
POPULATION: 2,354,000
CAPITAL: Riga
CURRENCY: 100 santims = 1 Latvian lat (LVL)
OFFICIAL LANGUAGE: Lettish
OTHER LANGUAGES: Lithuanian, Russian
MAIN RELIGION: Christianity 100%
EXPORTS: Oil products, timber, metals, dairy products, furniture, textiles

LITHUANIA
AREA: 65,201 sq. km
(25,174 sq. mi)
POPULATION: 3,585,000
CAPITAL: Vilnius
CURRENCY: 100 centas = 1 Lithuan litas (Lt)
OFFICIAL LANGUAGE: Lithuanian
OTHER LANGUAGES: Polish, Russian
MAIN RELIGION: Christianity 100%
EXPORTS: Electronics, petroleum products, food, chemicals

BELARUS
AREA: 207,599 sq. km
(80,154 sq. mi)
POPULATION: 10,402,000
CAPITAL: Minsk
CURRENCY: Belarussian rubel (BR)
OFFICIAL LANGUAGE: Belarussian
OTHER LANGUAGE: Russian
MAIN RELIGION: Christianity 68%
EXPORTS: Machinery and transport equipment, chemicals, food

POLAND
AREA: 312,758 sq. km
(120,756 sq. mi)
POPULATION: 38,609,000
CAPITAL: Warsaw
CURRENCY: 100 groszy = 1 zloty (Zl)
OFFICIAL LANGUAGE: Polish
MAIN RELIGION: Christianity 95%
EXPORTS: Machinery and transport equipment, manufactured goods, food, fuels

CZECH REPUBLIC
AREA: 78,866 sq. km
(30,450 sq. mi)
POPULATION: 10,281,000
CAPITAL: Prague
CURRENCY: 100 haleru = 1 koruna (Kc)
OFFICIAL LANGUAGE: Czech
OTHER LANGUAGE: Slovak
MAIN RELIGION: Christianity 47%
EXPORTS: Manufactured goods, machinery and transport equipment, chemicals, fuels, minerals, metals, agricultural products

SLOVAKIA
AREA: 49,011 sq. km (18,923 sq. mi)
POPULATION: 5,397,000
CAPITAL: Bratislava
CURRENCY: 100 haleru = 1 koruna (Sk)
OFFICIAL LANGUAGE: Slovak
OTHER LANGUAGE: Hungarian
MAIN RELIGION: Christianity 72%
EXPORTS: Machinery and transport equipment, chemicals, fuels, minerals and metals, agricultural products

UKRAINE
AREA: 603,701 sq. km
(233,089 sq. mi)
POPULATION: 49,812,000
CAPITAL: Kiev
CURRENCY: 100 kopiykas = 1 hryvna
OFFICIAL LANGUAGE: Ukrainian
OTHER LANGUAGES: Russian, Romanian, Polish, Hungarian
MAIN RELIGIONS: Christianity 90%, Judaism 2%
EXPORTS: Coal, electricity, metals, chemicals, machinery and transport equipment, grain, meat

HUNGARY
AREA: 93,030 sq. km
(35,919 sq. mi)
POPULATION: 10,187,000
CAPITAL: Budapest
CURRENCY: 100 filler = 1 forint (Ft)
OFFICIAL LANGUAGE: Hungarian
MAIN RELIGION: Christianity 92%
EXPORTS: Raw materials, machinery and transport equipment, manufactured goods, food, agriculture, fuels, energy

MOLDOVA

AREA: 33,701 sq. km
(13,012 sq. mi)
POPULATION: 4,461,000
CAPITAL: Chişinău
CURRENCY: 100 bani = 1 leu (L)
OFFICIAL LANGUAGE: Moldovian
OTHER LANGUAGES: Russian, Gagauz
MAIN RELIGIONS: Christianity 99%, Judaism 1%
EXPORTS: Food, wine, tobacco, textiles, shoes, machinery, chemicals

ICELAND
AREA: 102,828 sq. km
(39,702 sq. mi)
POPULATION: 272,600
CAPITAL: Reykjavik
CURRENCY: 100 aurar = 1 Icelandic krona (IKr)
OFFICIAL LANGUAGE: Icelandic
MAIN RELIGION: Christianity 99%
EXPORTS: Fish and fish products, animal products, minerals

NORWAY
AREA: 400,906 sq. km
(154,790 sq. mi)
POPULATION: 4,439,000
CAPITAL: Oslo
CURRENCY: 100 oere = 1 Norwegian krone (NKr)
OFFICIAL LANGUAGE: Norwegian
OTHER LANGUAGES: Lapp, Finnish
MAIN RELIGION: Christianity 91%
EXPORTS: Petroleum and petroleum products, metals and metal products, fish and fish products, chemicals, natural gas, ships

SWEDEN
AREA: 449,792 sq. km
(173,665 sq. mi)
POPULATION: 8,912,000
CAPITAL: Stockholm
CURRENCY: 100 oere = 1 Swedish krona (SKr)
OFFICIAL LANGUAGE: Swedish
OTHER LANGUAGES: Lapp, Finnish
MAIN RELIGION: Christianity 96%
EXPORTS: Machinery, motor vehicles, paper products, pulp and wood, iron and steel products, chemicals, petroleum and petroleum products

FINLAND
AREA: 337,032 sq. km
(130,128 sq. mi)
POPULATION: 5,159,000
CAPITAL: Helsinki
CURRENCY: 100 pennia = 1 markka (FmK)
OFFICIAL LANGUAGES: Finnish, Swedish
OTHER LANGUAGES: Lapp, Russian
MAIN RELIGION: Christianity 90%
EXPORTS: Paper and pulp, machinery, chemicals, metals, timber

DENMARK
AREA: 43,069 sq. km
(16,629 sq. mi)
POPULATION: 5,357,000
CAPITAL: Copenhagen
CURRENCY: 100 ore = 1 Danish krone (DKr)
OFFICIAL LANGUAGE: Danish
OTHER LANGUAGES: Faroese, Greenlandic, German
MAIN RELIGION: Christianity 93%
EXPORTS: Meat and meat products, dairy products, transport equipment, ships, fish, chemicals, industrial machinery

ASIA

RUSSIA

AREA: 17,075,383 sq. km
(6,592,812 sq. mi)
POPULATION: 146,394,000
CAPITAL: Moscow
CURRENCY: 100 copecks = 1 rouble (R)
OFFICIAL LANGUAGE: Russian
MAIN RELIGIONS: Christianity 75%, Islam,
Buddhism
EXPORTS: Petroleum and petroleum products,
natural gas, timber and timber products, metals,
chemicals, manufactured goods

TURKEY

AREA: 780,574 sq. km
(301,380 sq. mi)
POPULATION: 65,600,000
CAPITAL: Ankara
CURRENCY: 100 kurus = 1 Turkish lira (TL)
OFFICIAL LANGUAGE: Turkish
OTHER LANGUAGES: Kurdish, Arabic
MAIN RELIGION: Islam 99%
EXPORTS: Manufactured goods, food,
mining products

CYPRUS

AREA: 9,251 sq. km (3,572 sq. mi)
POPULATION: 754,100
CAPITAL: Nicosia
CURRENCY: 100 cents = 1 Cypriot pound (£C);
100 kurus = 1 Turkish lira (TL)
OFFICIAL LANGUAGES: Greek, Turkish
OTHER LANGUAGE: English
MAIN RELIGIONS: Christianity 78%, Islam 18%
EXPORTS: Citrus fruit, potatoes, grapes, wine,
cement, clothing, shoes

GEORGIA

AREA: 69,699 sq. km
(26,911 sq. mi)
POPULATION: 5,067,000
CAPITAL: Tbilisi
CURRENCY: Lari
OFFICIAL LANGUAGE: Georgian
OTHER LANGUAGES: Russian, Armenian, Azeri
MAIN RELIGIONS: Christianity 83%, Islam 11%
EXPORTS: Citrus fruit, tea, wine, machinery,
metals, textiles, chemicals, fuel re-exports

ARMENIA

AREA: 29,800 sq. km
(11,506 sq. mi)
POPULATION: 3,410,000
CAPITAL: Yerevan
CURRENCY: 100 luma = 1 dram
OFFICIAL LANGUAGE: Armenian
OTHER LANGUAGE: Russian
MAIN RELIGION: Christianity 94%
EXPORTS: Gold and jewellery, aluminium,
transport equipment, electrical equipment

AZERBAIJAN

AREA: 86,599 sq. km
(33,436 sq. mi)
POPULATION: 7,909,000
CAPITAL: Baku
CURRENCY: 100 gopiks = 1 manat
OFFICIAL LANGUAGE: Azerbaijani
OTHER LANGUAGES: Russian, Armenian
MAIN RELIGIONS: Islam 94%, Christianity 5%
EXPORTS: Oil, gas, chemicals, oil field equipment,
textiles, cotton

KAZAKSTAN

AREA: 2,715,097 sq. km
(1,048,300 sq. mi)
POPULATION: 16,825,000
CAPITAL: Astana
CURRENCY: 100 tiyn = 1 tenge
OFFICIAL LANGUAGE: Kazak
OTHER LANGUAGE: Russian
MAIN RELIGIONS: Islam 47%, Christianity 46%
EXPORTS: Oil, metals, chemicals, grain, wool,
meat, coal

UZBEKISTAN

AREA: 449,601 sq. km
(173,591 sq. mi)
POPULATION: 24,103,000
CAPITAL: Tashkent
CURRENCY: Som (UKS)
OFFICIAL LANGUAGE: Uzbek
OTHER LANGUAGES: Russian, Tajik
MAIN RELIGIONS: Islam 88%, Christianity 9%
EXPORTS: Cotton, gold, natural gas, mineral
fertilizer, metals, textiles, food

TURKMENISTAN

AREA: 488,098 sq. km
(188,455 sq. mi)
POPULATION: 4,367,000
CAPITAL: Ashkhabad
CURRENCY: 100 tenesi = 1 manat
OFFICIAL LANGUAGE: Turkmen
OTHER LANGUAGES: Russian, Uzbek
MAIN RELIGIONS: Islam 89%, Christianity 9%
EXPORTS: Natural gas, cotton, petroleum products,
electricity, textiles, carpets

KYRGYZSTAN

AREA: 198,500 sq. km
(76,641 sq. mi)
POPULATION: 4,547,000
CAPITAL: Bishkek
CURRENCY: 100 tiyin = 1 Kyrgyzstani som (KGS)
OFFICIAL LANGUAGE: Kyrgyz
OTHER LANGUAGE: Russian
MAIN RELIGIONS: Islam 75%, Christianity 20%
EXPORTS: Wool, chemicals, cotton, metals, shoes,
machinery, tobacco

TAJIKISTAN

AREA: 143,100 sq. km
(55,251 sq. mi)
POPULATION: 6,103,000
CAPITAL: Dushanbe
CURRENCY: 100 tanga = 1 Tajikistani ruble (TR)
OFFICIAL LANGUAGE: Tajik
OTHER LANGUAGE: Russian
MAIN RELIGION: Islam 85%
EXPORTS: Cotton, aluminium, fruit and
vegetables, textiles

SYRIA

AREA: 185,180 sq. km
(71,498 sq. mi)
POPULATION: 17,214,000
CAPITAL: Damascus
CURRENCY: 100 piastres = 1 Syrian pound (£S)
OFFICIAL LANGUAGE: Arabic
OTHER LANGUAGES: Kurdish, Armenian, Aramaic,
Circassian, French
MAIN RELIGIONS: Islam 90%, Christianity 10%
EXPORTS: Petroleum, textiles, cotton, fruit and
vegetables, wheat, barley, chickens

IRAQ

AREA: 437,521 sq. km
(168,927 sq. mi)
POPULATION: 22,428,000
CAPITAL: Baghdad
CURRENCY: 1,000 fils = 1 Iraqi dinar (ID)
OFFICIAL LANGUAGES: Arabic, Kurdish (in
Kurdish regions)
OTHER LANGUAGES: Assyrian, Armenian
MAIN RELIGIONS: Islam 97%, Christianity 3%
EXPORTS: Crude oil and refined products,
fertilizer, sulphur

IRAN

AREA: 1,647,064 sq. km
(635,932 sq. mi)
POPULATION: 65,180,000
CAPITAL: Tehran
CURRENCY: 100 dinars = 1 rial (R)
OFFICIAL LANGUAGE: Farsi (Persian)
OTHER LANGUAGES: Turkic, Kurdish
MAIN RELIGION: Islam 99%
EXPORTS: Petroleum, carpets, fruit, nuts,
animal skins

LEBANON

AREA: 10,228 sq. km (3,949 sq. mi)
POPULATION: 3,563,000
CAPITAL: Beirut
CURRENCY: 100 piastres = 1 Lebanese pound (£L)
OFFICIAL LANGUAGES: Arabic, French
OTHER LANGUAGES: Armenian, English
MAIN RELIGIONS: Islam 70%, Christianity 30%
EXPORTS: Agricultural products, chemicals,
textiles, metals, jewellery

ISRAEL

AREA: 20,699 sq. km (7,992 sq. mi)
POPULATION: 5,750,000
CAPITAL: Jerusalem
CURRENCY: 100 new agorot = 1 new Israeli
shekel (NIS)
OFFICIAL LANGUAGES: Hebrew, Arabic
OTHER LANGUAGES: English
MAIN RELIGIONS: Judaism 82%, Islam 14%,
Christianity 2%
EXPORTS: Machinery, cut diamonds, chemicals,
textiles, agricultural products, metals

JORDAN

AREA: 89,549 sq. km
(34,575 sq. mi)
POPULATION: 4,562,000
CAPITAL: Amman
CURRENCY: 1,000 fils = 1 Jordanian dinar (JD)
OFFICIAL LANGUAGE: Arabic
OTHER LANGUAGE: English
MAIN RELIGIONS: Islam 96%, Christianity 4%
EXPORTS: Phosphates, fertilizer, potash,
agricultural products, manufactured goods

SAUDI ARABIA

AREA: 2,240,350 sq. km
(865,000 sq. mi)
POPULATION: 21,505,000
CAPITAL: Riyadh
CURRENCY: 100 halalas = 1 Saudi riyal (SR)
OFFICIAL LANGUAGE: Arabic
MAIN RELIGION: Islam 100%
EXPORTS: Petroleum and petroleum products

KUWAIT

AREA: 17,819 sq. km (6,880 sq. mi)
POPULATION: 1,992,000
CAPITAL: Kuwait
CURRENCY: 1,000 fils = 1 Kuwaiti dinar (KD)
OFFICIAL LANGUAGE: Arabic
OTHER LANGUAGE: English
MAIN RELIGIONS: Islam 85%, Christianity 8%,
Hinduism and Parsi 2%
EXPORTS: Oil

BAHRAIN

AREA: 661 sq. km (255 sq. mi)
POPULATION: 692,100
CAPITAL: Manama
CURRENCY: 1,000 fils = 1 Bahraini dinar (BD)
OFFICIAL LANGUAGE: Arabic
OTHER LANGUAGES: English, Farsi, Urdu
MAIN RELIGION: Islam 100%
EXPORTS: Petroleum and petroleum
products, aluminium

QATAR

AREA: 11,395 sq. km (4,400 sq. mi)
POPULATION: 723,600
CAPITAL: Doha
CURRENCY: 100 dirhams = 1 Qatari riyal (QR)
OFFICIAL LANGUAGE: Arabic
OTHER LANGUAGE: English
MAIN RELIGION: Islam 95%
EXPORTS: Petroleum products, steel, fertilizer

UNITED ARAB EMIRATES

AREA: 77,701 sq. km
(30,000 sq. mi)
POPULATION: 2,345,000
CAPITAL: Abu Dhabi
CURRENCY: 100 fils = 1 Emirian dirham (Dh)
OFFICIAL LANGUAGE: Arabic
OTHER LANGUAGES: Persian, English, Hindi, Urdu
MAIN RELIGION: Islam 96%
EXPORTS: Crude oil, natural gas, dried fish, dates

OMAN

AREA: 212,380 sq. km
(82,000 sq. mi)
POPULATION: 2,477,000
CAPITAL: Muscat
CURRENCY: 1,000 baiza = 1 Omani rial (RO)
OFFICIAL LANGUAGE: Arabic
OTHER LANGUAGES: English, Baluchi, Urdu,
Indian languages
MAIN RELIGIONS: Islam 86%, Hinduism 13%
EXPORTS: Petroleum, fish, copper, textiles

YEMEN

AREA: 527,969 sq. km
(203,849 sq. mi)
POPULATION: 16,943,000
CAPITAL: Sanaa
CURRENCY: 1 Yemeni rial (YRI)
OFFICIAL LANGUAGE: Arabic
MAIN RELIGION: Islam 99%
EXPORTS: Crude oil, cotton, coffee, animal skins,
vegetables, dried and salted fish

Afghanistan

Area: 649,507 sq. km
(250,775 sq. mi)
Population: 25,825,000
Capital: Kabul
Currency: 100 puls = 1 afghani (AF)
Official Languages: Afghan, Persian, Pashto
Other Languages: Uzbek, Turkmen
Main Religions: Islam 99%, Hinduism and
Judaism 1%
Exports: Fruit, nuts, hand-woven carpets,
wool, cotton, animal skins, precious and
semi-precious gemstones

Pakistan

Area: 803, 944 km
(310,403 sq. mi)
Population: 138,124,000
Capital: Islamabad
Currency: 100 paisa = 1 Pakistani rupee (PRe)
Official Languages: Urdu, English
Other Languages: Punjabi, Sindhi,
Pashto, Baluchi
Main Religion: Islam 97%
Exports: Cotton, textiles, clothing, rice,
leather, carpets

India

Area: 3,095,472 sq. km
(1,195,063 sq. mi)
Population: 1,000,849,000
Capital: New Delhi
Currency: 100 paisa = 1 Indian rupee (Re)
Official Languages: Hindi, English
Other Languages: Hindustani, Bengali, Telugu,
Marathi, Tamil, Urdu, Gujarati, Malayalam,
Kannada, Oriya, Punjabi, Assamese, Kashmiri,
Rajasthani, Sindhi, Sanskrit
Main Religions: Hinduism 80%, Islam 14%,
Christianity 3%
Exports: Clothing, gemstones and jewellery,
engineering equipment, chemicals, leather goods,
cotton yarn, fabric

Nepal

Area: 140,798 sq. km
(54,362 sq. mi)
Population: 24,303,000
Capital: Kathmandu
Currency: 100 paisa = 1 Nepalese rupee (NR)
Official Language: Nepali
Main Religions: Hinduism 90%, Buddhism 5%,
Islam 3%
Exports: Carpets, clothing, leather goods, jute
(fibre) goods, grain

Bhutan

Area: 41,440 sq. km
(16,000 sq. mi)
Population: 1,952,000
Capital: Thimphu
Currency: 100 chetrum = 1 ngultrum (Nu);
Indian currency is also legal tender
Official Language: Dzongkha
Other Languages: Tibetan and Nepali
Main Religions: Buddhism 75%, Hinduism 25%
Exports: Timber, handicrafts, cement, fruit,
electricity, gemstones, spices

Bangladesh

Area: 142,776 sq. km
(55,126 sq. mi)
Population: 127,118,000
Capital: Dhaka
Currency: 100 poisha = 1 taka (Tk)
Official Language: Bengali
Other Language: English
Main Religions: Islam 88%, Hinduism 11%,
Buddhism and Christianity 1%
Exports: Garments, jute (fibre) and jute goods,
leather, shrimp

Maldives

Area: 298 sq. km (115 sq. mi)
Population: 300,300
Capital: Male
Currency: 100 laris = 1 rufiyaa (Rf)
Official Language: Divehi (Maldivian)
Other Language: English
Main Religion: Islam 100%
Exports: Fish, clothing

Sri Lanka

Area: 65,610 sq. km
(25,332 sq. mi)
Population: 19,145,000
Capital: Colombo
Currency: 100 cents = 1 Sri Lankan rupee (SLRe)
Official Languages: Sinhala, Tamil
Other Language: English
Main Religions: Buddhism 69%, Hinduism 15%,
Christianity 8%, Islam 8%
Exports: Textiles, tea, diamonds and other
precious gemstones, petroleum products, rubber
products, agricultural products, marine products

Myanmar (Burma)

Area: 678,034 sq. km
(261,789 sq. mi)
Population: 48,082,000
Capital: Yangon (Rangoon)
Currency: 100 pyas = 1 kyat (K)
Official Language: Burmese
Main Religions: Buddhism 89%,
Christianity 4%, Islam 4%
Exports: Pulses and beans,
rice, timber

Laos

Area: 236,799 sq. km
(91,428 sq. mi)
Population: 5,408,000
Capital: Vientiane
Currency: 100 at = 1 new kip (NK)
Official Language: Lao
Other Languages: French, English
Main Religions: Buddhism 60%, animism 34%,
Christianity 2%
Exports: Electricity, timber products, coffee,
tin, textiles

Vietnam

Area: 337,912 sq. km
(130,468 sq. mi)
Population: 77,312,000
Capital: Hanoi
Currency: 100 xu = 1 new dong (D)
Official Language: Vietnamese
Other Languages: French, Chinese, English,
Khmer, tribal languages
Main Religions: Buddhism 55%, Christianity 7%,
Taoism, indigenous religions, Islam
Exports: Petroleum, rice, agricultural products,
marine products, coffee

Thailand

Area: 513,998 sq. km
(198,455 sq. mi)
Population: 60,609,000
Capital: Bangkok
Currency: 100 satangs = 1 baht (B)
Official Language: Thai
Other Languages: English, Chinese, Malay
Main Religions: Buddhism 95%, Islam 4%
Exports: Machinery, manufactured goods,
agricultural products, fish

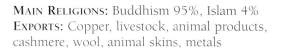

CAMBODIA

AREA: 181,036 sq. km
(69,898 sq. mi)
POPULATION: 11,627,000
CAPITAL: Phnom Penh
CURRENCY: 100 sen = 1 new riel (CR)
OFFICIAL LANGUAGE: Khmer
OTHER LANGUAGE: French
MAIN RELIGIONS: Buddhism 95%, Islam 2%
EXPORTS: Timber, rubber, soya beans, sesame

MALAYSIA

AREA: 333,403 sq. km
(128,727 sq. mi)
POPULATION: 21,376,000
CAPITAL: Kuala Lumpur
CURRENCY: 100 sen = 1 ringgit (M$)
OFFICIAL LANGUAGE: Malay
OTHER LANGUAGES: English, Chinese languages,
Tamil, Teluga, regional languages
MAIN RELIGIONS: Islam 53%, Buddhism 17%,
Confucianism 12%, Christianity 9%,
Hinduism 7%
EXPORTS: Electronic equipment, petroleum and
petroleum products, palm oil, timber and timber
products, rubber, textiles

PHILIPPINES

AREA: 299,536 sq. km
(115,651 sq. mi)
POPULATION: 79,346,000
CAPITAL: Manila
CURRENCY: 100 centavos = 1 Philippine peso (P)
OFFICIAL LANGUAGES: Pilipino, English
OTHER LANGUAGES: Regional languages
MAIN RELIGIONS: Christianity 92%, Islam 5%,
Buddhism 3%
EXPORTS: Electronics, textiles, coconut products,
copper, fish

SINGAPORE

AREA: 583 sq. km (225 sq. mi)
POPULATION: 3,532,000
CAPITAL: Singapore
CURRENCY: 100 cents = 1 Singapore dollar (S$)
OFFICIAL LANGUAGES: Chinese, Malay, Tamil,
English
MAIN RELIGIONS: Buddhism 28%, Islam 15%,
Christianity 13%, Taoism 13%, Hinduism 5%
EXPORTS: Computer equipment, rubber and
rubber products, petroleum products,
telecommunications equipment

BRUNEI

AREA: 5,765 sq. km
(2,226 sq. mi)
POPULATION: 323,300
CAPITAL: Bandar Seri Begawan
CURRENCY: 100 sen = 1 Bruneian dollar (B$)
OFFICIAL LANGUAGE: Malay
OTHER LANGUAGES: English, Chinese
MAIN RELIGIONS: Islam 63%, Buddhist 14%,
Christianity 8%, indigenous religions
EXPORTS: Crude oil, liquefied natural gas,
petroleum products

INDONESIA

AREA: 2,019,358 sq. km
(779,675 sq. mi)
POPULATION: 216,109,000
CAPITAL: Jakarta
CURRENCY: 100 sen = 1 Indonesian rupiah (Rp)
OFFICIAL LANGUAGE: Bahasa Indonesia
OTHER LANGUAGES: English, Dutch, Javanese,
regional languages
MAIN RELIGIONS: Islam 88%, Christianity 9%,
Hinduism 2%, Buddhism 1%
EXPORTS: Manufactured goods, fuels, food,
raw materials

EAST TIMOR

AREA: 19,000 sq.km (7,000 sq. miles)
POPULATION: 650,000
CAPITAL: Dili
CURRENCY: 100 sen = 1 rupiah (Rp)
OFFICIAL LANGUAGE: Bahasa Indonesia
OTHER LANGUAGES: Tetum, Portuguese
MAIN RELIGION: Christianity 90%
EXPORTS: Oil, minerals, coffee

CHINA

AREA: 9,583,000 sq. km
(3,700,000 sq. mi)
POPULATION: 1,246,872,000
CAPITAL: Beijing
CURRENCY: 100 fen = 1 yuan (Y)
OFFICIAL LANGUAGE: Mandarin
OTHER LANGUAGES: Cantonese, Shanghainese,
Fuzhou, Hokkien-Taiwanese
MAIN RELIGIONS: Daoism (Taoism) 20%,
Buddhism 6%, Islam 3%, Christianity 1%
EXPORTS: Textiles, clothing, shoes, toys,
machinery, weapons

MONGOLIA

AREA: 1,565,000 sq. km
(604,247 sq. mi)
POPULATION: 2,618,000
CAPITAL: Ulaanbaatar
CURRENCY: 100 mongos = 1 tughrik (Tug)
OFFICIAL LANGUAGE: Khalkha Mongol
OTHER LANGUAGES: Turkic, Russian, Chinese

MAIN RELIGIONS: Buddhism 95%, Islam 4%
EXPORTS: Copper, livestock, animal products,
cashmere, wool, animal skins, metals

NORTH KOREA

AREA: 120,717 sq. km
(46,609 sq. mi)
POPULATION: 21,386,000
CAPITAL: P'yŏngyang
CURRENCY: 100 chon = 1 North Korean
won (Wn)
OFFICIAL LANGUAGE: Korean
MAIN RELIGIONS: Chondogya 14%, Buddhism 2%,
Christianity 1%
EXPORTS: Minerals, metal products, agricultural
and fishery products, manufactured goods

SOUTH KOREA

AREA: 98,477 sq. km
(38,022 sq. mi)
POPULATION: 46,885,000
CAPITAL: Seoul
CURRENCY: 100 chon = 1 South Korean won (W)
OFFICIAL LANGUAGE: Korean
OTHER LANGUAGE: English
MAIN RELIGIONS: Christianity 49%, Buddhism
47%, Confucianism 3%
EXPORTS: Electronic and electrical equipment,
machinery, steel, motor vehicles, ships, textiles,
clothing, shoes, fish

TAIWAN

AREA: 35,967 sq. km
(13,887 sq. mi)
POPULATION: 22,113,000
CAPITAL: Taipei
CURRENCY: 100 cents = 1 New Taiwan
dollar (NT$)
OFFICIAL LANGUAGE: Mandarin
OTHER LANGUAGES: Taiwanese, Hakka
MAIN RELIGIONS: Buddhism 43%, Daoism
(Taoism) 21%, Christianity 5%, Confucianism
EXPORTS: Electrical machinery, electronic goods,
textiles, shoes, food, timber products

JAPAN

AREA: 371,973 sq. km
(143,619 sq. mi)
POPULATION: 126,182,000
CAPITAL: Tokyo
CURRENCY: 100 sen = 1 yen (¥)
OFFICIAL LANGUAGE: Japanese
MAIN RELIGIONS: Shinto and Buddhism 84%
EXPORTS: Machinery, motor vehicles,
consumer electronics

AFRICA

MOROCCO

AREA: 446,550 sq. km
(172,413 sq. mi)
POPULATION: 29,662,000
CAPITAL: Rabat
CURRENCY: 100 centimes = 1 Moroccan
dirham (DH)
OFFICIAL LANGUAGE: Arabic
OTHER LANGUAGES: Berber, French
MAIN RELIGIONS: Islam 99%, Christianity 1%
EXPORTS: Food, beverages, consumer goods,
phosphates

ALGERIA

AREA: 2,378,907 sq. km
(918,497 sq. mi)
POPULATION: 31,134,000
CAPITAL: Algiers
CURRENCY: 100 centimes = 1 Algerian dinar (DA)
OFFICIAL LANGUAGE: Arabic
OTHER LANGUAGES: French, Berber
MAIN RELIGIONS: Islam 99%, Christianity and
Judaism 1%
EXPORTS: Petroleum, natural gas

TUNISIA

AREA: 164,149 sq. km
(63,378 sq. mi)
POPULATION: 9,514,000
CAPITAL: Tunis
CURRENCY: 1,000 milliemes = 1 Tunisian
dinar (TD)
OFFICIAL LANGUAGE: Arabic
OTHER LANGUAGE: French
MAIN RELIGIONS: Islam 98%, Christianity 1%,
Judaism 1%
EXPORTS: Agricultural products, chemicals

LIBYA

AREA: 1,759,540 sq. km
(679,360 sq. mi)
POPULATION: 4,993,000
CAPITAL: Tripoli
CURRENCY: 1,000 dirhams =
1 Libyan dinar (LD)
OFFICIAL LANGUAGE: Arabic
OTHER LANGUAGES: Italian,
English
MAIN RELIGION: Islam 97%
EXPORTS: Crude oil, refined
petroleum products, natural gas

CAPE VERDE ISLANDS

AREA: 4,033 sq. km (1,557 sq. mi)
POPULATION: 405,800
CAPITAL: Praia
CURRENCY: 100 centavos = 1 Cape Verdean
escudo (CVEsc)
OFFICIAL LANGUAGE: Portuguese
OTHER LANGUAGE: Cape Verde creole
MAIN RELIGION: Christianity 97%
EXPORTS: Fish, bananas, animal skins

EGYPT

AREA: 1,002,071 sq. km
(386,900 sq. mi)
POPULATION: 67,274,000
CAPITAL: Cairo
CURRENCY: 100 piastres = 1 Egyptian pound (£E)
OFFICIAL LANGUAGE: Arabic
OTHER LANGUAGES: English, French
MAIN RELIGIONS: Islam 94%, Christianity 6%
EXPORTS: Crude oil and petroleum products,
cotton, textiles, metal products, chemicals

MAURITANIA

AREA: 1,030,807 sq. km
(397,955 sq. mi)
POPULATION: 2,582,000
CAPITAL: Nouakchott
CURRENCY: 5 khoums = 1 ouguiya (UM)
OFFICIAL LANGUAGES: Hasaniya Arabic, Wolof
OTHER LANGUAGES: French, Pular, Soninke
MAIN RELIGION: Islam 100%
EXPORTS: Iron ore, fish, fish products

MALI

AREA: 1,239,709 sq. km
(478,652 sq. mi)
POPULATION: 10,429,000
CAPITAL: Bamako
CURRENCY: 100 centimes = 1 CFA
franc (CFAF)
OFFICIAL LANGUAGE: French
OTHER LANGUAGES: Regional
languages
MAIN RELIGIONS: Islam 90%,
indigenous religions 9%,
Christianity 1%
EXPORTS: Cotton, livestock, gold

BURKINA FASO

AREA: 274,201 sq. km
(105,869 sq. mi)
POPULATION: 11,576,000
CAPITAL: Ouagadougou
CURRENCY: 100 centimes = 1 CFA franc (CFAF)
OFFICIAL LANGUAGE: French
OTHER LANGUAGES: Tribal languages
MAIN RELIGIONS: Islam 50%, indigenous religions
40%, Christianity 10%
EXPORTS: Cotton, gold, animal products

NIGER

AREA: 1,188,999 sq. km
(459,073 sq. mi)
POPULATION: 9,963,000
CAPITAL: Niamey
CURRENCY: 100 centimes = 1 CFA franc (CFAF)
OFFICIAL LANGUAGE: French
OTHER LANGUAGES: Hausa, Djerma
MAIN RELIGIONS: Islam 80%, indigenous
religions 14%, Christianity 1%
EXPORTS: Uranium ore, livestock, cowpeas, onions

CHAD

AREA: 1,283,998 sq. km
(495,752 sq. mi)
POPULATION: 7,558,000
CAPITAL: N'Djamena
CURRENCY: 100 centimes = 1 CFA franc (CFAF)
OFFICIAL LANGUAGES: French, Arabic
OTHER LANGUAGES: Sara, Sango
MAIN RELIGIONS: Islam 50%, Christianity 25%,
indigenous religions and animism 25%
EXPORTS: Cotton, cattle, textiles, fish

SUDAN

AREA: 2,505,825 sq. km
(967,500 sq. mi)
POPULATION: 34,476,000
CAPITAL: Khartoum
CURRENCY: 100 piastres = 1 Sudanese pound (£Sd)
OFFICIAL LANGUAGE: Arabic
OTHER LANGUAGES: Nubian, Ta Bedawie, Nilotic,
Nilo-Hamitic, regional languages, English
MAIN RELIGIONS: Islam 70%, indigenous
religions 25%, Christianity 5%
EXPORTS: Gum, livestock, cotton, sesame, peanuts

ERITREA

AREA: 117,599 sq. km
(45,405 sq. mi)
POPULATION: 3,985,000
CAPITAL: Asmara
CURRENCY: 100 cents = 1 nafka
OFFICIAL LANGUAGES: Arabic, Tigrinya, Tigre
OTHER LANGUAGES: African languages
MAIN RELIGIONS: Islam 50%, Christianity 50%
EXPORTS: Salt, animal skins, oilseed

ETHIOPIA

AREA: 1,221,897 sq. km
(471,775 sq. mi)
POPULATION: 59,681,000
CAPITAL: Addis Ababa
CURRENCY: 100 cents = 1 birr (Br)
OFFICIAL LANGUAGE: Amharic
OTHER LANGUAGES: African languages,
Arabic, English
MAIN RELIGIONS: Islam 50%, Christianity 40%,
animism 10%
EXPORTS: Coffee, leather products, gold

DJIBOUTI

AREA: 22,999 sq. km
(8,880 sq. mi)
POPULATION: 447,500
CAPITAL: Djibouti
CURRENCY: 100 centimes = 1 Djiboutian
franc (DF)
OFFICIAL LANGUAGES: French, Arabic
OTHER LANGUAGES: Somali, Afar
MAIN RELIGIONS: Islam 94%, Christianity 6%
EXPORTS: Animal skins, coffee

SOMALIA

AREA: 637,539 sq. km
(246,154 sq. mi)
POPULATION: 7,141,000
CAPITAL: Mogadishu
CURRENCY: 100 cents = 1 Somali shilling (So.Sh.)
OFFICIAL LANGUAGE: Somali
OTHER LANGUAGES: Arabic, Italian, English
MAIN RELIGION: Islam 99%
EXPORTS: Bananas, livestock, fish, animal skins

SENEGAL

AREA: 197,161 sq. km
(76,124 sq. mi)
POPULATION: 10,052,000
CAPITAL: Dakar
CURRENCY: 100 centimes = 1 CFA franc (CFAF)
OFFICIAL LANGUAGE: French
OTHER LANGUAGES: Regional languages
MAIN RELIGIONS: Islam 92%, indigenous
religions 6%, Christianity 2%
EXPORTS: Fish, peanuts, petroleum products,
phosphates, cotton

GAMBIA

AREA: 10,368 sq. km (4,003 sq. mi)
POPULATION: 1,337,000
CAPITAL: Banjul
CURRENCY: 100 butut = 1 dalasi (D)
OFFICIAL LANGUAGE: English
OTHER LANGUAGES: African languages
MAIN RELIGIONS: Islam 90%, Christianity 9%,
indigenous religions 1%
EXPORTS: Peanuts, fish, palm kernels

GUINEA-BISSAU

AREA: 36,125 sq. km
(13,948 sq. mi)
POPULATION: 1,235,000
CAPITAL: Bissau
CURRENCY: 100 centimes = 1 CFA franc (CFAF)
OFFICIAL LANGUAGE: Portuguese
OTHER LANGUAGES: Criolo, African languages
MAIN RELIGIONS: Indigenous religions 50%,
Islam 45%, Christianity 5%
EXPORTS: Cashews, fish, peanuts, palm kernels,
timber

GUINEA

AREA: 245,856 sq. km
(94,925 sq. mi)
POPULATION: 7,539,000
CAPITAL: Conakry
CURRENCY: 100 centimes = 1 Guinean franc (FG)
OFFICIAL LANGUAGE: French
OTHER LANGUAGES: Tribal languages
MAIN RELIGIONS: Islam 85%, Christianity 8%,
indigenous religions 7%
EXPORTS: Bauxite, alumina, diamonds, gold,
coffee, pineapples, bananas, palm kernels

SIERRA LEONE

AREA: 71,740 sq. km
(27,699 sq. mi)
POPULATION: 5,297,000
CAPITAL: Freetown
CURRENCY: 100 cents = 1 leone (Le)
OFFICIAL LANGUAGE: English
OTHER LANGUAGES: Mende, Temne, Krio
MAIN RELIGIONS: Islam 60%, indigenous
religions 30%, Christianity 10%
EXPORTS: Diamonds and other minerals, coffee,
cocoa, fish

LIBERIA

AREA: 111,370 sq. km
(43,000 sq. mi)
POPULATION: 2,924,000
CAPITAL: Monrovia
CURRENCY: 100 cents = 1 Liberian dollar (L$)
OFFICIAL LANGUAGE: English
OTHER LANGUAGES: Niger-Congo languages
MAIN RELIGIONS: Indigenous religions 70%,
Islam 20%, Christianity 10%
EXPORTS: Iron ore, rubber, timber, coffee

CÔTE D'IVOIRE (IVORY COAST)

AREA: 322,463 sq. km
(124,503 sq. mi)
POPULATION: 15,818,000
CAPITALS: Abidjan (seat of government),
Yamoussoukro (official)
CURRENCY: 100 centimes = 1 CFA franc (CFAF)
OFFICIAL LANGUAGE: French
OTHER LANGUAGES: Regional languages
MAIN RELIGIONS: Islam 60%, Christianity 22%,
indigenous religions 18%,
EXPORTS: Cocoa, coffee, timber, petroleum, cotton,
bananas, pineapples, palm oil

GHANA

AREA: 238,539 sq. km
(92,100 sq. mi)
POPULATION: 18,888,000
CAPITAL: Accra
CURRENCY: 100 pesewas = 1 new cedi (₵)
OFFICIAL LANGUAGE: English
OTHER LANGUAGES: African languages
MAIN RELIGIONS: Indigenous religions 38%, Islam
30%, Christianity 24%
EXPORTS: Cocoa, gold, timber, tuna, bauxite,
aluminium

TOGO

AREA: 56,599 sq. km
(21,853 sq. mi)
POPULATION: 5,082,000
CAPITAL: Lomé
CURRENCY: 100 centimes = 1 CFA franc (CFAF)
OFFICIAL LANGUAGE: French
OTHER LANGUAGES: Regional languages
MAIN RELIGIONS: Indigenous religions 70%,
Christianity 20%, Islam 10%
EXPORTS: Phosphates, cotton, cocoa, coffee

BENIN

AREA: 112,621 sq. km
(43,483 sq. mi)
POPULATION: 6,306,000
CAPITALS: Cotonou (de facto), Porto-Novo (legal)
CURRENCY: 100 centimes = 1 CFA franc (CFAF)
OFFICIAL LANGUAGE: French
OTHER LANGUAGES: Fon, Yoruba, regional languages
MAIN RELIGIONS: Indigenous religions 70%, Islam 15%, Christianity 15%
EXPORTS: Cotton, crude oil, palm products, cocoa

NIGERIA

AREA: 923,773 sq. km
(356,669 sq. mi)
POPULATION: 113,829,000
CAPITAL: Abuja
CURRENCY: 100 kobo = 1 naira (₦)
OFFICIAL LANGUAGE: English
OTHER LANGUAGES: Regional languages
MAIN RELIGIONS: Islam 50%, Christianity 40%, indigenous religions 10%
EXPORTS: Oil, cocoa, rubber

CAMEROON

AREA: 475,501 sq. km
(183,591 sq. mi)
POPULATION: 15,456,000
CAPITAL: Yaoundé
CURRENCY: 100 centimes = 1 CFA franc (CFAF)
OFFICIAL LANGUAGES: English, French
OTHER LANGUAGES: African languages
MAIN RELIGIONS: Indigenous religions 51%, Christianity 33%, Islam 16%
EXPORTS: Petroleum products, timber, cocoa beans, aluminium, coffee, cotton

EQUATORIAL GUINEA

AREA: 28,037 sq. km
(10,825 sq. mi)
POPULATION: 465,800
CAPITAL: Malabo
CURRENCY: 100 centimes = 1 CFA franc (CFAF)
OFFICIAL LANGUAGES: Spanish, French
OTHER LANGUAGES: Pidgin English, regional languages
MAIN RELIGION: Christianity 85%
EXPORTS: Coffee, timber, cocoa

CENTRAL AFRICAN REPUBLIC

AREA: 622,374 sq. km
(240,376 sq. mi)
POPULATION: 3,445,000
CAPITAL: Bangui
CURRENCY: 100 centimes = 1 CFA franc (CFAF)
OFFICIAL LANGUAGE: French
OTHER LANGUAGES: Sangho, Arabic, Hunsa, Swahili
MAIN RELIGIONS: Christianity 50%, indigenous religions 24%, Islam 15%
EXPORTS: Diamonds, timber, cotton, coffee, tobacco

SÃO TOMÉ AND PRÍNCIPE

AREA: 963 sq. km (372 sq. mi)
POPULATION: 154,900
CAPITAL: São Tomé
CURRENCY: 100 centavos = 1 dobra (Db)
OFFICIAL LANGUAGE: Portuguese
MAIN RELIGION: Christianity 100%
EXPORTS: Cocoa, copra (dried coconut flesh), coffee, palm oil

GABON

AREA: 265,001 sq. km
(102,317 sq. mi)
POPULATION: 1,226,000
CAPITAL: Libreville
CURRENCY: 100 centimes = 1 CFA franc (CFAF)
OFFICIAL LANGUAGE: French
OTHER LANGUAGES: African languages
MAIN RELIGIONS: Christianity 60%, animism 40%, Islam 1%
EXPORTS: Crude oil, timber, manganese, uranium

CONGO

AREA: 342,002 sq. km
(132,047 sq. mi)
POPULATION: 2,717,000
CAPITAL: Brazzaville
CURRENCY: 100 centimes = 1 CFA franc (CFAF)
OFFICIAL LANGUAGE: French
OTHER LANGUAGES: African languages
MAIN RELIGIONS: Christianity 50%, animism 48%, Islam 2%
EXPORTS: Crude oil, timber, sugar, cocoa, coffee, diamonds

DEMOCRATIC REPUBLIC OF THE CONGO (ZAIRE)

AREA: 2,344,872 sq. km
(905,356 sq. mi)
POPULATION: 50,482,000
CAPITAL: Kinshasa
CURRENCY: Congolese franc (CF)
OFFICIAL LANGUAGE: French
OTHER LANGUAGES: Lingala, Swahili, Kingwana, Kikongo, Tshiluba
MAIN RELIGIONS: Christianity 70%,

Kimbanguism 10%, Islam 10%
EXPORTS: Copper, coffee, diamonds, crude oil

UGANDA

AREA: 236,037 sq. km
(91,134 sq. mi)
POPULATION: 22,805,000
CAPITAL: Kampala
CURRENCY: 100 cents = 1 Ugandan shilling (USh)
OFFICIAL LANGUAGE: English
OTHER LANGUAGES: Luganda, Swahili, Bantu and other regional languages
MAIN RELIGIONS: Christianity 66%, indigenous religions 18%, Islam 16%
EXPORTS: Coffee, cotton, tea

KENYA

AREA: 582,646 sq. km (224,960 sq. mi)
POPULATION: 28,809,000
CAPITAL: Nairobi
CURRENCY: 100 cents = 1 Kenyan shilling (KSh)
OFFICIAL LANGUAGES: English, Swahili
OTHER LANGUAGES: Indigenous languages
MAIN RELIGIONS: Christianity 66%, indigenous religions 26%, Islam 7%
EXPORTS: Tea, coffee, petroleum products

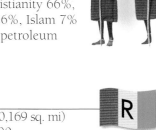

RWANDA

AREA: 26,338 sq. km (10,169 sq. mi)
POPULATION: 8,155,000
CAPITAL: Kigali
CURRENCY: 100 centimes = 1 Rwandan franc (RF)
OFFICIAL LANGUAGES: Kinyarwanda, French
OTHER LANGUAGE: Kiswahili
MAIN RELIGIONS: Christianity 74%, indigenous religions 25%, Islam 1%
EXPORTS: Coffee, tea, minerals

BURUNDI

PRONUNCIATION: boo-run-dee
AREA: 10,759 sq. miles (27,866 sq. km)
POPULATION: 5,736,000
CAPITAL: Bujumbura
CURRENCY: 100 centimes = 1 Burundi franc (FBu)
OFFICIAL LANGUAGES: Kirundi, French
OTHER LANGUAGE: Swahili
MAIN RELIGIONS: Christianity 67%, indigenous religions 32%, Islam 1%
EXPORTS: Coffee, tea, cotton, animal skins

TANZANIA

AREA: 945,091 sq. km (364,900 sq. mi)
POPULATION: 31,271,000
CAPITALS: Dar es Salaam (seat of government), Dodoma (official)

CURRENCY: 100 cents = 1 Tanzanian shilling (TSh)
OFFICIAL LANGUAGES: Swahili, English
MAIN RELIGIONS: Christianity 45%, Islam 35%, indigenous religions 20%
EXPORTS: Coffee, cotton, tobacco, tea, cashew nuts, sisal (fibre)

ANGOLA

AREA: 1,246,699 sq. km (481,351 sq. mi)
POPULATION: 11,178,000
CAPITAL: Luanda
CURRENCY: 100 lwei = 1 kwanza (NKz)
OFFICIAL LANGUAGE: Portuguese
OTHER LANGUAGES: Bantu and other African languages
MAIN RELIGIONS: Christianity 53%, indigenous religions 47%
EXPORTS: Oil, diamonds, refined petroleum products, gas, coffee, sisal (fibre), fish and fish products, timber, cotton

ZAMBIA

AREA: 752,615 sq. km (290,585 sq. mi)
POPULATION: 9,664,000
CAPITAL: Lusaka
CURRENCY: 100 ngwee = 1 Zambian kwacha (ZK)
OFFICIAL LANGUAGE: English
OTHER LANGUAGES: Regional languages
MAIN RELIGIONS: Christianity 75%, Islam and Hinduism 24%, indigenous religions 1%
EXPORTS: Copper, zinc, cobalt, lead, tobacco

ZIMBABWE

AREA: 390,624 sq. km (150,820 sq. mi)
POPULATION: 11,164,000
CAPITAL: Harare
CURRENCY: 100 cents = 1 Zimbabwean dollar (Z$)
OFFICIAL LANGUAGE: English
OTHER LANGUAGES: Regional languages
MAIN RELIGIONS: Syncretic (part Christianity, part indigenous religions) 50%, Christianity 25%, indigenous religions 24%
EXPORTS: Tobacco, manufactured goods, gold, textiles

MALAWI

AREA: 118,485 sq. km (45,747 sq. mi)
POPULATION: 10,001,000
CAPITAL: Lilongwe
CURRENCY: 100 tambala = 1 Malawian kwacha (MK)
OFFICIAL LANGUAGES: English, Chichewa
OTHER LANGUAGES: Regional languages
MAIN RELIGIONS: Christianity 75%, Islam 20%, indigenous religions 5%
EXPORTS: Tobacco, tea, sugar, coffee, peanuts, timber products

MOZAMBIQUE

AREA: 771,421 sq. km (297,846 sq. mi)
POPULATION: 19,125,000
CAPITAL: Maputo
CURRENCY: 100 centavos = 1 metical (Mt)
OFFICIAL LANGUAGE: Portuguese
OTHER LANGUAGES: Regional languages
MAIN RELIGIONS: Indigenous religions 50%, Christianity 30%, Islam 20%
EXPORTS: Shrimp, cashews, cotton, sugar, copra (dried coconut flesh), citrus fruit

NAMIBIA

AREA: 824,451 sq. km (318,321 sq. mi)
POPULATION: 1,649,000
CAPITAL: Windhoek
CURRENCY: 100 cents = 1 Namibian dollar (N$)
OFFICIAL LANGUAGE: English
OTHER LANGUAGES: Afrikaans, German, regional languages
MAIN RELIGION: Christianity 90%
EXPORTS: Diamonds, copper, gold, zinc, lead, uranium, cattle, processed fish

BOTSWANA

AREA: 569,582 sq. km (219,916 sq. mi)
POPULATION: 1,465,000
CAPITAL: Gaborone
CURRENCY: 100 thebe = 1 pula (P)
OFFICIAL LANGUAGE: English
OTHER LANGUAGE: Setswana
MAIN RELIGIONS: Indigenous religions 50%, Christianity 50%
EXPORTS: Diamonds, copper and nickel, meat

SOUTH AFRICA

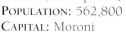

AREA: 1,221,043 sq. km (471,445 sq. mi)
POPULATION: 43,427,000
CAPITALS: Bloemfontein (judicial), Cape Town (legislative), Pretoria (administrative)
CURRENCY: 100 cents = 1 rand (R)
OFFICIAL LANGUAGES: Afrikaans, English, Xhosa, Zulu and other regional languages
MAIN RELIGIONS: Christianity 68%, Hinduism, Islam
EXPORTS: Gold, diamonds and other minerals and metals, food, chemicals

SWAZILAND

AREA: 17,366 sq. km (6,705 sq. mi)
POPULATION: 986,000
CAPITAL: Mbabane, Lobamba (legislative)
CURRENCY: 100 cents = 1 lilangeni (E)
OFFICIAL LANGUAGES: English, Swazi
MAIN RELIGIONS: Christianity 60%, indigenous religions 40%
EXPORTS: Sugar, wood pulp, cotton, asbestos

LESOTHO

AREA: 30,344 sq. km (11,716 sq. mi)
POPULATION: 2,129,000
CAPITAL: Maseru
CURRENCY: 100 lisente = 1 loti (L)
OFFICIAL LANGUAGES: English, Sesotho
OTHER LANGUAGES: Zulu, Xhosa
MAIN RELIGIONS: Christianity 80%, indigenous religions 20%
EXPORTS: Wool, mohair, wheat, cattle, peas, beans, maize, animal skins, baskets

COMOROS

AREA: 1,862 sq. km (719 sq. mi)
POPULATION: 562,800
CAPITAL: Moroni
CURRENCY: 100 centimes = 1 Comoran franc (CF)
OFFICIAL LANGUAGES: Arabic, French
OTHER LANGUAGE: Comoran
MAIN RELIGIONS: Islam 86%, Christianity 14%
EXPORTS: Vanilla, cloves, perfume oil, copra

MADAGASCAR

AREA: 587,042 sq. km (226,657 sq. mi)
POPULATION: 14,874,000
CAPITAL: Antananarivo
CURRENCY: 100 centimes = 1 Malagasy franc (FMG)
OFFICIAL LANGUAGES: French, Malagasy
MAIN RELIGIONS: Indigenous religions 52%, Christianity 41%, Islam 7%
EXPORTS: Coffee, vanilla, cloves, shellfish, sugar, petroleum products

SEYCHELLES

AREA: 277 sq. km (107 sq. mi)
POPULATION: 79,200
CAPITAL: Victoria
CURRENCY: 100 cents = 1 Seychelles rupee (SRe)
OFFICIAL LANGUAGES: English, French
OTHER LANGUAGE: Seychelles creole
MAIN RELIGION: Christianity 98%
EXPORTS: Fish, cinnamon, copra (dried coconut flesh), petroleum products

MAURITIUS

AREA: 1,865 sq. km (720 sq. mi)
POPULATION: 1,183,000
CAPITAL: Port Louis
CURRENCY: 100 cents = 1 Mauritian rupee (MauR)
OFFICIAL LANGUAGE: English
OTHER LANGUAGES: Mauritian creole, French, Hindi, Urdu, Hakka, Bojpoori
MAIN RELIGIONS: Hinduism 52%, Christianity 28%, Islam 17%
EXPORTS: Textiles, sugar, light manufactured goods

Australia and Oceania

Australia

Area: 7,686,884 sq. km (2,967,909 sq. mi)
Population: 18,784,000
Capital: Canberra
Currency: 100 cents = 1 Australian dollar ($A)
Official Language: English
Other Languages: Aboriginal languages
Main Religion: Christianity 76%
Exports: Coal, gold, meat, wool, wheat, machinery and transport equipment

Papua New Guinea

Area: 461,693 sq. km (178,260 sq. mi)
Population: 4,705,000
Capital: Port Moresby
Currency: 100 toea = 1 kina (K)
Official Languages: English, pidgin English, Motu
Other Languages: Regional languages
Main Religions: Christianity 66%, indigenous religions 34%
Exports: Gold, copper ore, oil, timber, palm oil, coffee, cocoa, lobster

New Zealand

Area: 268,676 sq. km (103,736 sq. mi)
Population: 3,663,000
Capital: Wellington
Currency: 100 cents = 1 New Zealand dollar (NZ$)
Official Language: English
Other Language: Maori
Main Religion: Christianity 67%
Exports: Wool, lamb, mutton, beef, fish, cheese, chemicals, forestry products, fruit and vegetables, manufactured goods

Solomon Islands

Area: 29,785 sq. km (11,500 sq. mi)
Population: 455,500
Capital: Honiara
Currency: 100 cents = 1 Solomon Islands dollar (SI$)
Official Language: English
Other Language: Melanesian pidgin
Main Religions: Christianity 96%, indigenous religions 4%
Exports: Fish; timber, palm oil, cocoa, copra (dried coconut flesh)

Western Samoa

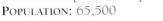

Area: 2,850 sq. km (1,100 sq. mi)
Population: 230,000
Capital: Apia
Currency: 100 sene = 1 tala (WS$)
Official Languages: Samoan (Polynesian), English
Main Religion: Christianity 99%
Exports: Coconut oil and cream, taro (food plant), copra (dried coconut flesh), cocoa

Vanuatu

Area: 14,763 sq. km (5,700 sq. mi)
Population: 189,100
Capital: Port Vila
Currency: 100 centimes = 1 vatu (VT)
Official Languages: English, French
Other Language: Bislama
Main Religions: Christianity 77%, indigenous religions 8%
Exports: Copra, beef, cocoa, timber, coffee

Fiji

Area: 18,272 sq. km (7,055 sq. mi)
Population: 813,000
Capital: Suva
Currency: 100 cents = 1 Fijian dollar (F$)
Official Language: English
Other Languages: Fijian, Hindustani
Main Religions: Christianity 52%, Hinduism 38%, Islam 8%
Exports: Sugar, clothing, gold, processed fish, timber

Tonga

Area: 699 sq. km (270 sq. mi)
Population: 109,100
Capital: Nuku'alofa
Currency: 100 seniti = 1 pa'anga (T$)
Official Languages: Tongan, English
Main Religion: Christianity 70%
Exports: Squash (vegetable), vanilla, fish, root crops, coconut oil

Kiribati

Area: 717 sq. km (277 sq. mi)
Population: 85,500
Capital: Tarawa
Currency: 100 cents = 1 Australian dollar ($A)
Official Language: English
Other Language: Gilbertese
Main Religion: Christianity 94%
Exports: Copra (dried coconut flesh), seaweed, fish

Marshall Islands

Area: 181 sq. km (70 sq. mi)
Population: 65,500
Capital: Majuro
Currency: 100 cents = 1 United States dollar (US$)
Official Language: English
Other Languages: Marshallese, Japanese
Main Religion: Christianity 98%
Exports: Coconut oil, fish, livestock, coffee

Federated States of Micronesia

Area: 689 sq. km (266 sq. mi)
Population: 131,500
Capital: Palikir
Currency: 100 cents = 1 United States dollar (US$)
Official Language: English
Other Languages: Regional languages
Main Religion: Christianity 97%
Exports: Fish, copra (dried coconut flesh), bananas, black pepper

Nauru

Area: 22 sq. km (8.5 sq. mi)
Population: 10,600
Capital: None. Government offices in Yaren district
Currency: 100 cents = 1 Australian dollar ($A)
Official Language: Nauruan
Other Language: English
Main Religion: Christianity 100%
Export: Phosphates

Palau

Area: 495 sq. km (191 sq. mi)
Population: 18,500
Capital: Koror
Currency: 100 cents = 1 United States dollar (US$)
Official Language: English
Other Languages: Palauan, Sonsorolese, Angaur, Japanese, Tobi
Main Religions: Christianity 67%, Modekngei religion 33%
Exports: Shellfish, tuna, copra, handicrafts

Tuvalu

Area: 23 sq. km (9 sq. mi)
Population: 10,600
Capital: Funafuti Island
Currency: 100 cents = 1 Tuvaluan dollar ($T) or 1 Australian dollar ($A)
Official Languages: Tuvaluan, English
Main Religion: Christianity 98%
Exports: Copra (dried coconut flesh)

*T*erritories and Dependencies

*T*HE COUNTRIES LISTED BELOW govern land outside their national borders. These areas of land are known as territories or dependencies. Some territories are governed directly by the country to which they belong. Others receive only protection and financial assistance, and have their own governments and laws. Some major territories are listed here.

*U*NITED *S*TATES OF *A*MERICA

AMERICAN SAMOA: South Pacific Ocean; 197 sq. km (76 sq. mi); population 63,800
GUAM: Western Pacific Ocean; 541 sq. km (209 sq. mi); population 151,800
MIDWAY: Central Pacific Ocean; 5 sq. km (2 sq. mi); no permanent population
NORTHERN MARIANA ISLANDS: North Pacific Ocean; 477 sq. km (184 sq. mi); population 69,400
PUERTO RICO: Caribbean Sea; 113 sq. km (70 sq. mi); population 3,888,000
VIRGIN ISLANDS OF THE UNITED STATES: Caribbean Sea; 345 sq. km (133 sq. mi); population 119,900
WAKE ISLAND: North Pacific Ocean; 7.7 sq. km (3 sq. mi); population 126

*U*NITED *K*INGDOM

ANGUILLA: Caribbean Sea; 91 sq. km (35 sq. mi); population 11,600
BERMUDA: North Atlantic Ocean; 52 sq. km (20 sq. mi); population 62,500
BRITISH INDIAN OCEAN TERRITORY: Indian Ocean; 60 sq. km (23 sq. mi); no permanent population
BRITISH VIRGIN ISLANDS: Caribbean Sea; 153 sq. km (59 sq. mi); population 19,200
CAYMAN ISLANDS: Caribbean Sea; 306 sq. km (118 sq. mi); population 39,400
FALKLAND ISLANDS AND DEPENDENCIES (SOUTH GEORGIA AND SOUTH SANDWICH ISLANDS): South Atlantic Ocean; 16,240 sq. km (6,270 sq. mi); population 2,800
GIBRALTAR: Southern Spain; 6 sq. km (2.25 sq. mi); population 29,200
GUERNSEY: English Channel; 78 sq. km (30 sq. mi); population 65,400
ISLE OF MAN: Irish Sea; 572 sq. km (221 sq. mi); population 75,700
JERSEY: English Channel; 116 sq. km (45 sq. mi); population 89,730
MONTSERRAT: Caribbean Sea; 104 sq. km (40 sq. mi); population 12,860

PITCAIRN ISLANDS: South Pacific Ocean; 47 sq. km (18 sq. mi); population 50
ST. HELENA AND DEPENDENCIES (ASCENSION ISLAND AND TRISTAN DA CUNHA): South Atlantic Ocean; 308 sq. km (119 sq. mi); population 7,150
TURKS AND CAICOS ISLANDS: Caribbean Sea; 430 sq. km (166 sq. mi); population 16,900

*F*RANCE

FRENCH GUIANA: Northern South America; 90,976 sq. km (35,126 sq. mi); population 168,000
FRENCH POLYNESIA: South Pacific Ocean; 3,266 sq. km (1,261 sq. mi); population 242,100
GUADELOUPE: Caribbean Sea; 1,507 sq. km (582 sq. mi); population 421,000
MARTINIQUE: Caribbean Sea; 1,101 sq. km (425 sq. mi); population 411,600
MAYOTTE: Mozambique Channel, Africa; 373 sq. km (144 sq. mi); population 149,400
NEW CALEDONIA: South Pacific Ocean; 19,081 sq. km (7,367 sq. mi); population 197,400
RÉUNION: Indian Ocean; 2,510 sq. km (969 sq. mi); population 717,800
ST-PIERRE AND MIQUELON: North Atlantic Ocean; 241 sq. km (93 sq. mi); population 7,000
WALLIS AND FUTUNA ISLANDS: South Pacific Ocean; 275 sq. km (106 sq. mi); population 15,200

*T*HE *N*ETHERLANDS

ARUBA: Caribbean Sea; 179 sq. km (69 sq. mi); population 68,700
NETHERLANDS ANTILLES: Caribbean Sea; 961 sq. km (371 sq. mi); population 207,900

*N*ORWAY

JAN MAYEN ISLAND: North Atlantic Ocean; 373 sq. km (144 sq. mi); no permanent population
SVALBARD: Arctic Ocean; 62,052 sq. km (23,958 sq. mi); population 2,505

*D*ENMARK

FAEROE ISLANDS: North Atlantic Ocean; 1,399 sq. km (540 sq. mi); population 41,100
GREENLAND: North Atlantic Ocean; 2,175,000 sq. km (840,000 sq. mi); population 59,900

*A*USTRALIA

CHRISTMAS ISLAND: Indian Ocean; 135 sq. km (52 sq. mi); population 2,380
COCOS (KEELING) ISLANDS: Indian Ocean; 23 sq. km (9 sq. mi); population 636
HEARD AND MCDONALD ISLANDS: Indian Ocean; 293 sq. km (113 sq. mi); no permanent population
NORFOLK ISLAND: South Pacific Ocean; 34 sq. km (13 sq. mi); population 1,905

*N*EW *Z*EALAND

COOK ISLANDS: South Pacific Ocean; 238 sq. km (92 sq. mi); population 20,200
NIUE: South Pacific Ocean; 259 sq. km (100 sq. mi); population 2,105
TOKELAU: South Pacific Ocean; 10 sq. km (4 sq. mi); population 1,475

*D*ISPUTED *T*ERRITORIES

GAZA STRIP (PALESTINE): Middle East; disputed by Israel and Palestine, Palestinian interim self-government; 378 sq. km (146 sq. mi); population 1,113,000
KASHMIR: Southern Asia; disputed by India and Pakistan; 138,992 sq. km (53,665 sq. mi); population 7,718,700
TURKISH FEDERATED STATE OF CYPRUS: Mediterranean Sea; disputed by Turkey and Cyprus; 3,424 sq. km (1,322 sq. mi); population 177,120
WEST BANK (PALESTINE): Middle East; disputed by Israel and Palestine, Palestinian interim self-government; 5,640 sq. km (2,100 sq. mi); population 1,612,000
WESTERN SAHARA: Northwestern Africa; disputed by Morocco and separatist movement; 266,001 sq. km (102,703 sq. mi); population 239,400

Glossary

acid rain ~ Rain that has combined with pollution in the atmosphere to form an acid. Acid rain can kill plants and damage buildings.

adaptation ~ A change that occurs in a plant's structure or in an animal's body or behaviour to allow it to cope better with its environment.

agriculture ~ The use of land to grow crops and raise animals. Agriculture is another word for farming.

altitude ~ The height of a place or object above sea level.

ancestor ~ A member of a person's family who lived a long time ago.

Antarctic Circle ~ A line of latitude at 66.5° south which marks the boundary of Earth's southern polar region. South of this line there is continuous daylight in midsummer and continuous darkness in midwinter.

archipelago ~ A large group of islands.

Arctic Circle ~ A line of latitude at 66.5° north which marks the boundary of Earth's northern polar region. North of this line there is continuous daylight in midsummer and continuous darkness in midwinter.

arid ~ Having low rainfall and, as a result, little vegetation. Very arid areas are called deserts.

atoll ~ A low, ring-shaped, sandy island enclosing a lagoon. An atoll is usually formed by the growth of a coral reef on top of an undersea mountain.

axis ~ An imaginary line through the centre of the Earth around which the planet rotates.

basin ~ 1. A wide, bowl-shaped dip in the landscape.
2. An area of land that is drained by a river and its tributaries.

bay ~ A body of water partly enclosed by land.

bight ~ A curve or recess in a stretch of coastline that forms a large bay.

border ~ A line that separates one country from another.

canal ~ An artificial waterway created to carry water for irrigation or shipping.

canyon ~ A deep, steep-sided valley formed by a river.

cape ~ A piece of land that juts out into a lake or sea.

capital ~ The city where a state or country's government is located. Sometimes a country has more than one capital, because parts of its government are located in different cities.

cartographer ~ A person who makes maps. The art of making maps is known as cartography.

channel ~ A narrow stretch of water between two land masses.

climate ~ The pattern of weather that occurs in a place over an extended period of time. Earth can be divided into a number of climatic zones.

compass ~ 1. An instrument with a magnetic needle that indicates the direction north.
2. An arrow or similar icon that indicates the direction north on a map.

coniferous ~ Coniferous trees are evergreen trees that produce seeds inside cones and usually have thin, needle-shaped or scaly leaves.

continent ~ One of Earth's seven major land masses: Europe, Asia, Africa, North America, South America, Australia and Antarctica.

coral ~ A rocky material formed by the skeletons of tiny marine creatures, especially corals.

crop ~ A plant that is grown in large quantities by farmers. Crops include foods such as cereals and vegetables as well as other plants such as cotton and tobacco.

crust ~ The hard, thin rocky layer that covers the Earth's surface. The crust has split into sections called plates.

culture ~ The shared traditions and way of life of a people.

currency ~ The kind of money used in a country.

dam ~ A wall or barrier built across a river to hold back the water and create an artificial lake called a reservoir.

deciduous ~ Deciduous trees shed their leaves every year, usually in autumn. The tree remains bare during winter but grows new leaves in spring.

deforestation ~ The cutting down of forest trees for timber, or to clear land for farming or building.

delta ~ A fan-shaped area formed when soil and silt carried by a river collect at the river mouth.

dependency ~ A region or land mass governed by another country.

descendants ~ The offspring of a person, including his or her children, grandchildren and so on.

desert ~ A dry area with low rainfall and sparse vegetation that is adapted to withstand drought.

earthquake ~ A shaking of the ground caused by movement of part of the Earth's crust.

ecosystem ~ A community of plants and animals and the environment to which they are adapted.

endangered ~ An animal or plant species that is in danger of becoming extinct.

environment ~ The natural surroundings of a community of plants and animals, particularly the shape of the land, the climate and the soil.

Equator ~ An imaginary line that circles the globe midway between the North and South poles. The Equator divides the world into the Northern and Southern hemispheres.

ethnic group ~ A group of people sharing the same origin, language and culture.

evergreen ~ An evergreen tree is a tree that bears leaves all year round.

evolution ~ A process of gradual change, especially in living things.

exports ~ Goods that are sold to other countries.

extinct ~ An extinct species of animal or plant is one that no longer exists because all the individual animals or plants of that kind have died.

federation ~ A group of independent states or territories that agree to become one country.

fertile ~ Fertile land is land with good soil. Plants grow well in fertile land if there is good rainfall or irrigation.

fjord ~ A deep, steep-sided valley gouged out by a glacier and later flooded by the sea to form a narrow inlet.

forestry ~ The science of using and managing forest resources.

fossil ~ The remains or traces of a prehistoric plant or animal, usually found between layers of rock.

fossil fuel ~ Fuel found deep underground that formed from the decayed remains of prehistoric plants and animals. The most common fossil fuels are coal, oil and natural gas.

gazetteer ~ An index of place names.

geyser ~ A natural spring that spouts a column of hot water and steam.

glacier ~ A large mass of ice that moves slowly down the side of a mountain or along a valley and is constantly replenished by snow falling on top of the mountain.

gorge ~ A deep, steep-sided, rocky valley.

grassland ~ A large area of land covered with grass plants.

Greenwich Meridian ~ An imaginary line that extends from the North Pole to the South Pole through Greenwich, England, and that marks 0° longitude.

gulf ~ A large bay.

hemisphere ~ One half of the world. The Earth is divided into Northern and Southern hemispheres by the Equator, and into Eastern and Western hemispheres by the Greenwich Meridian (0°) and the 180° line, an imaginary line that is 180° east or west of the Greenwich Meridian.

high-tech industries ~ Industries that produce electronic goods such as computers.

hydroelectricity ~ Electricity produced using the power of running water.

iceberg ~ A large block of ice floating in the sea. Icebergs break off the ends of glaciers and ice sheets. The part of an iceberg below the surface of the sea is usually eight times as big as the part above the surface.

ice-cap ~ A permanent sheet of ice and snow covering an area. Ice-caps are found in polar regions and on some high mountain tops.

immigrant ~ A person who has settled in a country but originally came from another country.

independent ~ Not governed by another country.

inlet ~ A narrow bay.

irrigation ~ The process of providing water to farmland by artificial means, such as pumping water from rivers, lakes and dams, or diverting water through channels and pipes.

island ~ An area of land surrounded by water.

■

kingdom ~ A country whose ruler or head of state is a king or queen.

■

lagoon ~ 1. A shallow area of salt water separated from the sea by a strip of land. 2. Inland bodies of water that were previously part of a river.

land mass ~ A large area of land not covered by water.

latitude ~ Distance north or south of the Equator measured in degrees.

livestock ~ Animals, such as cattle and sheep, raised by farmers.

longitude ~ Distance east or west of the Greenwich Meridian measured in degrees.

■

marsh ~ An area of wet land where plants adapted to water grow. Also called a swamp or wetland.

manufacturing ~ The making of useful products from raw materials.

migration ~ The movement of people or animals to another country or region. Many animals migrate to find food or avoid severe weather.

mineral ~ A natural substance occurring in the Earth's crust that is neither plant nor animal. Well-known minerals include chalk, clay and many metals.

■

native people ~ The original human inhabitants of a region or country.

nomad ~ A person who does not live in one place but continually moves around. Nomads often move in search of food and water for themselves and their animals.

North Pole ~ *See* **pole**.

■

oasis ~ A patch of land in a desert where there is water and more vegetation than elsewhere.

■

peninsula ~ A long strip of land that extends outwards from a larger land mass and is almost surrounded by water.

plain ~ An area of flat or rolling land with shallow river valleys.

plantation ~ An area of land where a particular tree crop is grown. Such crops include forest trees, rubber trees and coconut palms.

plate ~ One of the sections of the Earth's crust.

plateau ~ An area of flat or rolling land with deep river valleys, gorges and canyons.

pole ~ Points on the Earth's surface that represent the ends of the axis around which our planet is constantly rotating. The North Pole is the most northern point on Earth. The South Pole is the most southern point. The regions around the poles are known as the polar regions.

population ~ 1. The people who live in a place. 2. The total number of people living in a place.

populous ~ A populous country is a country with a large population.

principality ~ A country whose ruler or head of state is a prince or princess.

■

radioactive ~ Giving out invisible rays of high-energy particles. Some natural substances, such as uranium, are radioactive.

rainforest ~ A type of dense forest that grows in regions of high rainfall.

range ~ 1. A chain of mountains. 2. An area of open grassland where animals graze.

raw materials ~ Natural substances that can be turned into useful products. Examples include timber, coal and coffee beans. Raw materials are also known as resources.

reef ~ A ridge of rock, sand or coral lying just below the surface of the sea.

republic ~ A country led by an elected representative called a president.

reservoir ~ An artificial lake created to store water, usually by building a dam across a river.

resources ~ Substances or materials that occur naturally in a place and are of value to the area's inhabitants. Resources that can never be used up, such as water and waves, are called renewable resources. Resources that will eventually be used up, such as coal and other minerals, are known as non-renewable resources.

river basin ~ An area of land drained by a river and its tributaries.

rural ~ Relating to the countryside. The term rural industries means agricultural industries.

■

savannah ~ Open grassland with scattered trees. Most savannahs are found in tropical areas that have a distinct summer wet season.

scale ~ On a map, an indication of how distances on the map relate to actual distances.

scrub ~ An area of land covered with shrubs and low trees.

sea level ~ The average height of the surface of the sea, which is used as a base point for measuring altitude.

South Pole ~ *See* **pole**.

species ~ Animals or plants of the same type.

steppe ~ A large, grassy plain, usually without trees, as found in parts of eastern Europe and central Asia.

strait ~ A narrow strip of water that connects two larger bodies of water.

swamp ~ An area of wet land containing plants adapted to growing in water. Also called a marsh or wetland.

■

technology ~ The use of scientific knowledge to carry out tasks or solve problems. Using machines in industry is an example of technology.

temperate ~ Neither hot nor cold. Most of the Earth's temperate regions are located between the tropics and the polar regions.

territory ~ 1. A large area of land. 2. All the land and sea governed by a country or state. 3. A region or land mass governed by another country.

textiles ~ Woven or knitted fabrics.

time zone ~ A region in which everyone uses the same time. The world is divided into 24 time zones. The time in each zone is usually one hour earlier than in the zone to the east.

trade ~ The exchange of goods, usually by buying and selling.

tributary ~ A stream or river that flows into a larger stream or river.

Tropic of Cancer/Capricorn ~ *See* **tropics**.

tropics ~ 1. The hot, wet regions of the Earth that lie near the Equator. 2. Either of two lines of latitude: the Tropic of Cancer, at 23.5° north, and the Tropic of Capricorn, at 23.5° south. Because the Earth is tilted at an angle of 23.5°, these lines mark the point at which the Sun is directly overhead in summer.

tundra ~ A cold, barren area where much of the soil is frozen and the vegetation consists only of mosses, lichens and other small plants adapted to withstand intense cold. Tundra is found near the Arctic Circle and on mountain tops.

■

urban ~ Relating to cities. A country's urban population is the number of people that live in its cities.

■

valley ~ A long, narrow gap between hills or mountains along which a river usually flows.

vegetation ~ The community of plants that is characteristic of a particular region.

volcano ~ A mountain that has been built up from lava, molten rock that erupts through a hole in the Earth's crust.

■

wetland ~ An area of wet land containing plants adapted to growing in water. Also called a swamp or marsh.

woodland ~ An area of land covered with widely spaced trees and shrubs.

Index and Gazetteer

*A*cknowledgments

Weldon Owen would like to thank the following people for their assistance in the production of this book:
Helen Bateman, Anthony Burton, Alastair Campbell, Jo Collard, Melanie Corfield, Simon Corfield, Sharon Dalgleish, Libby Frederico, Kathy Gammon, Kathy Gerrard, Janine Googan, Greg Hassall, Lynn Humphries, Chris Jackson, Megan Johnston, Ralph Kelly, Jennifer Le Gras, Rosemary McDonald, Kylie Mulquin, Nicholas Rowland, Rachel Smith, Julie Stanton, Dawn Titmus, Greg Tobin, Wendy van Buuren, Michael Wyatt.

Cartographic sources: U.S. Central Intelligence Agency; International Boundaries Research Unit, Durham University, United Kingdom; U.S. Geographer General

Photographic credits: 14 bottom left, **David Weintraub**/The Photo Library – Sydney; 14 bottom centre, **Stephen Wilkes**/The Image Bank; 14 bottom right, **Mats Wibe Lund**/Icelandic Photo; 15 centre far right, **David Hardy**/SPL/The Photo Library – Sydney; 15 bottom left, **Francois Gohier**/Ardea London; 15 bottom centre, **B. McDairmant**/Ardea London; 15 bottom right, **International Photo Library**; 16 top far right, **Robert Harding** Picture Library; 16 bottom, **David W. Hamilton**/The Image Bank; 17 top left, **Jeffrey C. Drewitz**/The Photo Library – Sydney; 17 top centre left, **Sobel/Klonsky**/The Image Bank; 17 top centre, **Horizon International**; 17 top centre right, **Staffan Widstrand**/Bruce Coleman Limited; 17 top right, **Christer Fredriksson**/Bruce Coleman Limited; 19 top centre, **Alain Compost**/Bruce Coleman Limited; 27 top, **Horizon International**; 27 centre, **Shone/Gamma/Picturemedia**; 27 bottom, **Witt/Sipa Press**/The Photo Library – Sydney.